# Marian Apparitions in Cultural Contexts



*Marian Apparitions in Cultural Contexts* provides an analysis of collective phenomena, specifically mass visions of the Virgin Mary, from a psychoanalytical perspective. It draws from Jung's compensation theoretical model with the aim of merging depth-psychology and historical material from the Zeitoun case. Offering an original interpretation of this phenomenon from a Jungian psychological perspective, the book provides stimulating insights to any person interested in these supernatural events, whether general readers with active curiosity or scholars with broad intellectual interests.

A review of the literature points to a prevailing socio-political approach to examining visions of the Virgin Mary, while a psychoanalytical approach is generally lacking. Musso draws from Jung's compensation theoretical model in *Flying Saucers* with the aim of merging depth-psychology and historical material. Common themes and symbols are extracted and interpreted from the empirical material and analysed along with Egyptian social and political data. The book concludes with a discussion on how depth-psychological principles grounded in empirical and historical material could be applied in order to explicate cases of mass visions.

An original interdisciplinary exploration of cultural phenomena, *Marian Apparitions in Cultural Contexts* will be of value to academics and students in the fields of psychoanalysis, analytical psychology, political science, and religious studies. This book will also be of interest among Jungian scholars and practitioners in applications of depth-psychology to cultural phenomena.

**Valeria Céspedes Musso** is an analyst in training at the C.G. Jung Institute Zürich, Küsnacht and an independent researcher and lives in Frankfurt, Germany.

## Research in Analytical Psychology and Jungian Studies

Series Advisor: Andrew Samuels

*Professor of Analytical Psychology, Essex University, UK*

The *Research in Analytical Psychology and Jungian Studies* series features research-focused volumes involving qualitative and quantitative research, historical/archival research, theoretical developments, heuristic research, grounded theory, narrative approaches, collaborative research, practitioner-led research, and self-study. The series also includes focused works by clinical practitioners, and provides new research informed explorations of the work of C. G Jung that will appeal to researchers, academics, and scholars alike.

Books in this series:

**Jung and Kierkegaard**
Researching a Kindred Spirit in the Shadows
*Amy Cook*

**Consciousness in Jung and Patañjali**
*Leanne Whitney*

**Shame and the Making of Art**
A Depth Psychological Perspective
*Deborah E. Cluff*

**Modern Myths and Medical Consumerism**
The Asclepius Complex
*Antonio Karim Lanfranchi*

**The Archetypal Pan in American Culture**
Hypermasculinity and Terror
*Sukey Fontelieu*

**Marian Apparitions in Cultural Contexts**
Applying Jungian Concepts to Mass Visions of the Virgin Mary
*Valeria Céspedes Musso*

For more information about this series please visit: https://www.routledge.com/Research-in-Analytical-Psychology-and-Jungian-Studies/book-series/JUNGIANSTUDIES.

# Marian Apparitions in Cultural Contexts

## Applying Jungian Concepts to Mass Visions of the Virgin Mary

Valeria Céspedes Musso

Routledge
Taylor & Francis Group
LONDON AND NEW YORK

First published 2019 by Routledge

2 Park Square, Milton Park, Abingdon, Oxfordshire OX14 4RN
52 Vanderbilt Avenue, New York, NY 10017

*Routledge is an imprint of the Taylor & Francis Group, an informa business*

First issued in paperback 2020



*British Library Cataloguing-in-Publication Data*
A catalogue record for this book is available from the British Library

*Library of Congress Cataloging-in-Publication Data*
Names: Musso, Valeria Céspedes, author.
Title: Marian apparitions in cultural contexts : applying Jungian concepts to mass visions of the Virgin Mary / Valeria Céspedes Musso.
Description: Abingdon, Oxon ; New York, NY : Routledge, 2019. | Series: Research in analytical psychology and Jungian studies series
Identifiers: LCCN 2018018774 (print) | LCCN 2018032791 (ebook) | ISBN 9780429485862 (E-book) | ISBN 9781138599215 (hbk) | ISBN 9780429485862 (ebk)
Subjects: LCSH: Mary, Blessed Virgin, Saint—Apparitions and miracles. | Mary, Blessed Virgin, Saint—Devotion to. | Jungian psychology. | Psychology, Religious.
Classification: LCC BT650 (ebook) | LCC BT650 .M87 2018 (print) | DDC 232.91/7—dc23
LC record available at https://lccn.loc.gov/2018018774

ISBN: 978-1-138-59921-5 (hbk)
ISBN: 978-0-367-48932-8 (pbk)

Typeset in Sabon
by Apex CoVantage, LLC

This book is for Alberto

# Contents

# Acknowledgements

I would like to express my sincere gratitude to several people who generously offered their help and support, in one way or another, during my travelling along the long path which led to the preparation of this book. First of all, I am greatly indebted to Dr Roderick Main, for accompanying me through this process, and whose advice and continuous encouragement have been essential. I thank Dr Kevin Lu and Dr Matt Ffytche for their positive feedback and numerous valuable suggestions regarding my work. I would like to thank the University of Essex and the Department of Psychosocial and Psychoanalytic Studies for allowing me to benefit both from the very stimulating intellectual atmosphere which characterizes their seminars and workshops and from the intellectually enriching exchange of ideas during several conversations with members of the department. I am also grateful to the Goethe University of Frankfurt which allowed me to frequently use its library and bibliographic searching facilities. I thank Dr Elizabeth Brodersen for her encouragement and friendly support, and for our many discussions on the feminine. Last, but not least, this book could not have been written without the constant support and encouragement of my husband, Alberto Musso, to whom I am very grateful.

# Introduction

The year 1968 was a year of chaos, turmoil, and revolt, with seismic societal and political shifts taking place in many parts of the globe. In the United States, a tide of change emerged especially among marginalized Americans advocating increasing socio-political and economic equality, ushering in the civil rights movements, against the background of widespread protests and violence which led to several deaths, including the assassinations of two great American leaders of peace, Martin Luther King Jr. (who died in April 1968) and Robert Kennedy (killed two months later). The peace movement began to grow as more Americans protested against the war in Vietnam while many American soldiers returned home in black body bags. In April, Columbia University students occupied five buildings in protest against the university's participation in the Defence Analysis. A second wave of feminism, known as the women's liberation movement, spread across the United States as feminist publications were launched, organizations were founded, and liberation activists protested the Miss America pageant. At the Olympics, U.S. medallists performed a black power salute during the "Star-Spangled Banner" ceremony. In Europe, protests and revolutions also spread across the continent. May 6 came to be known as "Bloody Monday" marking one of the most violent days in Paris as students revolted, and later that month 9 million workers went on strike throughout France. Czechoslovakia enjoyed a brief period of freedom known as the "Prague Spring" before violent protests broke out, leading to clashes between students and Warsaw Pact troops. In Mexico, the police and military reacted violently to student-led protests as hundreds were killed and injured.

As these world events unfolded, the appearances of the Virgin Mary began in full view of thousands of people in Egypt. It was April 2, 1968 when the first apparition took place on top of St Mary's Coptic Church in Zeitoun (a district of Cairo, Egypt), followed by several other similar apparitions at irregular intervals taking place during the next 18 months. As soon as it was declared by bystanders that the luminescent figure on top of St Mary's Church represented a vision of the Virgin Mary, thousands of believers began to gather on the street to catch a glimpse of the image. Muslims,

Copts, and Jews, as well as other people holding different belief systems, Egyptians and foreigners alike, were drawn by the tales of the Virgin appearing nightly. Perhaps also fascinated by many stories of spontaneous healing from serious illnesses, thousands of people gathered at the church in hope of catching a glimpse of the Blessed Virgin. Even President Nasser secretly went to the church to witness the apparitions. The sheer mass of people was so large that the police had to tear down trees in the surrounding area in order to accommodate it. To give an idea of the dimension of the phenomenon, according to one estimate 250,000 people gathered in one evening ("Apparition", 1969). Sometimes the apparition would last for a few minutes, while other times it would persist long enough for eyewitnesses to inform and bring relatives and friends to the church. The crowds at the apparition site were diverse; one professor at American University in Cairo overhead her students discussing the apparitions, and she also noted that some of her colleagues expressed frustrations over intellectuals and professors visiting the apparition site (Nelson 1973, p. 6). By the time the visions ended in 1970, an estimated 500,000 people had witnessed the apparitions at Zeitoun. In order to understand how the apparitions at Zeitoun could attract the attention of hundreds of thousands of people over a short period of time, it can be useful to highlight some important events preceding the first apparition.

The unexpected military defeat of Egypt in the June 1967 War with Israel transformed the then-confident President Gamal Adbel Nasser and Egyptians, who before the defeat had developed a strong sense of national identity inculcated over the years by the president's vision of a strong Egyptian state since taking power in 1952 after deposing and exiling King Faruq. The shock of the defeat had reverberated throughout Egypt as Egyptians could not believe that the Israelis could go up against the mighty Egyptian army. As one Egyptian recounts, "I felt ashamed for not feeling concerned about the Israeli threat before our defeat in 1967, and my shame doubled because of my excess of optimism in the first days of that war" (Hafny 2013). The optimism was fuelled by Nasser in his speeches and interviews; Nasser's own optimism came from the belief that the Soviet Union would back Egypt and also that the United States would restrain Israel from engaging in war. It is uncertain what Nasser's intentions were, whether he wanted war or preferred to avoid a conflict by the use of diplomacy, although certain actions during the week before the war, including the removal of the United Nations Emergency Force (UNEF), the blockage of the Straits of Tiran, and moving the Egyptian army to the Sinai, indicate that he was preparing for war before the Israelis took pre-emptive action (Mor 1991, p. 359; see Chapter 2). Acknowledging and taking responsibility for his defeat, Nasser submitted his resignation. Shortly afterwards, a mass demonstration in support of Nasser took place in Cairo, demanding the withdrawal of his resignation. Nasser withdrew his resignation, but the image of the charismatic hero was shattered. The consequences of Nasser's missteps and misperception of events were very costly in terms of his prestige within Egypt and the Arab world.

It was against this backdrop of socio-economic and political upheaval that the apparitions began. The 1967 defeat is often considered to mark a turning point in Egyptian history, but I posit that the apparitions at Zeitoun were events of no lesser importance in that they represented a major impetus to Egypt's religious, spiritual, and cultural life which changed the way they thought about religion in the late 1960s and into the 1970s. The June 1967 War and the Zeitoun apparitions were historical events which put into question in the minds of Egyptians the issue of religion and its place in society. These events also put into question the secular and socialist ideology of the Nasser regime.

The year 1968 was a year in which a generation revolted against oppressive power structures which required citizens to conform to strict social norms, such as the expectation that women would stay at home and raise children, inevitably leading to the systemic discrimination of minority groups, lack of worker rights etc. The events of the year inspired an international movement, as each local or national protest against a respective authority or government inspired other groups to organize the next revolt, ultimately transforming societal and political structures in many countries. There seemed to have been a rebirth taking place in these societies as many traditions and ideals, such as the social norms mentioned previously, were challenged and questioned. From a Jungian perspective, it could be argued that a psychological disturbance such as collective anxiety or tension may have been behind these global events. For example, anxiety was a common condition in the post-World War II (WWII) era due to "psychosocial stressors, especially family- and work-related problems" (Horwitz 2010). In the midst of turmoil on a global scale, the Virgin appears in Egypt. The Marian apparitions at Zeitoun were the only mass visions that took place during this period.[1] As I argue in the coming pages, the image of the Virgin Mary represents the feminine principle. Mass visions of the Virgin Mary may not have been reportedly seen in countries such as the United States and the United Kingdom, but the manifestation of the feminine could have appeared in another form, reflecting an archetype symbolizing renewal or rebirth (see Chapter 5). This book attempts to interpret from a Jungian perspective the mass visions of the Virgin Mary at Zeitoun, also addressing the question as to why they appeared at this time and in this particular place.

My interest in the Virgin began when I was a child. News spread of the appearance of the Virgin Mary in my neighbourhood while I was growing up in El Monte, California. I remember my excitement at the prospect of meeting the Virgin in person as my mother Rosa dressed my 6-year-old little body. What would she look like? What would she do? I imagined a fairy-godmother-like woman prancing around in a long, sparkly, pink dress under a rainbow surrounded by beautiful angels, fairies, and unicorns. When we reached the location, which was only a few blocks from our home, a small crowd had already gathered at the site. A group of mostly Mexican-American women were fervently praying towards the front yard's tree. On the tree, someone had nailed a photographic image of the Virgin Mary, and that was it. After waiting some time for the miraculous and unexplainable to occur, my mother left, and as we walked home she expressed her scepticism regarding the validity of the claim of the apparition. Not fulfilling my naïve expectations, I also left the site rather disappointed. Despite this disappointing experience, my mother never lost her faith in the Virgin Mary, and I often saw her pray to the image. I wondered, what was the appeal of this woman whose image could also be found on the living room furniture of every one of my numerous aunts and my mother's friends? The Virgin was called on to watch over their children, their home, their husbands, and prayed on in times of financial crisis and difficulties as well as for infertility. Mary was the protective mother, and she was seen as holy, innocent, and pure. Mary's opposite is perhaps Santa Muerte, a Mexican female deity and personification of death; however, she was considered taboo, as exemplified by the fact that candles and images of Santa Muerte were typically relegated to the back of Mexican shops. In retrospect, I came to realize that the Virgin was sacrosanct, and there was much reverence of Mary by the women in my community; and, given this level of veneration, I wondered who the Virgin Mary was, and why she was so important to many. These were questions that would later revisit me, re-emerging, quite potently, as I undertook the interpretation of the apparitions under study.

To the best of my knowledge, a systematic study of the Marian visions at Zeitoun has never been undertaken, with the possible exception of some modest investigations published in booklets mainly aiming at documenting eyewitness accounts (Palmer 1969; Zaki 1982). The Zeitoun visions of the late 1960s represent a fascinating apparitional phenomenon, not least due to its links to the biblical past, the goddess Isis, the tense socio-political and economic circumstances, and the vast number of people holding a wide variety of belief systems who witnessed the visions. As discussed in Chapter 1, numerous systematic studies of Marian apparitions have been published; however, most of them only address the socio-political and economic aspects, while research addressing the psychological aspect of the phenomenon is sparse. The present study is an attempt to rectify this gap in the literature. More precisely, the aim of this thesis is to present a depth-psychological approach to investigating the mass visions of the Virgin Mary at Zeitoun while at the same time preserving the necessary historical analysis of the phenomenon. I propose to achieve this objective by introducing a Jungian approach, starting by the adoption of aspects of Jung's theory of compensation in *Flying Saucers* (1959). Moreover, the theoretical approach in his paper is expanded by applying other Jungian concepts such as the repression of the religious function and the psycho-political state of masculine and feminine elements of the *coniunctio*. It will be argued that a historical analysis of the period under study is an essential component of a thorough psychological examination of the cultural phenomenology of Marian apparitions. Although the present investigation mainly represents a case study on the Marian apparition at Zeitoun set within the time period of the 1960s, the research extends to the future events in Egypt in the final sections of the study.

Carl Jung did not undertake a study of Marian apparitions, but in *Answer to Job* (1958a) he discusses the psychological need behind the increased number of apparitions in the 19th and 20th centuries, and the impact this popular movement had on the Roman Catholic Church to declare the dogma of the Assumption of the Virgin Mary (Jung 1958a, paras. 748\749). It would have been interesting to see, in my opinion, Jung's interpretation of mass visions of the Virgin Mary like the Zeitoun apparitions since he was very interested in the psychological significance of the Virgin Mary (see Chapter 5 for a discussion on the Assumption of the Virgin and the quaternity). As we will see in the second part of this study, the Virgin is more than just the loving and protective mother, as a symbol she possesses the power to change individuals and transform societies from within.

## Structure of research

It can be useful to summarize the organizational structure of this work. The research is divided into two parts. The first part focuses on the literature review, the historical events surrounding the apparitions, and the methodological aspects of this study, while the second includes the empirical and interpretative analysis. Each chapter hones in on a specific element of the study, but my hope is that the material will converge convincingly in the last chapter.

Chapters 1–3 lay the groundwork by covering the relevant historical background on previous Marian apparitions, the methodology adopted, and the empirical analysis, before moving on from the concrete and logical to the abstract and interpretative analysis of the second part of this research. Chapter 1 begins with a brief overview of Marian apparitions throughout the centuries, focusing specifically on the apparitions of the 19th and 20th centuries. In addition, previous explanations on the phenomenology of the Marian apparitions are examined. I draw attention to the lack of convincing investigations addressing the psychological meaning behind the phenomenon in the literature. The chapter ends with a presentation of Michael Carroll's (1986) contributions on the subject of the Marian apparitions from a psychoanalytic perspective.

In Chapter 2, I propose a methodological approach to investigating collective visions, specifically Marian apparitions, building on the contributions of Jungians and post-Jungians. I argue that a Jungian hermeneutic can be useful in the study of Marian apparitions given Carl Jung's openness to investigate similar phenomena. I incorporate some of the aspects of Jung's approach in *Flying Saucers* (1959) and supplement some of its weaknesses, for instance its lack of direct referencing. I end the chapter with a short discussion of the criticism sometimes levelled against the idea of applying psychoanalytic interpretations to historical events.

In Chapter 3, I introduce the factual details of the Zeitoun apparitions and the typically reported sequence of events. In the second part of the chapter, I present the social and political events that may have been connected to the apparitions at Zeitoun. Four key aspects of Egyptian history under President Nasser's rule are examined, specifically, Pan-Arabism, the economic recession, the June 1967 War, and internal socio-political changes.

While reading several accounts of the Zeitoun apparitions, I asked myself if there was a way to translate published eyewitness accounts into empirical data, and created a database which classifies and synthesizes the eyewitness descriptions of the apparitions. This material is presented in Chapter 4 and includes a combination of the quantitative and the qualitative information extracted from the statements of the seers. After examining the main features of the database, this information is used to identify the common themes and symbols. Also included in the primary sources is material found in a 1986 survey of eyewitnesses of the Zeitoun apparitions which helped to supplement information lacking in the case studies from the database.

Chapters 5 and 6 represent the centrepiece of this study. They place under psychological analysis the images of the apparitional event. While Chapter 3 on the historical research is grounded in concrete material, Chapter 5 enters a world of myths and fantasies as every main aspect, figure, or image of the apparition is observed from multiple angles, whether from a real, imagined, religious, or mythological perspective. In Chapter 5, the image of the oft-seen loving and caring Mary transforms herself into a nymph or mermaid as the virginity aspect of the image is interpreted using the method of amplification. There are two main parts to this chapter: the first part amplifies the virgin aspect of Mary while in the second part the mother aspect is amplified. Symbols extracted from the database in Chapter 4, such as the doves, Christ Child, and olive branch, are also amplified. As these symbols are interpreted, a psychological meaning of each emerges revealing themes such as renewal, unity, and rebirth.

The psychological meaning of the symbols is then integrated and analysed in Chapter 6 along with the historical material. I examine several explanations offered by eyewitnesses and bystanders. This examination is followed by my interpretation of the apparitional phenomenon at Zeitoun. Given its complexity, I offer several ways to interpret the visions at Zeitoun, taking into consideration the events surrounding Egypt in the 1950s and 1960s. I conclude the chapter by asking whether integration or synthesis of the uniting symbol of the feminine as the Virgin Mary occurred since the mass visions continued to appear.

The Virgin Mary at Zeitoun has been "buried in history" for too long. This topic is relevant because it illuminates aspects of the Virgin Mary not typically associated with her, especially the renewal aspect of the archetype of the virgin discussed in Chapter 5. This aspect of the Virgin Mary is much needed especially under the current political climate not only in Egypt and the Middle East, but throughout the world.

## Note

1 Other Marian apparitions did take place in the 1960s, but most were not in the scale of the Zeitoun apparition.

# Chapter 1

# Marian apparition research

## Introduction

This chapter provides an overview of Marian apparitions, highlighting the features of the Zeitoun apparitions which are unique compared to other apparitions, as well as a discussion of the main explanations offered to interpret them. The chapter is divided into three sections. In the first section, a brief overview on the phenomenology of Marian apparitions is presented, which includes apparitions approved by Christian churches and categorizations of the visions of the Virgin Mary. In the second section, I review previous explanations and theories about the apparitions of the Virgin Mary. The focus will be limited to contributions of scholars who offered explanations from anthropological, historical, political, and psychological perspectives to the phenomenon of apparitions, with special focus on hypotheses which propose a relationship between the visions and their respective society. As we will see in this section, most scholarly investigations on Marian apparitions focus only on the social, historical, or "outer-world" events of the phenomenon, and they do not address psychological factors which may be at the root of these phenomena. Finally, in the third section, a review of Michael Carroll's work on Marian apparitions from a psychoanalytic perspective is presented.

## Overview on Marian apparitions

This section provides a brief historical overview of Marian apparitions, specifically focusing on reported apparitions in the last two centuries. In addition, it includes classifications of the types of Marian visions as well as those officially recognized by Christian churches (Catholic and/or Coptic).

### *Records on Marian apparitions and historical trends*

The first known apparition of the Virgin Mary dates back to January 2 in A.D. 40 (Varghese 2000, p. 34). This apparition is described as a bilocation since Mary was still alive when she appeared to the Apostle St James in

Caesaraugusta (present day Zaragoza), Spain. The apparition of the Virgin Mary instructed St James "to build a church under her patronage and name", a theme which is repeated in other apparitions of the Virgin Mary throughout history (ibid., p. 34). Many of the apparitions which took place after the Apostolic Age were not documented, and reports of Marian apparitions in the first ten centuries of Christian history survived in three ways: 1) via popular shrines and pilgrimage sites that trace their origins to an apparition or vision; 2) personal accounts of the apparition from ecclesiastical authorities; and 3) accounts of Marian apparitions by the laity (Varghese 2000, pp. 34–35).

Church historians estimate that about 21,000 apparitional events have been reported throughout history (Bromley and Bobbitt 2011, p. 7; Horsfall 2000, p. 376). Pope Pius XII called the 1800s the century of Marian predilection, as many apparitions took place in France in that century, the most famous one arguably being represented by the Marian visions in 1858 of 14-year-old Bernadette Soubirious at Lourdes (Miller and Samples 1992). The popularity of the Virgin Mary in the 20th century is a result of the secret messages given to the visionaries at Fatima in 1917, which were in part made public later on in the 1940s (Horsfall 2000, p. 377); the messages received are an important source of inspiration for the network of divergent Marian devotion (Margry 2009, p. 246). There were two types of messages which distinguished 19th century apparitions from those taking place in the 20th century. For example, the La Salette (1846) messages reflected the conflicts surrounding the industrial revolution and modernity, while the Fatima messages were directed against the undermining of society, the ideology of socialism and communism, secularism in general, and "the deterioration of the Roman Catholic belief" such as birth control, abortion, homosexuality, etc. (Bromley and Bobbitt 2011, p. 9; Margry 2009, p. 246).

According to the Marian Library of the International Marian Research Institute (Dayton, Ohio; in Miracle Hunter), during the period from 1900 to 2009, 535 Marian apparitions have been recorded (512 of which are not officially recognized by the Catholic Church, i.e. on which no decision has been made or on which a negative decision has been taken by the Catholic Church). Interestingly, over the past two centuries, there has been an increase in the number of reported Marian apparitions throughout the world. Specifically, and according to the data taken from the Marian Library, there have been spikes in reported Marian apparitions in three time periods: the 1930s, the 1950s, and the period between the mid-1980s and the mid-1990s (see Figure 1.1). During the first two time periods, the 1930s and the 1950s, most of the reported Marian apparitions came from Europe, while in the more recent period mentioned recorded apparitions were more widespread geographically, increasing especially in countries in Central and South America, Asia, and North America, although Europe still maintained a significant percentage of reported Marian apparitions. A case by case

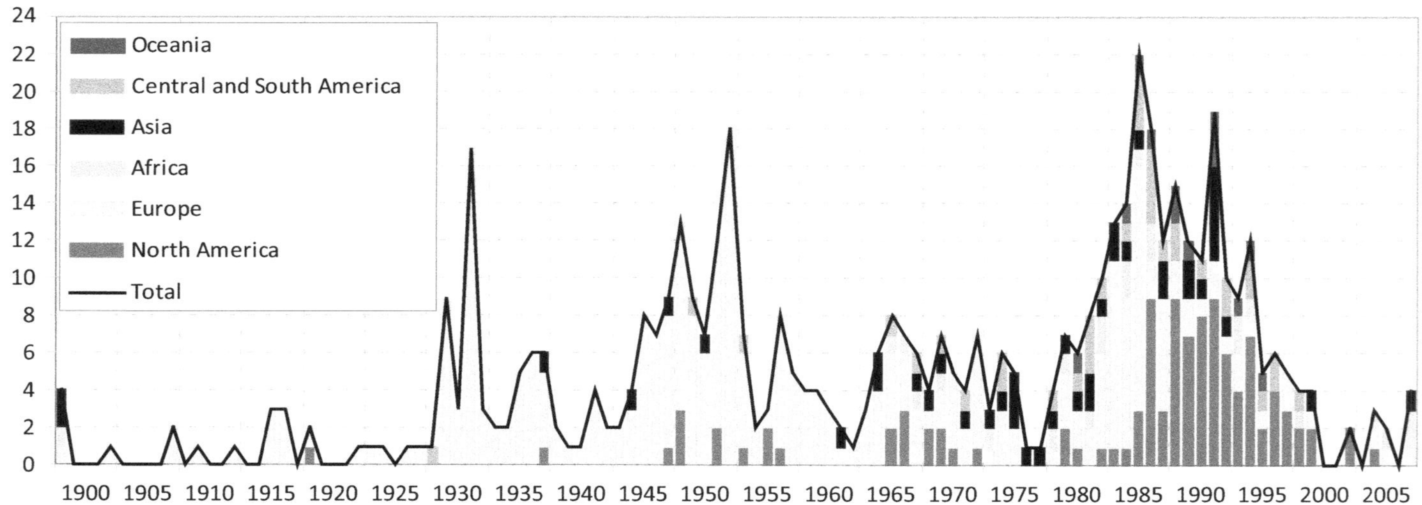


*Figure 1.1* Marian apparitions from 1900 to 2009 by geographic area

Source: Marian Library of the International Marian Research Institute, Dayton, Ohio (in Miracle Hunter).

Note: "Oceania" includes Australia, New Zealand, and Samoa. "North America" includes Canada and the United States.

Total: 524 apparitions, of which 25 (5%) in Africa; 43 (8%) in Asia; 298 (57%) in Europe; 110 (21%) in North America; 35 (7%) in Central and South America; 12 (2%) in Oceania.

analysis of the appearances in Figure 1.1 might suggest that some type of psychological disturbance had taken place in these countries at certain time periods, such as political instability in the Latin American world. Overall, beyond some periods which saw relatively high numbers of reported Marian apparitions, it is noticeable that the number of apparitions increased significantly from the 1930s onwards, being relatively low during the first three decades of the 20th century. One author on Marian apparitions places this great increase from 1945 onwards, particularly in the Western world, noting that the "frequency, content, structure . . . diverge from those of the preceding centuries" (Margry 2009, p. 245). I argue along the line that what lies behind the worldwide phenomena of Marian apparitions is a psychic disturbance caused by collective distress or anxiety. The connection between the phenomenology of Marian apparitions and collective distress is posited by many of the authors in the next section (Blackbourn 1993; Christian 1987; Ventresca 2003).

### *Apparitions recognized by the Christian churches (Catholic and/or Coptic)*

Despite the thousands of apparitions that have been reported since A.D. 40, only a fraction of those have been recognized and approved by either the Catholic Church or the Coptic Church. An approved apparition may be explained as follows, "To accept an apparition or believe it to be authentic generally means . . . to judge it to be of divine origins, whereas to reject it or believe it to be inauthentic means to judge it to have a purely natural or perhaps even a demonic nature" (Zimdars-Swartz 1991, p. 11). Each claim is investigated by a local bishop or by a special commission appointed by him to interview visionaries and to study the situation (Horsfall 2000, p. 377). In the past, the local priests and bishops used aggressive interrogation methods in their investigations. The three children at Fatima were held and interrogated by priests; at La Salette, the young visionaries were called liars and threatened with imprisonment; in Marpingen, the seers were separated from their families and confined to the institution, kept under close observation and visitors were restricted (Bromley and Bobbitt 2011, p. 24). A negative decision may also be taken and this means that a proclamation cannot be made, pilgrimages are discouraged, and shrines are prevented from being established (Zimdars-Swartz, p. 10). Historically, there has been reluctance by the Roman Catholic Church to acknowledge Marian apparitions due, for example, to the contentious and political character of the messages from the visionaries creating a divergent Marian devotion; for example, visionary Ida Peerdeman received a message in 1951, following Pope Pius XII's official proclamation of the Virgin's bodily assumption into heaven, introducing the theme of Mary as Co-Redemptrix, a bone of contention within the Catholic Church for centuries (Margry 2009, pp. 245–246, 250). The Catholic

Church was very cautious about its acknowledgement of the apparitions, and for the hundreds of reported visions in Italy in 1948, it did not give its stamp of approval to any of the apparitions; as Ventresca (2003) observes, the Church's response was consistent with its centuries-old attitude towards the supernatural, with apparitions considered as a potential challenge to its authority in maintaining "a direct, immediate rapport between the Virgin Mary and the so-called 'ordinary folk'" (Ventresca 2003, p. 446). Moreover, historically, the Christian church wrestled over the role Mary played in Jesus's origin story, being aware that some of the titles that were applied to Mary were the same that were applied to her pagan forerunners; therefore, churchmen discouraged the laity's adoration of Mary due to her strong ties to the Great Goddess (Walker 1983, pp. 602–603).

A majority of reported apparitions have not been investigated by diocesan commissions because they have simply failed to attract widespread public attention for very long and eventually they faded in memory (Zimdars-Swartz 1991, p. 10). According to Sandra L. Zimdars-Swartz (1991), out of hundreds of apparitions recorded in the last two centuries, seven have gained a particular widespread international attention, all of which have been recognized and approved by the Catholic Church: Rue du Bac (France, 1830), La Salette (France, 1846), Lourdes (France, 1858), Pontmain (France, 1870), Fatima (Portugal, 1917), Beauraing (Belgium, 1932–1933), and Banneux (Belgium, 1933). From this list, Lourdes and Fatima, most particularly, have been points of reference for investigations of later apparitions such as Marpingen in Germany, Ezquioga in Spain, Bayside in New York, and Clearwater in Florida, as we will see later. According to the list from the Marian Library, there are 33 fully approved apparitions and seven semi-approved apparitions. The Marian apparition at Zeitoun, Egypt was approved on May 4, 1968 by the Pope of the Coptic Orthodox Church and by Cardinal Stephanos, the patriarch of the Catholic Copts (Varghese 2000, p. 86). Official pronouncements or approvals of Marian visions are made by the Coptic Orthodox Church which occurred in a "Coptic Orthodox environment" since there is no "corporate unity" between Rome and the Coptic Orthodox Church (Johnston 1980, p. 14).

## *Seers of the apparitions of the Virgin Mary*

One of the features characterizing Marian apparitions is that most seers, or people who have witnessed apparitions, are female. Based on a list created by The Marian Library, I developed a chart showing the percentage of Female seers, Male seers, and Unspecified. In Unspecified, the gender of the seer or seers was not clear since the chart indicated words such as "3 children", "several people", and "1 religious person", for instance. We can see from Figure 1.2 that out of 418 unapproved apparitions documented from 1900 to 2009, 52% of seers were female and 28% were male. Moreover, despite not being able to quantify them, it is clear from their list that a large portion of the seers were children.

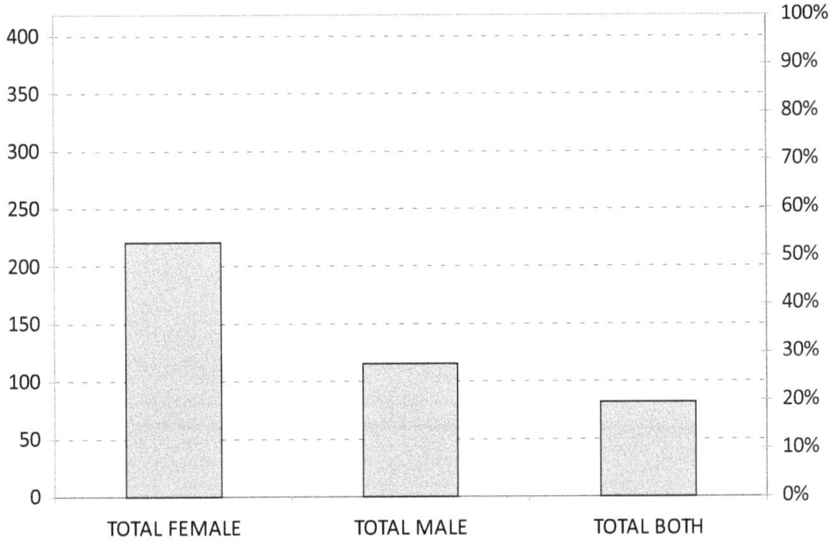


*Figure 1.2* Apparitions by gender (1900–2009)

Source: Ohio Institute.

Note: Unapproved apparitions only.

The visions not only seem to appear more frequently to women and the young, but the seers are often described as lacking any exceptional quality and as "simple, naïve, sincere, and pious" (examples include Jeanne-Louise in Kerizinen, Bernadette in Lourdes, Rosa in San Damiano, and Melanie and Maximin in La Salette); moreover, the seers from early apparitional events were most often from poor and modest families with limited formal education and seers from the modern era "were described as leading conventional lives built around their roles as housewives and mothers" (Bromley and Bobbitt 2011, p. 12). A final interesting characteristic about the seers is that many of them were experiencing individual and family problems at the time of the visions. For instance, Mary Ann Van Hoof (Necedah) was bedridden due to serious illnesses. She survived an abusive first marriage, aborted a pregnancy, and experienced the death of an infant; Rosa (San Damiano) was also bedridden, had poor health, and was often in and out of hospitals; Louise (Kerizinen) suffered from chronic health problems throughout her childhood (Bromley and Bobbitt 2011, pp. 9–10).

### Categorizations of Marian apparitions

William A. Christian Jr. (1981) examines apparitions in late medieval and Renaissance Spain, with particular attention to the regions of Catalonia and Castile. One of the interesting contributions made by Christian is his categorization of Marian apparitions. Christian traces the origins of Marian shrines in both of these regions and discusses a survey published in 1657 categorizing the legends associated with the shrines in Catalonia. In that survey, 14 *legendary* apparitions are documented. Christian categorizes two types of apparitions: "real" and "legendary". Real apparitions are defined as those "stories for which there is no contemporary report", while those in which there is documentation after the supposed event are labelled as legendary apparitions (Christian 1981, p. 7). For instance, just like there was a written documentation 800 years after Our Lady of Pilar in Zaragoza, likewise a legend can be found prior to the erection of a Marian shrine. Christian adds, "[s]uch legends were created to justify, illustrate, or dignify a preexisting devotion . . . [b]ut legends in turn can have a dramatic impact, and may even stimulate 'real' apparitions of an imitative nature" (Christian 1981, p. 7). The apparition at Zeitoun would be categorized as "legendary" as a 40-year-old legend is connected to the church in which the visions appear (see Chapter 6). Ruth Harris notes that some Marian shrines were founded on the basis of a miraculous apparition (Harris in Kselman 2001).

A more simplistic yet important categorization of apparitions can be found in Zimdars-Swartz (1991) where the more well-known apparitions of the last two centuries are examined. She focuses on six apparitions: three apparitions taking place before WWII (La Salette, Lourdes, and Fatima) and three which occurred after WWII (San Damiano, Garabandal, and Medjugorie). In her study, she concludes that much of the patterns in the pre-WWII apparitions could also be found in the post-WWII apparitions. The main theme emerging from both categories is Mary as the divine intermediator, an image prescribed to the Mary at Zeitoun (see third section and Chapter 6).

## Interpretations and explanations

This section reviews previous explanations and interpretations offered on the apparitions of the Virgin Mary. There is a wealth of scholarly work (in addition to the not so scholarly work) on visions of the Virgin Mary and the Marian cult. For the purpose of the present study, I think it is particularly interesting to focus on the works relating to the phenomenology of Marian apparitions which address the historical, socio-political, religious, and economic component of the visions. This section is divided into two parts: the first part introduces socio-political and religious explanations for Marian apparitions, while the second part, albeit not directly addressing approaches to interpret the visions, examines associations of post-WWII Marian apparitions with apocalyptic themes.

### *Socio-political and religious interpretations*

One of the most fascinating works on Marian apparitions was carried out by the historian David Blackbourn (1993), standing out for his careful and laborious investigation of the material relating to the Marpingen phenomena, especially in his usage of archival material and economic data. Blackbourn investigated Marian apparitions that took place in Marpingen, Germany, in 1876, when three children, all 8-year-olds, saw a woman in white while picking blueberries. During this period, the village of Marpingen was facing religious persecution by the Prussian state as well as suffering from "the effects of severe agricultural and industrial recession" (Blackbourn 1993, p. 91). Following an industrial and economic boom in 1873, the new German Empire's economy crashed and fell into a Great Depression (Blackbourn 1993, p. 91). Religious persecution took on the form of the *Kulturkampf* or the culture-clash/culture-war which consisted of legislative measures that passed between 1871 and 1876 as part of a "preventive" strategy against the Catholic minority in Prussia. The Protestant Prussian state co-opted the liberal anticlerical in order to help pass laws such as the "May Law" of 1873 which allowed state control over education and appointment of the clergy. According to Blackbourn, "The great state-building process of the nineteenth century Europe, whether it took place within a monarchical, imperial, or republican form, challenged the authority and jurisdiction of the church" (Blackbourn 1993, p. 27). The apparitions of the 1860s and early 1870s were cases that shadowed political upheaval with the creation of new states redrawing the map of Europe and reshaped by flared "war, church-state conflicts", and faltered "economies"; these crises were the backdrop that fed "a mood of desperation" in Marpingen (Blackbourn 1993, pp. 35, 399). The apparitions of the Virgin in Marpingen were spontaneous and reactive rather than organized and active; however, the civil authorities viewed apparition gatherings as a potential danger (Blackbourn 1993, p. 38). Writing from a historical perspective, Blackbourn argues that as a backlash to the anticlerical legislations, the Catholic Church utilized the apparition crowds as an organized movement against the state. As quoted by one critic,

> [i]n a 19th century world defined by secularization and the emergence of modern-states, the Virgin Mary proved a potent weapon for Catholics in their struggle against both secularization and the hostility of the nascent nation-states of Europe to Church temporal power and influence.
>
> (Ventresca 2003, p. 443)

Like Blackbourn, William A. Christian Jr. (1987) identifies social and political factors as well as Catholic persecution as the backdrop of Marian apparitions centred in Ezquioga in Northern Spain using newspaper accounts to investigate the phenomenon. In 1931 the Second Republic was proclaimed, and the fall of the monarchy impacted the social structure of Spanish society which included changes in "gender relations, clerical regulation of public morality and education, the relationship between parents and children, and of workers and employers" (Christian 1987, p. 141). The fall of the monarchy disrupted the entire social order, argues Christian (1987), "that included the model of royalty/subject for the divine/human relation, and by extension it jarred the belief in God" (Christian 1987, p. 141). The visions at Ezquioga started in the spring of 1931 and continued until the summer of 1931 in the midst of these regime changes. The visions were seen by both children and adults. The first vision took place on April 23, 1931, just nine days after the Republic was proclaimed when a girl in a group of children playing outside claimed to have heard the voice of the Virgin say, "Do not mistreat my son" (Christian 1987, p. 141). At that time, the crucifix had been taken down at the town hall and broken by anarchists in anticipation of the separation of church and state. As tensions increased between the Republicans and Catholics, the number of seers also began to increase. The majority of the seers came from farm and rural areas. In July one of the first messages that the Virgin Mary provided (to a 7-year-old girl) was to "pray the rosary daily" (Christian 1987, p. 143). Not only was the Virgin Mary addressing the crisis, she was also providing a solution through prayer. In the month of July, there had been over 100 visionaries and "up to 80,000 persons prayed the rosary" (Christian 1987, p. 143). Three weeks prior to those apparitions in July, a newspaper correspondent recognizing the collective distress of the Spanish people, reported,

> The simple and plain folk have understood that we are in the midst of a sea of dangers . . . from which we will hardly be able to emerge without divine help; and in sacrifice they have gone to the feet of the Virgin to pray for Spain.
>
> (Christian 1987, p. 155)

The Virgin Mary seems to have been placed in the position as "intermediator" as the hope was that through prayer she could intervene in the problems of the collective. As another newspaper correspondent wrote,

> Difficult times, times of trial, sorrowful omens, disquieting doubts, bitter disillusions, anguished frights. . . . What's happening? What's going to happen? . . . we must turn our eyes to God and to our conscience. And begin a crusade of prayer, fervent persevering prayer; crusade of penance and redress.
>
> (Christian 1987, p. 155)

Christian argues that because of "a complex turning point in Basque history" which had impacted the social and political order, the Marian apparitions had been seen as a great power to tap into in order to shape and define Catholicism against the new Republican government which favoured modernity; moreover, as Christian writes,

> Local priests took on the difficult task of combating new ideas and morality (the concomitants of changing relations of power) with religious sodalities, sermons, and revival missions. The advert of the Republic was seen as tipping the scales in favour of the long-term, ongoing encroachment of modernism.
>
> (Christian 1987, pp. 142–143)

In order for Catholics, including priests and bishops, to counteract the wave of modernity, the apparitions were used as a tool to galvanize the laity and drive a strong oppositional movement. As seen in the Marpingen and Ezquioga cases, the imminent threats against the local Catholic churches forced the religious institution to co-opt the apparitional movement, a phenomenon that seemed to emerge, especially in 19th-century Marian apparitions, when the Roman Catholic Church was under threat by the inevitability of the modern secular state.

Evidently, for Blackbourn and Christian, the rise of Marian visions were a consequence, whether directly or indirectly, of social, political, and especially religious tensions in the country where they took place. In Ruth Harris's (1999) treatment of the Marian apparitions in Lourdes in 1858, we can extract the patterns of social and political contexts affecting Lourdes, which are reminiscent of the cases presented by Blackbourn and Christian. At the time of the apparitions, in the area of Lourdes there were breakouts of cholera and a famine due to crop failure (Harris in Bromley and Bobbitt 2011, p. 9). Harris links the Marian apparitions to the social and political context, such as France's defeat by Prussia, the disaster of the civil war, and the papacy's "loss of its temporal domains to the newly unified Italy" as well as population growth and the disappearance of common land (Harris 1999, p. 16; Kselman 2001, p. 338). In his study of the 1917 apparitions at Fatima, Paul Christopher Manuel (2002) states that political scientists and historians have treated Marian apparitions as "a case of popular reaction against modernity, without any enduring consequences" (Manuel 2002, p. 3); according to Manuel, his work is in line with recent scholarship offered by David Blackbourn, William Christian, and Ruth Harris, suggesting that "social scientists need to treat the consequences of wide-scale popular religiosity more completely – not as a theological reality, but as a political one" (Manuel 2002, p. 3). Not surprisingly, a key focus of Manuel's research is centred on the political context and identifies "widespread societal anxiety, foreign war, and conflicts over church-state issues" as features of the Fatima apparitions (Manuel 2002, p. 4). Specifically, Portugal intervened in World War I, and horror stories from the battlefield were told by soldiers who had returned home, including stories of Portuguese troops left abandoned and neglected as food supplies and replacements were slow to arrive as well as the defeat by the German army in which 7,425 soldiers were killed (Manuel 2002, p. 5). Similar to the events in Marpingen and Ezquioga, ideological differences ensued between the Republicans and Catholics, and with the overthrow of King Manuel in 1910 and the inauguration of its first Republican state, those in power "all but declared war on the Catholic Church" (i.e. restrictive anticlerical laws were passed, many seminaries were closed, the observance of holy days was eliminated, Church property was nationalized, etc.) (Manuel 2002, p. 5). Manuel states that at the time of the First Republic there was not a general negative view of the clergy, as many people took refuge in their faith and the Church given that a large part of the population felt adversely affected by the secular elites; moreover, Manuel argues that popular anticlericalism subsides when the Church is under attack by its government and the converse occurs when it's not (Manuel 2002, p. 6).

Robert A. Ventresca (2003) argues that the Marian apparitions throughout post-WWII Italy were a response to political and ideological tensions. Drawing on the works of Blackbourn (1993) and Christian (1987), Ventresca tries to establish a link between the anxieties of individuals and the collective "created by the rise of Communism and the possibility of a Left victory in the polls" (Ventresca 2003, p. 449). According to Ventresca, the question for historians is not whether the apparitions are true or not, but to question why seers claim to experience apparitions and miracles (Ventresca 2003, p. 440). Ruth Harris (1999) shares a similar perspective on the study of supernatural phenomenon such as Marian apparitions in which she observes that historians of the modern era are "ill at ease with, if not actually repelled by" such phenomena which are "usually seen as little more than superstitious remnants on the road to extinction" (Harris 1999, p. 12). In approaching his study, Ventresca weaves together the larger political narrative of 1948 Italy with the social and political dimensions employing Ruth Harris's sympathetic approach in *Lourdes* (1999), an approach which Ventresca writes is

> more anthropology than history, in that it seeks to suspend preconceived notions of individual or collective behaviour, and so assesses the apparitions on their own terms . . . [this approach] begins from the basic assumption that . . . the apparitions are genuine spiritual experiences for the faithful involved, either as participants or observers.
>
> (Ventresca 2003, p. 441)

Prior to and after the Italian 1948 election, hundreds of apparitions took place and drew hundreds if not thousands of people to the sites reported in Rome, Gimigliano, Lucca, Ponsacco, and elsewhere throughout the country (Ventresca 2003, p. 452). According to Ventresca, the popular devotion of the apparitions was "neither the product of individual or collective delusion, nor deliberate intervention of the Church fathers for electoral purposes"; instead, Ventresca argues that,

> the wave of apparitions and movements in Italy on the eve of the 1948 vote, one might argue, reflected an individual and collective search for meaning, order and protection on the part of ordinary Italians who feared the fate that awaited them should the Popular Front win the April election. The anxiety created by the rise of Communism and the possibility of a Left victory at the polls in April help to explain why so many people in every corner of Italy reported seeing visions. Just as important, it helps to explain why so many who did not see the Virgin appear or a statue move or an icon cry in 1948, still believed in the divine nature of the phenomena.
>
> (Ventresca 2003, p. 450)

The divisions of the modern and pre-modern world in which the former is characterized as rational, secular, and scientific and the latter as irrational and superstitious, argues Ventresca, can no longer hold (Ventresca 2003, p. 452). And despite the consequences of modernity, 1948 Italian Catholics in the modern era "clung to its traditional beliefs about supernatural beings and their powers to intercede before God on behalf of his people" (Ventresca 2003, p. 452).

### *Apocalyptic themes of 20th-century Marian apparitions*

In her investigations of Marian apparitions, Sandra L. Zimdars-Swartz (1991) suggests that a "transcultural apocalyptic ideology" has developed in modern apparitions. In her study, Zimdars-Swartz examines six apparitions and she concludes that much of the patterns in the three pre-WWII apparitions (La Salette, Lourdes, and Fatima) could be found also in the three post-WWII apparitions (San Damiano, Garabandal, and Medjugorie). However, the post-WWII apparitions had grown more apocalyptic in their nature, which appears to be the case particularly drawing on messages and literature from Fatima and La Salette (Zimdars-Swartz 1991, p. 20), thus creating an apocalyptic worldview with the underlying principle being, as she states, "images of intercession and intervention". "It is assumed here that a divinely appointed figure may, on the heavenly plane, intercede with God or Christ, and on the earthly plane, intervene in history to change an otherwise predetermined course of events" (Zimdars-Swartz 1991, p. 247). The Virgin Mary as an intermediator, messenger, and intervener seems to be a prevalent universal characteristic of Marian apparitions. Edith and Victor Turner (1982) also suggest that the Virgin Mary intervenes in times of political and economic crisis appealing to the lower and middle classes who feel that big businesses are examples of the grievous sins from which humanity must turn away.

In his paper, *Holy People in Peasant Europe*, Christian (1973) writes about three apparitional phenomena pointing to the universality of the Virgin Mary's message. The two interesting key themes featuring in his study were: 1) the Church's management of the seers and the universality of the messages (which was briefly discussed earlier); and 2) that the Virgin's message is not specifically aimed for the locale, but for the salvation of the human race. Christian states that these apparitions as well as the apparitions in La Salette, Lourdes, Pontmain, Fatima, Ezquioga, and Beauraing "all have included prescriptions for salvation. They also include more somber warnings of a great chastisement should the world not amend" (Christian 1973, p. 108). Christian does not elaborate on the apocalyptical messages of the apparitions further than this in his article, but he recognizes the apocalyptic theme emerging out of these apparitions.

In line with the investigation by Zimdars-Swartz, in the article, "Marian Piety and the Cold War in the United States", Kselman (1986) investigates the appeal of Marian apparitions in the United States after WWII. Kselman suggests that the Marian devotion in the United States can be traced to events happening in the world, i.e. Communism and the Cold War, and that this brought about a 19th-century revivalism of Marian apparitions such as the cult of Lourdes and especially the messages from Fatima. In 1950, Mary Ann Van Hoof from Necedah, Wisconsin attracted thousands of Catholic pilgrims to her farm in hopes to witness a miracle while Van Hoof communicated with the Virgin Mary and relayed her message (Kselman 1986, p. 403). As Kselman notes,

> Our Lady of Necedah repeated the warnings about Russia issued by Our Lady of Fatima, and added details that stressed Mary's direct concern with America and referred explicitly to the need to combat the enemy within Mary's warnings were combined with promises that, with enough prayer, peace could be preserved.
>
> (Kselman 1986, p. 419)

Kselman's analysis is carried out within the context of American religious history and he does not use the term "apocalyptic" in his study. However, three apocalyptic characteristics can be drawn from this investigation: 1) Mary acts as mediator between people and God or Christ; 2) political events threaten or undermine the Church and the laity; and 3) the messages contain apocalyptic undertones, i.e. if the crowds or audience of Mary's message do not pray, a disaster might occur.

Marina Warner (1976) and Andrew Greeley (1977) have also made contributions to the study of the cult of the Virgin Mary and emphasize the significance of her role. However, they question whether Marian devotion would survive the 21st century:

> The Virgin Mary has inspired some of the loftiest architecture, some of the most moving poetry, . . . the most beautiful paintings. . . . But the reality her myth describes is over; the moral code she affirms has been exhausted. The Catholic Church might succeed . . . in accommodating her . . ., but it is more likely that . . . the Virgin will recede into legend.
>
> (Warner 1976, pp. 338–339)

Is Mary still relevant now, as Greeley poses the question, "Is the Lady of Bethlehem an anachronism?" (Greeley 1977, pp. 219–220). I agree with Warner's revised 2013 position on the cult of the Virgin Mary that it [i.e. the Cult of the Virgin] is more entrenched than ever (Warner 2013); in fact, reports of Mary's appearances continue into 21st century such as in the mass visions in 2009 in Warraq, Egypt, and apparitions will continue to emerge so long as there is a psychological disturbance creating a need by the feminine aspect of the collective.[1] E. A. Matter (2001) argues that Marian devotion has become more fervent in the last quarter of the century (Matter 2001, p. 126). In Matter's investigation, she analyses Marian apparitions, Mary's cult, and her followers as reported in the media and popular press, scholarly works, and books. In her paper, she observes that "the visions of the Virgin Mary are associated with particular times of cultural stress" (Matter 2001, p. 127), and that the Virgin Mary in Fatima became a reference point for the latter part of the 20th century which "set the apocalyptic tone for later and less well-accepted manifestations" (Matter 2001, p. 128). More provocatively, Wojcik (1997) argues that apocalyptic sentiment has always abided in American culture. He presents different forms of apocalypticism stemming from "folk" or popular belief by way of oral narratives, prophecies of visionaries, charismatic leaders, etc. He argues that the nuclear age and other potential catastrophes have influenced apocalyptic thought and associates these prophecies with visions of the Virgin Mary. In a similar vein, Echeverria and Perry (1988) postulate that messages derived from Fatima, and backed by the Blue Army,[2] were used to "exploit the fear of nuclear destruction" (Echeverria and Perry 1988, p. 302) in Yugoslavia and Central America.

The first part of this section discussed studies of scholars whose hypotheses of Marian apparitions consist of anxieties caused by a backlash against modernity, secularization, change of political regime/power, and anticlericalism, changes and events which plagued the 19th century. Scholars in the second section suggest that the post-WWII apparitions were an extension of pre-WWII apparitions; that is, the messages from modern Marian apparitions stemmed from those received at Fatima and La Salette and have transformed into one of a catastrophic and destructive nature, and which express the salvation of the world and the consecration of Communist Russia.

## Psychoanalytic and depth-psychological explanations

This section introduces literature on Marian apparitions written from a psychoanalytic point of view, concentrating on the work of Michael P. Carroll (1986). As far as I am aware, this is the only work that directly investigates the psychological nature of Marian apparitions. For this reason, I believe, it deserves to be closely examined.

### *A Freudian approach*

Carroll's book, *The Cult of the Virgin Mary: Psychological Origins* (1986) is divided into two parts: part 1 deals with the cult of the Virgin Mary, and part 2 deals with Marian apparitions. Part 1 of Carroll's book attempts to provide a bridge of understanding from Marian apparitions to the cult of the Virgin Mary. According to Carroll, the cult of the Virgin Mary in Spain and Southern Italy could be understood via Freud's theory of the father ineffective-family complex. Carroll defines this complex as "a family-type characterized by the concentration of de facto authority within the home in the hands of the mother, and is usually considered to be a result of the widespread economic marginality of males" (Carroll 1986, p. 50). Within these two regions and among the proletariat, the prevalence of the father ineffective-family produced in sons a strong but strongly repressed desire for the mother (Carroll 1986, p. 112), and that devotion to the mother was originally expressed in the Cybele cult. This devotion was later redirected to a new goddess, the Virgin Mary, as more people belonging to this group began joining the Catholic Church in large numbers (Carroll 1986, p. 112).

In the second part of the book, Carroll presents what he interprets as two categories of Marian apparitions: *hallucinations* and *illusions*. There are two conditions that infer the presence of a hallucination: 1) "the subject must perceive a stimulus and believe that it really exists (that is, is not imaginary)" and 2) "independent observers must be unable to detect a stimulus of any sort that corresponds, however loosely, to that perceived by the subject" (Carroll 1986, p. 117). That is, a person who sees the image of the Virgin Mary, while everybody else can neither see the image nor notice anything unusual in the surrounding area, would be categorized as experiencing a hallucination. Carroll cites Freud's study on a religious hallucination in which he suggested two hypotheses: "first, that the occurrence of such a hallucination serves as a mechanism for the discharges of excess of sexual energy, and second, that the content of the apparition was shaped by the seer's desire to gratify an unconscious wish" (Carroll 1986, pp. 140–142). Carroll draws from Freud's case study in "A Seventeenth-Century Demonological Neurosis" (1923), in which Christoph Haizmann experienced apparitions including the Virgin Mary, but Freud was concerned with his apparition of the Devil. Freud concluded that the Devil was a projection of the image of

Haizmann's father, and that this image was shaped by "his unconscious *hostility* toward his father, a hostility that had been formed during the Oedipal period and had long since been repressed" (Carroll 1986, p. 141, italics in original). Furthermore, in the case of Haizmann, he had a strong libidinal drive for material comfort and when blocked, Carroll states,

> reactivated his repressed hostility toward his father. That this hostility was reactivated, rather than some other 'infantile' impulse, was mainly activated due to the fact that this hostility had already been activated to some degree by his father's recent death.
>
> (Carroll 1986, p. 142)

Next, Carroll presents a second categorization of Marian apparitions, consisting of illusions. The definition can be described as "the misperception of a physical stimulus whose existence can be verified by independent observers" (Carroll 1986, p. 117). In other words, a person sees the Virgin Mary while other people, though not seeing the image, might for instance see a light surrounding the location of the apparition. According to Carroll, a Marian apparition falls into the category of an illusion with the concatenation of these four factors:

> first, they confront an unusual stimulus of some sort; second, they are experiencing great anxiety over the future; third, someone makes the explicit suggestion that an apparition of the Virgin Mary is in progress; and fourth, their religious worldview legitimates the belief that an apparition of the Virgin Mary might be a sign from God and He is on their side.
>
> (Carroll 1986, p. 218)

From this perspective, the apparitions at Zeitoun would fall into the category of illusions. Carroll dedicates most of his discussion to the category of hallucinations because the majority of reported apparitions are by individual seers; three Marian apparitions categorized as illusions are examined, including the apparition at Zeitoun.

One of the strengths of Carroll's contribution is that he elaborates on the cultural and historical dimension of the phenomenon under discussion by explaining the cooptation by the Catholic Church of the Cybele cult into the Marian cult in Europe, specifically Spain and Southern Italy. The connection between the cult of the Virgin Mary and the phenomenon of Marian apparitions can be explained in three ways: 1) in terms of a prevailing religious worldview which legitimates the belief in the reality of so-called hallucinations; 2) historical circumstances "within a traditionally Catholic area can easily insure that the predilection of the population toward religious hallucination is checked" (Carroll 1986, p. 133); and 3) an imitation hypothesis (i.e. an imitation of a well-known apparition in the region) (Carroll 1986, p. 134). Carroll states in the conclusion of his book that the Marian cult is likely to continue to flourish "in those areas where the prevailing form of the family is especially strong and strongly repressed" such as Southern Italy and Spain since the father-ineffective family is predominant in those areas (Carroll 1986, p. 222). Moreover, he argues that there is no reason to believe "that apparitions of the Virgin Mary, at least in predominantly Catholic areas, will cease, since the processes producing these apparitions are as likely to operate in the future as in the past" (Carroll 1986, p. 224). He ends by saying that so long as there is a Marian cult, there will be people who speak to the Goddess "face to face" (Carroll 1986, p. 224).

There are several ideas and questions that arise from Carroll's analysis of Marian apparitions on which a Jungian analysis may provide some original insight. First, Carroll develops the backbone of his approach by focusing on Marian apparitions which took place in Spain and Southern Italy. Although the father ineffective-family approach is a strong argument, it may not be robust enough to be applied to other Marian apparitions, whether those categorized as illusions or those labelled as hallucinations, which took place in regions where this complex may not exist to a significant degree. The apparitions categorized as hallucinations would not apply to mass visions such as the Zeitoun apparitions since independent observers can detect the perceived stimulus. As Carroll states in his book and as examined by Wolf (1969), the Islamic world does not suffer from a father ineffective-family complex (Carroll 1986, pp. 72–73). Since my study focuses on a Marian apparition which took place in the Islamic world, Carroll's approach is not likely to apply since many of the eyewitnesses at Zeitoun were of the Muslim faith. Second, Carroll applies the mechanism of Freud's analysis to those apparitions that fall into the category of hallucinations, i.e. that they stem from sexual tension or wish fulfilment. However, Carroll has not shown how Freud's theory on hallucinations could be applied to those experiencing so-called illusions, and I think that a theory (which explains the mechanism of the psychic or inner-world and which induces a so-called hallucination) should also be found in the case of illusions. What seems to define an illusion is the concomitant emergence of the four conditions mentioned earlier, but I think this explanation is too narrow because from this perspective, the illusion only occurs when triggered by the outer-world. Therefore, according to Carroll, individual seers who experience an apparition are influenced by psychic conditions while multiple seers experiencing an apparition are mostly influenced by external conditions. The question emerges about the robustness of such theory if applied to apparitions categorized as illusions. It seems that even if Carroll would have applied Freud's theory to interpret illusions, I think that sexual repression, or Freud's definition of the libido, is not the only type of excess energy to be discharged in an occurrence of a hallucination or illusion. As will be discussed in Chapter 2, Jung's concept of libido differs from Freud's in that it is psychic energy containing a spiritual or religious aspect; an aspect that may be more appropriate in investigating phenomena of a religious nature. Moreover, a Jungian perspective potentially avoids approaching apparitions as hallucinations, instead viewing them, following Jung, as a "vision", because the former "bears the stamp of a pathological concept, whereas a vision is a phenomenon that is by no means peculiar to pathological states" (Jung 1959, p. 1). At any rate, Carroll's approach seems to possibly apply, to a larger extent, to individual seers while his approach falls flat in his analysis of apparitions with multiple seers.

Against this background, and considering that mass visions of the Virgin Mary are likely to reflect multiple important aspects, I argue that a Jungian approach can offer valuable insights in the context of an interpretation of these events, based on the concept of the collective unconscious, expanded to recognize the culture and identity of a society (see Chapter 2), and complemented by an in-depth historical analysis from which the mass apparitions emerge.

## Conclusion

This first part of this chapter provides a historical overview of Marian apparitions over the centuries beginning with the first appearance of the Virgin Mary to St James presumably while Mary was still alive. Among other facts, it highlights the marked increase of reported Marian apparitions observed since the 1930s as well as some periods when a particularly high number of apparitions were reported (the 1930s, the 1950s, and the period from the mid-1980s to the mid-1990s). The latter fact suggests that a disturbance, possibly stemming from cultural and/or global distress, takes place around these periods characterized by peaks in the number of apparitions. Historically, a majority of reported Marian apparitions were not officially recognized by the Roman Catholic Church. Although it is likely the Christian churches on some occasions aligned with the apparition movement for their own political advantage by co-opting and orchestrating a religious movement against secular forces, there was a strong reluctance of Christian churches to recognize most apparitions if it contradicted canonical law.

The chapter concludes with a discussion of the main scholarly interpretations of Marian apparitions, the majority of which focuses on the sociopolitical and religious aspects of the phenomenon. Although such focus is arguably a necessary component in investigations of Marian apparitions, especially when involving mass visions, there is a lack of investigations addressing the psychological meaning behind the phenomenon in the literature; moreover, I think that the area of Mariology would be enriched if research focused on the psychological nature of these types of apparitions due, for instance, to their numinous symbolic nature. In this regards, to my knowledge, Carroll's (1986) work on the psychological origins of Marian apparitions is the only scholarly work available. Carroll applies Freudian principles to his analysis of the phenomenon, specifically the father-ineffective complex. While Carroll's work represents an interesting contribution to the literature on the cult of the Virgin Mary and Marian apparitions, I have highlighted some limitations of his approach to interpret Marian apparitions, particularly marked for the case of collective apparitions as was the Zeitoun case. Against this background, I propose a Jungian approach to the study of collective Marian apparitions, which in my opinion has the potential to provide useful insights along the way to interpret them from a depth-psychological perspective. More specifically, Jung's concept of the libido lends itself to investigate this phenomenon not to origins connected to repressed sexual energy, but psychic energy that may be related to a religious nature. In Chapter 2, I outline in detail the methodological approach that will be used to investigate the apparitions at Zeitoun in the present study.

## Notes

1 In Chapter 5, I argue with Warner that the Virgin Mary is a prototype of primal goddesses like Aphrodite and Cybele.

2 The World Apostolate of Fatima/Blue Army is a worldwide public association of the faithful, responding to the requests that Our Blessed Mother made to three shepherd children in Fatima, Portugal in 1917, to help save souls and bring peace to the world. www.wafusa.org/

Chapter 2

# A depth-psychological approach to the analysis of the collective visions

## Introduction

The Virgin Mary of Zeitoun, as it is often referred to, stands out among other Marian apparitions, like the famous ones in Lourdes and Fatima, in that the Virgin Mary was seen by thousands at a time during several apparitions over a period of two years. In Chapter 1, I present ways in which scholars, investigating Marian apparitions, have attempted to explain and interpret these phenomena from their respective fields, including from anthropological, historical, and political perspectives (Blackbourn 1993; Christian 1981; and Ventresca 2003). These investigations focus exclusively on the historical events surrounding the phenomenon without giving much consideration to the psychological workings that may be also underlying these events. Moreover, I argued that what are largely lacking in the field of Marian apparitions are explanations from a psychological perspective. Although there has been an attempt to analyse Marian apparitions from a psychological perspective (Carroll 1986), the Virgin Mary of Zeitoun has not been systematically and thoroughly researched, with at most marginal references in the literature. Collective Marian apparitions may be a topic marginally written on perhaps due to its intimidating supernatural content or the unwillingness to take seriously "occult phenomena".

The aim of this chapter is to offer a depth-psychological approach to investigating the mass visions of the Virgin Mary at Zeitoun. The methodology offered stems widely from the works of Jung and relies on theories of the psyche proposed by Jung and post-Jungians; specifically, I adopt a Jungian classical approach with a focus on Jung's later work on flying saucers.

The chapter begins by introducing Jung's contribution to studying these types of collective phenomena. Following a presentation of Jung's study of flying saucers and addressing weaknesses to his methodology, the approach imbedded in this study and its application to the study of collective visions is outlined. Lastly, I end the chapter with a discussion on the application, challenges, and limitations of psychoanalytic interpretations used as approaches to understand such phenomena within their respective historical contexts.

## An approach to understanding supernatural phenomena

Jung is known for introducing concepts such as the collective unconscious and archetypes, but his legacy also includes an openness to observing and understanding the occult, the mysterious, and the supernatural. This legacy, unfortunately, also includes the style and structure of Jung's writings which sometimes were mercurial in nature and difficult to follow. Moreover, the works of Jung appear to be characterized by a lack of a clear methodological structure usually found in modern scientific writings. In fact, criticisms have been advanced regarding the use of his source materials in that he was too impatient to trouble himself to adhere to high academic standards (Heisig 1979, p. 107). In Deirdre Bair's biography of Jung, she states that Jung insisted that he was an empiricist to the end of his life, instead of his work being based on case material, and therefore his writings often reflected something more philosophical than scientific (Bair 2003, p. 395). Jung, however, was convinced that "he had presented an adequate methodology that would protect his theories from the charge of philosophical naiveté and recommend them as scientifically sound" (Heisig 1979, p. 110). At the same time, it is difficult to extract a methodological approach from Jung's writings. According to Renos K. Papadopoulos (2006), this is due to him not clearly or specifically writing about his methodology (Papadopoulos 2006, p. 7). Moreover, Papadopoulos argues that Jung's methodology was "interwoven into the very fabric of his theories and his overall psychology" and that a special extraction procedure is required in order for it to be examined (Papadopoulos 2006, p. 7). Accordingly, as suggested by James W. Heisig (1979), one must approach Jung's writings patiently and slowly (Heisig 1979, p. 103), which might help in identifying the main elements of his methodology and reducing the risks of overlooking some aspects which are not fully explicit.

A very useful contribution extracting Jung's epistemology and methodology as well as illustrating his interest in the supernatural can be found in Papadopoulos's *The Handbook of Jungian Psychology* (2006). In the first chapter of this book, Papadopoulos pinpoints Jung's epistemological sensitivity by offering a few interesting examples that capture the development of Jung's approach, such as Jung's theory of complexes that emerge out of his work with the Word Association Test at the Burghlzöli and his analysis of James Joyce's novel *Ulysses*. However, more importantly and relevant to the study of supernatural phenomena was Jung's doctoral dissertation, entitled "On the Psychology and Pathology of the So-called Occult Phenomena" (1902). In this investigative undertaking, Jung observes the spiritualistic séances of a 15-year-old girl referred to with the initials S.W., later identified as Helene (Helly) Preiswerk, a cousin of Jung. Two features of particular interest for our discussion can be drawn from Papadopoulos's examination of this doctoral dissertation: 1) Jung

> attempted to look for the meaning behind the external formulations of verbalizations - the focus of his enquiry . . . was beyond the express language of the medium and on the meaning this language had for her, in her own specific circumstances and context;

and 2)

> Jung's interest was in the psychological meaning and implications of the fact that the medium believed she was communicating with spirits, and not whether the spirits existed.
>
> (Papadopoulos 2006, p. 18)

In the first feature, Jung did not accept Helene's alleged communications with spirits at face-value, but he sought the meaning that they had for her behind the language of the phenomena. Moreover, closely connected with the latter feature, Jung was not focused on the existence of the spiritualistic phenomenon itself, but rather on the medium's reaction to, and belief in, communicating with spirits. Further on, I will elaborate how these two features could be applied to seers of Marian visions.

The above-mentioned two features formed part of Jung's epistemological approach, argues Papadopoulos, and he continued to follow it "to investigate phenomena that could come under various headings, e.g., 'insanity', 'religion', 'politics', 'art', etc." (Papadopoulos 2006, p. 18). Another key feature of Jung's approach as identified by Papadopoulos in the doctoral dissertation is the "specific method of participant observation" (Papadopoulos 2006, p. 19). That is, Jung "always valued that knowledge was produced by experience and in the context of interaction with others" (Papadopoulos 2006, p. 19). Jung was aware that this was a key aspect of his approach, albeit he did not acknowledge it: "I have no method at all, when it comes to the individual case" and "all decisive moments in analysis have nothing to do with an intellectual method", but rather "originate in the indescribable human totality" (quoted in Bair 2003, pp. 382–383). However, the question emerges as to how a researcher can investigate a phenomenon that has already taken place and in which the researcher was not a "participant observer" like the séances of Helene or the encounter of two individuals in the consulting room? How did Jung investigate phenomena such as religion, politics, art, etc. and still gain insight? Jung says he has no method when it comes to the individual case, yet in a letter to a former patient he states:

> When I am speaking or writing about what I do, then I abstract from all my individual experience of what happens in analysis and I construct a method for the purpose of teaching.
>
> (quoted in Bair 2003, p. 382)

Jung believed his method, if he had to describe one, to consist of a "conceptual construction" which is "based on similar characteristics and patterns abstracted from individual patients and melded into a representative composite" (Bair 2003, p. 383). A similar approach to abstracting patterns and characteristics from patients to form representations could be found in Jung's later writing, *Flying Saucers* (1959) – an approach that I think may answer the above two questions, as I will discuss in the next section.

Jung was one of the pioneers in the analysis of the occult and the supernatural at a time when the field of psychoanalysis was establishing itself as a science. Inspired by the work of Théodore Flournoy's *From India to the Planet Mars* and modelling his dissertation on his work (Shamdasani 1998, p. 118), Jung's work paved the way by providing an approach to observe and examine supernatural phenomena by still maintaining scientific objectivity. In the following section, I introduce the methodological approach applied in the present study which includes key elements of Jung's epistemological approach to the study of the supernatural as summarized by Papadopoulos as well as incorporating several aspects of Jung's approach in *Flying Saucers* (1959).

## Jung's methodological approach in *Flying Saucers*

Jung's research on unidentified flying objects, or UFOs, in *Flying Saucers* (1959) provides a useful starting point to approaching the study of collective visions such as the Marian apparitions at Zeitoun. Jung's open-mindedness, and respect for complex phenomena like the supernatural left us with an approach, albeit skeletal and incomplete (see as follows), to research these types of phenomena. I adhere to Jung's epistemological approach as presented earlier, by following Jung's interest in the psychological meaning and implications of a phenomenon as well as the meaning behind the language of the phenomenon, such as the approach found in his study of séances as well as his study of flying saucers.

It is estimated that thousands of people witnessed the Marian apparitions at Zeitoun over a period of two years (Palmer 1969). Like the UFOs described in *Flying Saucers* (1959), the image of the Virgin Mary hovered over the dome at St Mary's Church in Zeitoun for many to see. The present study does not focus on the existence of the supernatural phenomenon itself, but on the contrary, my interest lies in the psychological meaning and implications of a phenomenon as well as the meaning behind the language of the phenomenon Accordingly, the material or primary sources used in this study are analysed only for this purpose. In *Flying Saucers* (1959) Jung examines the phenomenon of UFOs by analysing them in dreams, paintings, and as *visionary rumours*. Visionary rumours, as defined by Jung, differ from other rumours in that they are accompanied by a vision or collective vision and are kept alive by them (Jung 1959, p. 2). These rumours stem from an unusual emotion, while its "intensification into a vision and delusion of the senses, however, springs from a stronger excitation and therefore from a deeper source" (Jung 1959, p. 2). The most likely explanation, argues Jung, of a mass phenomenon like the UFO visions and Marian apparitions "lies in a psychic disturbance" (Jung 1959, p. 14). Subsequently, Jung argues that the "figures in a rumour can be subjected to the same principles of dream interpretation" by way of personal associations and then by way of mythical and cultural amplifications (Jung 1959, p. 15; Samuels, Shorter and Plaut 2007, p. 16). This technique was a hermeneutical approach originally developed for individuals in psychotherapy, defining the dream as "a *spontaneous self portrayal, in symbolic form, of the actual situation in the unconscious*" (Jung 1948d, para. 505, italics in original). Jung applied dream interpretation also to understand collective phenomena, and in this respect, I later discuss the challenges of adopting an individual lens to explain collective phenomena. He treated the contents and central statements of, for instance, the *visionary rumours* with the same principles that could be used in dream interpretation. According to this method, attention is drawn to the psychic aspect of the phenomenon and one reviews the contents of the rumour or its central statements (Jung 1959, p. 15); that is, one examines the description of the objects reportedly seen in the sky by eyewitnesses (e.g. different colours, spherical or disk-like shapes etc.). These round or disk-like figures are likened to what the unconscious produces in dreams, visions, etc. and they are to be regarded as *symbols* (Jung 1959, p. 14). These symbols represent visual forms which had not been thought of consciously, though they were present in the unconscious in invisible form until they went through the process of becoming conscious. The visible form or symbol expresses the meaning of the unconscious content, and, as Jung suggests, "the meaning has to be completed by amplificatory interpretation" (Jung 1959, p. 14). For example, in Jung's application of this method to interpret the round object aspect of the vision, he proposes an analogy with the symbol of totality or *mandala* or, as Jung has defined this image, the symbolic representation of the archetype of the *Self* (Jung 1959, pp. 15–16).

Gathering the central statement and contents from paintings, dreams, and the visionary rumours, Jung applies compensation theory to interpret the psychological meaning behind the UFO phenomenon. He offers the theory that the psyche is a self-regulating system working through a process of compensation according to which the unconscious aims to balance, adjust, and supplement any tendency towards one-sidedness arising from consciousness (Jung 1923a, para 693; Main 2004, p. 21; Samuels, Shorter and Plaut 2007, p. 32). Jung asserts that phenomena like visions and illusions occur when an individual is suffering from psychic dissociation; "that is, when there is a split between the conscious attitude and the unconscious contents opposed to it" (Jung 1959, p. 7). First, contents that are repressed, excluded, and inhibited by consciousness will gather in the unconscious, forming a counter-pole. Then, the counter-position of the unconscious inhibits the conscious position, and finally, once the repressed unconscious contents have gathered enough energy charge, they break into consciousness forming dreams, beliefs, illusions, visions, and so forth (Jung 1959, p. 7; Main 2004, p. 21; Samuels, Shorter and Plaut 2007, p. 32). The symbol associated with this mechanism is the bridge between the conscious and unconscious worlds, and if effective, the conscious mind will acknowledge and integrate it, putting an end to the division of opposites (Jung 1923a, paras. 825–827; Samuels, Shorter and Plaut 2007, p. 32). This implies that without the projection of a symbol the psyche is balanced, yet it is possible that "repressed unconscious contents" have not "gathered enough energy charge". The UFO or symbol, which Jung identifies as the representation of the "Self", is the central archetype that consistently appears in the examples presented in his paper (Jung 1959, p. 114). The archetype of the Self acts as the regulator of chaotic states, and it expresses "order, deliverance, salvation, and wholeness" (Jung 1959, p. 18). On the characteristics of the projected image, Jung argues,

> in contrast to its previous expressions, the archetype should now take the form of an object, a technological construction, in order to avoid the odiousness of a mythological personification. Anything that looks technological goes down without difficulty with modern man.
>
> (Jung 1959, p. 18)

To summarize, the function of compensation theory works accordingly: the UFO is a symbol which represents the archetype of the Self and it is the bridge between the conscious and unconscious worlds bringing balance to an otherwise chaotic state. Similarly, from such perspective Helene could be seen as using séances as a mechanism to deal with her developmental issues. Consequently, the séances had a teleological function for Helene in balancing her dichotomous personalities. Flying saucers, a modern-day representation of a saviour or intermediator, served as the symbol between consciousness and unconsciousness, the outer and inner worlds, and between world events and the collective anxiety.

What is central to Jung's argument in *Flying Saucers* is that events in the outer-world may be causing visionary rumours and UFO imagery in dreams and paintings. Jung states that the "basis for this kind of rumour is an *emotional tension* having its cause in a situation of collective distress or danger, or in a vital psychic need" and that this condition exists in so far as the world suffers from events like Russia's policies at that time, and its unpredictable consequences had put a strain (Jung 1959, p. 7, italics in original). The key factor seems to be represented by outer events and circumstances that seem to influence or play a role in the manifestations of UFOs in visionary rumours. Collective distress is also the emotional tension which dominates the dreamers and painters in Jung's cases. For example, in a dream reported by Jung, the dreamer admits that aspects of his dream are due to his "pre-occupation with the political future of Europe" and his fears of a coming World War in 1960–66 (Jung 1959, p. 59). Also, the painter of a plate reproduced in *Flying Saucers* (1959) admits that his painting depicts "the collapse of our civilization in chaos", and it expresses a deep-rooted and universal fear (Jung 1959, p. 83). This connection between the UFO phenomenon and collective distress runs throughout Jung's paper.

This leads us to another key aspect of Jung's methodological approach: connecting symbol to anxiety. In the present case, the symbol or image of the Virgin Mary may express the meaning of the unconscious content, and they may reflect the repressed contents and emotional tensions created by collective distress. Compensation theory is used as a way of establishing a connection between the conscious and unconscious. The visions represent the symbol; however, until its meaning is analyzed, the archetype is unknown.

I have presented a methodological approach extracted from Jung's *Flying Saucers* (1959). Aspects of this approach include subjecting figures in visionary rumours to the same principles of dream interpretation, using amplification to interpret the meaning of the figure, application of compensation theory, and identifying a link between a psychic need and outer-world or collective events which have created the emotional tension and anxiety. As mentioned earlier, I found this approach incomplete and in need of supplementation. Moreover, the challenges in applying analytical psychology to social phenomena need to be addressed. Next, I briefly address the weaknesses and challenges of the approach and introduce ways to strengthen the overall methodology.

## Methodological weaknesses and challenges in *Flying Saucers*

There are a few weaknesses in the methodological approach adopted in *Flying Saucers* (1959), primarily found in Chapter 1, "UFO as Rumours", which in my opinion need to be addressed before we proceed. First of all, there is a lack of references to primary sources. The description of UFO visions in Chapter 1 comes from reports, articles, documentary evidence, and American newspapers (Jung 1959, pp. 5–6, 8). However, Jung does not provide any direct referencing from seers of UFOs which he purportedly extracted from these reports or articles, except for an eyewitness called Mr Adamski who claimed to have flown to the moon in a UFO, though Jung questions the validity of this account (Jung 1959, p. 10). Applying a conceptual construction method (Papadopoulos 2006, p. 30), Jung extracted the common themes of the reports of UFO seers and analysed their symbolic representation against the background of the outer circumstances of that time. This leads us to the second weakness in Jung's approach: there are no direct statements or quotes from UFO seers describing their experiences that can lead a researcher to authenticate these accounts. Jung assumes that the reader will take his analysis at face-value. Lastly, and this is connected to the above-mentioned two weaknesses, Jung neglected to place eyewitness statements into their historical context; that is, he failed to juxtapose Russian policy, the threat of nuclear war, or overpopulation with a direct statement from the seer or seers. Instead, Jung tries to connect albeit loosely general historical themes to the symbol of the *Self* derived from unaccountable sources.

What is apparently lacking in the first chapter of *Flying Saucers* (1959) is a systematic approach to investigating this phenomenon which ensures that 1) the statements of eyewitness reports are well-documented and subject to verification, 2) the data and other type of sources of information used (e.g. eyewitness reports) provide a picture of the relevant aspects of the historical period in question, and 3) the historical period is not only clearly defined and described but is also aligned with the sources. The alignment and juxtaposition of points 1 and 2, I think, will provide a more tightly interwoven approach and perhaps draw a strong correlation between the two variables, strengthening Jung's theoretical argument.

In the chapter entitled "UFOs in Dreams", Jung compensates a lack of specific direct reports by actually subjecting seven dreams which included UFOs to the analytical method of dream interpretation. In this chapter, Jung does a better job juxtaposing the analysand's dream with his or her specific anxiety, not surprisingly, since dream interpretation is Jung's forte. Jung also applies this technique when he analyses paintings in the following chapter. Despite the fact that the dreams of the seven case histories are grounded on individuals' underlying anxieties, Jung also links these anxieties with the prevailing "breathless tempo of modern civilization" (Jung 1959, p. 43). The collective fear and anxiety that are gleaned from these vignettes are not grounded on a concrete or particular historical event like a famine, war, or genocide. Instead, these anxieties stem from transformations and changes of the age which could be very general and generic.

The challenges of applying individual psychological methods to social phenomena such as the approach used in *Flying Saucers* (1959) have been written on and debated.[1] A critique emerging from this debate relates to the issue of encroaching upon, instead of dialoguing with, other disciplines (Lu 2013, p. 387). Specifically, the issue rests on the "universalizing tendency" of the application of individual psychological methods to group phenomena; as Kevin Lu (2013) points out, it "provides a potentially monolithic interpretation of society and culture that does little to appreciate the specific and particular" (2013, p. 419). Lu provides Jung's "Wotan" as an example to illustrate his point, in relation to which he states that "Jung all too easily dismisses the economic, political, and even psychological factors converging to create National Socialism" (Lu 2013, p. 419). This is in line with the criticism presented earlier in the first chapter in *Flying Saucers* (1959). In order to address this point, the present work takes into account the socio-political and economic factors specific to this case, the usefulness of which is highlighted by adopting some aspects of a political science approach.[2]

At this junction, two concepts need to be addressed, the collective unconscious and the cultural unconscious. Jung defined the unconscious as a "psychological borderline concept, which covers all psychic contents and processes that are not conscious", and in the collective unconscious there are contents

> which do not originate in personal acquisitions but in the inherited possibility of psychic functioning in general, i.e., in the inherited structure of the brain. These are the mythological associations, the motifs and images that can spring up anew anytime anywhere, independently of historical tradition or migration
>
> (Jung 1923a, paras. 837 and 842)

As this study focuses on an event occurring within a specific and national historical context, it seems appropriate that the concept of *cultural unconscious* should be applied to this case. In his paper, "The Cultural Unconscious", Joseph Henderson defined the cultural unconscious as,

> an area of the historical memory that lies between the collective unconscious and the manifest pattern of the culture. It may include both these modalities, conscious and unconscious, but it has some kind of identity arising from the archetypes of the collective unconscious, which assists in the formation of myth and ritual.
>
> (Henderson 1990, p. 102)

Sam Kimbles (2003) places the location of the cultural unconscious between the personal and collective unconscious. Kimbles (2003) posits that the cultural unconscious "is a group level unconscious that is neither personal nor archetypal"; moreover, he says that since "the concept of the collective unconscious implies more homogeneity than the diversity we observe, it was necessary to posit a cultural level of the psyche" (Kimbles 2003, pp. 54–55). Thomas Singer (2016) defines the cultural complex as autonomous, and that it "[has] a life of their own in the psyche that is separate from the everyday ego of the individual or group" (Singer 2016, p. 7). Given this definition, the cultural complex as well as the cultural unconscious could be seen as a separate entity with its own set of psychological needs. Moreover, Thomas Singer and Sam Kimbles (2004) describe the cultural complex as "a synthetic idea" which draws from the tradition of analytical psychology "to build a new idea for the purpose of understanding the psychology of group conflict" (Singer and Kimbles 2004, p. 2). Though not a completely new idea to Henderson who had intuited the cultural aspect of the psyche in the late 1920s (Kimbles 2003, p. 53), to Jung the psyche had many levels to it and he was "keenly attuned to what [is] now called the cultural unconscious" (Singer and Kimbles 2004, p. 3). Moreover, the term "national consciousness" has been used by political scientists; for example, Benedict Anderson (1991) examines the origins of the "imagined communities" of nationality which were created out of capitalism and print technology (Anderson 1991, p. 46).

The analytical psychological concept of the cultural unconscious is a "work in progress"; Farhad Dala (1998) posits another layer of the psyche which he calls the "social unconscious" which includes the power relationships between discourses (Dala 1998, p. 212); subsequently, the layers of the unconscious become more nuanced as various groups are identified within a society such as the Christian Coptic minority in Egypt. In adopting the concept of the cultural unconscious, the nuances and differences of the cultural discourses within a society such as class and religion are considered as well as the shared imagination of communities within Egyptian culture.

## A Jungian approach to the study of mass visions of the Virgin Mary

There are three branches of Jungian analytical psychology identified and classified by Andrew Samuels (1985): archetypal, developmental, and classical. In contrast to the other branches of Jungian thought, the classical school focuses on symbolic transformation, and the interest is on approaching the numinous (Samuels 1985, p. 16). The developmental school focuses on the age-related development or psychological stages and valued transference and countertransference as the most important aspect (Hart 2008, p. 95; Samuels 1985, p. 16). Whereas in the classical school the "purpose of analysis is the individualization of the ego" in relation to the Self via the process of compensation, archetypal psychology "considers the purpose of analysis to be the 'relativization' of the ego by the imagination" (Adams 2008, pp. 112–113). A classical lens is better suited to approach this study due to Jung's work on the mass vision of UFOs. In my opinion, in *Flying Saucers* (1959) Jung provided a structure to analyse numinous objects such as the Zeitoun apparitions as constellated material which emerged out of the cultural unconscious. Moreover, the theory of compensation allows us to uncover or view an individual or collective's psychological state, and this function works to provide support, balance, and correction; in Chapter 6, I argue how the visions played a compensatory role. Applying the other approaches to the study of mass visions of the Virgin Mary may likely yield another interpretation due to their respective foci, especially the archetypal school, where the ego is "decentered", the theory of compensation is replaced, and the objective is no longer the integration of the psyche (Adams 2008, pp. 112–113).

The first step to approaching the study of the mass visions is the inclusion of a historical analysis surrounding the phenomenon, which I found to be lacking in *Flying Saucers* (1959), and what I deem an essential component of a thorough examination of the cultural phenomenology of Marian apparitions. I postulate that collective anxiety[3] may have stemmed from the Six-Day War of June 1967, and as is presented in Chapter 3, material specific to this time period is included in the historical analysis of this case. The presentation of the historical material is in line with the works of David Blackbourn (1993), William A. Christian Jr. (1973, 1981, and 1987) and Robert A. Ventresca (2003) – in their research on Marian apparitions in Germany, Spain, and Italy, respectively – they linked historical events through usage of such sources to collective anxiety. These particular studies do not address the psychological origins of the apparitions, but discussing the Marian apparition within its historical context is noteworthy, and it is an approach that this study may benefit from. For example, Blackbourn sourced the financial records from Marpingen, Germany to link economic instability to anxieties surrounding the events of the Marian apparitions. As presented in Chapter 3, the financial records of Egypt during the 1960s are also included in the historical analysis. This type of material provides a way to ground phenomenon like apparitions with tangible and concrete sources, and by including this component to supplement weaknesses to Jung's approach, we make a step in the direction of deriving a more general and comprehensive approach.

The next step in the approach is the examination of published eyewitness accounts. Chapter 4 introduces a database created to organize the number of eyewitness accounts and record the descriptions of the Zeitoun apparitions. I refer to this database as *case studies*. The case studies are based on data from 22 published eyewitness testimonies. While Jung analysed contents in dreams, paintings, and material from the concept labelled *visionary rumours*, the contents from published sources are extracted in the form of eyewitness testimonies as well as a survey of witnesses from the Zeitoun apparitions conducted in 1986. The case studies and 1986 survey assist in identifying the symbols and common themes of the Zeitoun phenomenon, and with this information the application of some of Jung's ideas from *Flying Saucers* (1959). An essential feature of the present study is represented by what people saw, this material being instrumental in uncovering the archetype or the meaning of the unconscious content, ergo extracting the descriptions of the apparition from the available data is vital. After extracting the main characteristics and descriptions of the UFOs given by testimonies and reports as well as from case studies from dreams and paintings, Jung proposes that the "aggregate", or the sum collection of the reports, is a representation of the Self or the archetype. The method Jung adopts to do this is "conceptual construction", as mentioned previously; that is, by collecting eyewitness reports and identifying the main themes surrounding the mass phenomenon.

In contrast to the dreams in Chapter 2 in *Flying Saucers*, which are presented as single-case histories with their own narrative and interpretation, the published materials for the present study will be researched using an approach similar to the *aggregating single-case research* method. With this method, several single-case studies are superimposed in order to discern a common pattern (Dreher 2000, pp. 54–56). This research tool is applied by Jung in his examination of "visionary rumours"; that is, he extracts the common themes and images from the various eyewitness testimonies. It should be noted that similar to the considerations of Jütteman's "qualitative-comparative procedure", the primary materials of this case are systematically compared to one another "for the purpose of investigating the origins of psychic, or psychically relevant . . . events, phenomena, conditions, or similar" (Dreher 2000, p. 57). Jung's "conceptual construction" approach and the *aggregating single-case research* method, according to these methods, may allow me to identify the symbol and to determine its symbolic representation or archetype.

Inclusion of quantitative and qualitative methods has been used by Michael P. Carroll (1986) in his research on the Mary cult in Southern Italy and Spain. Carroll (1986) utilizes quantitative methods to supplement historical as well as qualitative approaches. His qualitative data include in-depth analyses of eight Marian apparitions, of which, he argues, five fall into the category of hallucinations and three into the category of illusions (one of the latter is represented by the Zeitoun case). This approach allows Carroll to extract the pattern that is central to his concept of hallucinations: "the content of the apparition . . . appears to have been influenced by some of the idiosyncratic wishes and desires that characterize the particular seer" (Carroll 1986, p. 147). In contrast to the analysis of the hallucination types, when Carroll analyses Marian apparitions of the illusion type, he introduces a concatenation of factors instead of applying Freud's theory of the father ineffective-family complex. Carroll's approach is an interesting mixture of the quantitative and the qualitative methods; more precisely, he chooses a theoretical framework, employs a sampling method, as well as treats the Marian apparitions as case studies. The latter perspective not only provides the reader with a glimpse into the story behind the apparitions, but it also respects the narrative without trivializing or categorizing them into concepts or numbers.

These considerations provide an introduction to the next step in the approach of the present study, which involves identifying the narratives or explanations which emerge from the event. In Chapter 6, I identify three sets of explanation given by Egyptians and eyewitnesses of the Zeitoun apparitions. These sets of explanation represent the "analysand's" part of the story or interpretation of the vision (or dream or fantasy), and the patient's input is a crucial element to the analytical process because it assists the analyst in pinpointing the root of a neurosis or anxiety. For each set of explanations, an interpretation is offered based on the narrative and descriptions as well as its connection to the historical context. There are obvious limitations to this approach due to the challenges of working with published accounts (as explained later), and much is lost since the interaction between the analyst and analysand is missing. In this respect, the challenges in the application of individual psychology to social phenomena become evident.

In addition to analysing the three sets of explanation, I propose my interpretation of the Zeitoun phenomenon based on the primary sources and historical analysis. This additional element of interpretation allows the researcher to draw from the objective psyche, a "source of knowledge, insight, and imagination" (Samuels, Shorter and Plaut 2007, p. 100) similar to the way an analyst interprets the patient's dream; with the objective psyche a different perspective of the dream emerges apart from the dreamer, helping the patient to understand the meaning of the figures and symbols. The amplification method is applied to the extracted symbols and common themes from the database as the method of interpretation. In Chapter 5, I apply amplification to the symbols and common themes from the case studies and the 1986 survey. Amplification is also applied in Chapter 6 where I merge the interpreted material with the historical analysis. Jung used amplification as an interpretative tool, which is, as he said it,

> appropriate when dealing with some obscure experience which is so vaguely adumbrated that it must be enlarged and expanded by being set in a psychological context in order to be understood at all. That is why, in analytical psychology, we resort to amplification in the interpretation of dreams, for a dream is too slender a hint to be understood until it is enriched by the stuff of association and analogy and thus amplified to the point of intelligibility.
>
> (Jung 1937, para. 403)

In her book, *Interpretation of Fairy Tales* (1996), Marie-Louise von Franz lays out specific principles to approaching an interpretation of symbols found and illustrates this approach by using a Brother's Grimm story, "The Three Feathers". Von Franz stresses that "interpretation is an art or craft that can be learned only by practice and experience" and that some rules are needed as a guide in the interpretation process (von Franz 1996, p. 39). This form of discipline is deeply rooted in psychoanalysis and analytical psychology, the way being paved by Freud, Jung, and others, such that in the application process one may draw inspiration from their methods. However, the method of interpretation utilized by von Franz, which is clearly presented in her book, naturally lends itself to the study of the cultural unconscious. Fairy tales, like myths, are not the sole creation of individuals, but form part of a collective story of a particular group or culture.

Theories of the origin and meaning of myths have been put forth, and Robert A. Segal (1998) presents a discussion on the subject matter. However, Jung interprets myths as projections of the collective unconscious, and declares that myths are "the best medium for conveying the unconscious" (quoted in Segal 1998, pp. 6 and 11). In line with the same psychological explanation as Jung, von Franz states, "[i]n myths or legends, or any other more elaborate mythological material, we get at the basic patterns of the human psyche through an overlay of cultural material" (von Franz 1996, p. 1). According to von Franz's definition, amplification "*means enlarging through collecting a quantity of parallels*" (ibid., p. 43, italics in original). Von Franz stresses that the need for comparative material is "to know the comparative anatomy of all the symbols", and that the interpreter needs "*to know the average setup*" (ibid., p. 43, italics in original); von Franz's meaning of "comparative material" goes beyond using only fairy tales as a source for interpretation.

Once an understanding of the symbol is obtained via comparative material, the final and essential step is to interpret it using psychological language. As von Franz suggests, the task is to translate the amplified story into psychological language, and only then the interpretation is known (ibid., p. 44). Psychological interpretations of symbols are not absolute truths, but they offer explanations on what symbols and myths seem to represent (ibid., p. 45). Every archetype is an unknown psychic factor, but an archetypal image, von Franz states, "affords us the best clues to the understanding of the processes going on in the collective psyche" (von Franz 1996, p. 1). Archetypal images provide clues to understanding the collective thought buried underneath while at the same time surrounding a nation during a specific period of history.[4] In this sense, archetypal images could also act as a time-capsule waiting to be unearthed and reveal a foregone period or era. As Mircea Eliade states, "[i]mages, symbols, and myths are not irresponsible creations of the psyche; they respond to a need and fulfill a function, that of bringing to light the most hidden modalities of being" (Elide 1961, p. 12).

There have been several interpretations given to describe Jung's theory of the archetypes. George B. Hogenson (2004) argues that the reason for this is because, "*Jung did not have a theory of archetypes*" (Hogenson 2004, p. 33 italics in original). Hogenson elaborates further on this point and states that Jung "lacks a single, grounded, understanding of just what a theory of archetypes should entail" (Hogenson 2004, p. 40). There seems to be four categories of interpretations of archetypal theory: *biological and evolutionary*, *emergence*, *developmental*, and *imaginal*. Anthony Stevens's argument for an interpretation of archetypes as biological and evolutionary states "that the archetype corresponds to a genetically defined need that must be fulfilled to develop successfully" (Hogenson 2004, p. 40). Stevens argues that a complex arises when an innate need is in deficit (Hogenson 2004, p. 40). Also, the interpretation of Richard Gray (1996), I argue, can be seen as part of the biological and evolutionary category. Gray's interpretation stems from the idea of centration. As Gray states,

> They [the archetypes] approximate the activation of an instinct but are in practice much more diffuse. In the process of their expression, certain behavioral and affective elements are marshaled together to form an active archetypal center. Because the center partakes of the whole, one may never say that the archetype exists *per se*, but only that it exists as one of many centers of libidinal activity within the organism.
>
> (Gray 1996, p. 12)

When one sees the Self as the central archetype and whole system, then one sees the Self as moving towards "unfolding of the teleological self (the process of individuation)" (Gray 1996, p. 22). In both Stevens's and Gray's interpretations, whether the archetypal biological understanding is derivative of genetics as suggested by Stevens or compared to living organisms as suggested by Gray, the emphasis lies in the idea that the goal of the archetype is linked to development and evolution.

The second category, or the emergence perspective, originates from the work of George B. Hogenson, Peter Saunders, and Patricia Skar. Emergence is defined as "the notion that within certain kinds of systems, phenomena can come into being without any precursor state predicting the appearance of those phenomena" (Hogenson 2004, p. 45). This means that a phenomenon takes place when *new* properties appear unexpectedly in a system. Stevens's and Jean Knox's criticism of this theory is that the archetype-in-itself loses its place and location (Hogenson 2004, p. 46).

The developmental category of archetypal interpretations stems from the work of Jean Knox. Knox argues that much can be learned from cognitive science to enhance our understanding of archetypes. The template on which archetypal phenomena rests is "not quite *a priori*, but potentially prenatal, image schemas of developmental psychology" (Hogenson 2004, p. 46). Knox (2001) suggests the idea of image schema which is not innate but the formation of which is dependent upon innate mechanisms (Knox 2001, p. 629). Furthermore, Knox states, as quoted in Hogenson,

> The image schema would therefore seem to be a model that, for the first time, offers a developmentally sound description of the archetype-as-such and of the archetypal image. The abstract pattern itself, the image schema, is never experienced directly, but as a foundation or ground plan that can be likened to the concept of the archetype-as-such.
>
> (Hogenson 2004, p. 47)

In Knox's opinion, Jung may have viewed archetypes as having an innate predisposition with an organizing function (Knox 2001, p. 631).

Finally, according to the *imaginal* interpretation of archetypal theory, forwarded by James Hillman, "The *datum* with which archetypal psychology begins is the image" (Hogenson 2004, p. 45). Hillman suggests that archetypal psychology does not begin in the physiology of the brain, in language structure, the organization of society, or the analysis of behaviour, but instead begins in the process of imagination (Hogenson 2004, p. 45).

In *The Archetypes and the Collective Unconscious* (1936/37) Jung writes, that

> there exists a second psychic system of a collective, universal, and impersonal nature which is identical in all individuals. This collective unconscious does not develop individually but is inherited. It consists of pre-existent forms, the archetypes, which can only become conscious secondarily and which give definite form to certain psychic contents.
>
> (Jung 1936/37, para. 90)

Furthermore, Jung states that archetypes are closely analogous to instincts in that they are

> impersonal, universally distributed, hereditary factors of a dynamic or motivating character . . . are not vague and indefinite by nature, but are specifically formed motive forces which, long before there is any consciousness . . . pursue their inherent goals.
>
> (Jung 1936/37, para.91)

Like a neurosis of a personal nature, archetypes may also become constellated. Because archetypes have a dominating power, according to Jung, "it is not surprising that they are repressed with the most intense resistance. When repressed they do not hide behind any trifling thing but behind ideas and figures" (Jung 1954d, para. 130). Archetypes are altered when they become conscious and perceived and then take on their form from the individual consciousness (Jung 1954a, para. 6). As Jung states, "The archetype corresponding to the situation is activated and as a result those explosive and dangerous forces hidden in the archetype come into action, frequently with unpredictable consequences" (Jung 1936/37, para. 98). In summary, archetypes, residing in the collective unconscious, are dynamic patterns, primordial images that have a universal quality, are autonomous and "possess spontaneity and purposiveness, or a kind of consciousness and free will" (Jung 1958a, para. 557), and they become evoked, constellated, and activated (Edinger 1992).

How do we determine which specific archetype is constellated? The archetypal image points to clues, as already mentioned previously, to determine the unknown archetype constellated in the unconscious. As Jungian analyst Michael Vannoy Adams (2009) states,

> A concept is nondescript; it possesses no distinctive qualities. In contrast, the image possesses quite distinctive qualities that imply, with exquisite exactitude, an essence. It is in and through those distinctive qualities that it is possible accurately to ascertain what is essentially implicit in the image.
>
> (Adams 2009, p. 229)

In *On the Nature of the Psyche* (1954e), Jung stresses the "feeling-value" of the archetypes, and that

> [they] have, when they appear, a distinctly numinous character which can only be described as "spiritual", if "magical" is too strong a word. Consequently this phenomenon is of the utmost significance for the psychology of religion. In its effects it is anything but unambiguous. It can be healing or destructive, but never indifferent, provided of course that it has attained a certain degree of clarity. This aspect deserves the epithet "spiritual" above all else. It not infrequently happens that the archetype appears in the form of a *spirit* in dreams or fantasy products, or even comports itself like a ghost. There is a mystical aura about its numinosity, and it has a corresponding effect upon the emotions.
>
> (Jung 1954e, paras. 405 & 411, italics in original)

Examining the details and descriptions of the image analytically may determine the constellated archetype. In some cases, it may be unclear which archetype is constellated which is why Jung stressed the "feeling-value". The Virgin Mary dressed in blue is only one part of the analytical work; it is equally important, or more important, to look into the emotions surrounding the image as experienced by the dreamer, or in this case, the eyewitnesses. As discussed in Chapter 6, the visions of the Virgin Mary had been shown to be both a healing and a destructive force for many Egyptians.

Initially, I hypothesized that compensation theory was sufficient to interpret the Zeitoun phenomenon, but as I worked with the material and considered alternative interpretations, I came to the conclusion that applying other Jungian concepts would be beneficial to understand in more depth the phenomenon under study. Application of these concepts is in Chapter 6, while the amplification method is only applied in Chapter 5. One such concept which I felt would provide further insights in the analysis of the material is represented by the *religious function*, for example in the context of my analysis of the main features of the Egyptian government under Nasser which revealed its authoritarian nature. Jung's idea of religion should not be associated to religious dogma or creed, but rather to the experience of the *numinosum* from which the creed is originally derived (Jung 1938/40, para. 9). An experience of the *numinosum* seizes the individual independently of his will causing an alteration of consciousness (Jung 1938/40, para. 9).

Modernity and secularist forms of governance have left people living in these societies little time to reflect on the sacred. Lionel Corbett (1996) posits that "events of recent generations, such as genocide, environmental catastrophes and nuclear weapons, together with the advent of feminist thought, have forced us to abandon the traditional anthropomorphic images of the divine as an invisible Superior Being" (Corbett 1996, p. 2). Despite the rational spirit of our times, the "divine manifests itself to individuals in unique ways" (Corbett 1996, p. 1), and in Corbett's book *The Religious Function of the Psyche* (1996) he documents the ways in which the religious experience presents itself in the psychotherapeutic session.

The religious and numinous experiences arise from the autonomous level of the psyche (Corbett 1996, p. 8) and include experiences which could be destructive. Jung viewed the unconscious from a teleological point of view; that is, rather than being associated to causes, it is oriented to ends and purposes, a view which, Jung posited, existed in life and energy (Samuels, Shorter and Plaut 2007, p. 150; Jung 1934, para. 798). Suffering and depression were viewed by Jung as the damming up of energy, and when released it takes on a positive direction (Samuels 1993, pp. 73–74).

Adopting the concept of the teleology of the unconscious or in this case, the cultural unconscious, I am compelled to inquire the meaning behind the symbols such as the doves, tree, cross, and more importantly, the Virgin Mary and ask, "What for?" What are these symbols trying to convey? What is their purpose? Religion seems to have been a major theme in the Zeitoun narrative which prompted me to explore the connection between religion and the psychological.

The final aspect of my interpretation introduces the concept of the *coniunctio oppositorum*. Jung viewed the *coniunctio* as the symbol of psychic functioning, and he states,

> a union of opposites is performed under the likeness of a union of male and female (called the *coniugium, matrimonium, coniunctio, coitus*) follow by the death of the product of the union (*mortification, calcinatio, putrefaction*) and a corresponding *nigredo*. From this washing (*ablutio, baptisma*) either leads direct to the whitening (*albedo*), or else the soul (*anima*) released at the 'death' is reunited with the dead body and brings about a resurrection.
>
> (Jung 1952d, para. 334, italics in original)

## Using published texts as case studies

There are two specific points regarding the case material that need to be addressed: 1) the researcher was not a "participant observer" of the case material; and 2) the reflections of most eyewitnesses are not reported. Useful insights on how to deal with situations relating to the first point can be derived from the work of Lawrence R. Alschuler (2006) and his unique application of depth-psychology to social and political questions using the "case history" method. In *The Psychopolitics of Liberation*, Alschuler investigates the political consciousness of oppressed peoples by analysing four personal testimonies of people who had lived under oppression and achieved "liberated consciousness" and "psycho-political healing". Alschuler uses data from published personal testimonies as his case studies, which differ from "clients on the couch" analysis because, he says, he could neither incorporate the client's reactions to his interpretations nor communicate with them (Alschuler 2006, p. 85). Though the analysis of written texts is less reliable than face-to-face communication, admits Alschuler, the way was paved by Jungians following the example writings of Jung's *Symbols of Transformation*, where Frank Miller was unknown to Jung and whose fantasies where published by Théodore Flournoy, as well as Marie-Louise von Franz's analysis of Apuleius in *A Psychological Interpretation of The Golden Ass of Apuleius* and other present-day analysts who support the "appropriateness of using published documents as case studies" (Alschuler 2006, pp. 85–86). In this respect, it is also worthwhile to mention the proposal of Jung, from *Psychology and Alchemy* (1936, "to adopt the method we would use in deciphering a fragmentary text or one containing unknown words: we examine the text", following which he approached a series of dreams, which were not recalled under his observation, as if he were the dreamer himself (Jung 1952e, para 48–51).

## Subjectivity and depth-psychology

In their studies of the history of witchcraft, Lyndal Roper (1994) and Robin Briggs (1996) applied psychoanalytic thought to understand how witchcraft developed in early modern European societies. As their primary source, both Roper and Briggs used interrogations and confessions at the witch trials, focusing mainly, but not exclusively, on the village of Augsburg and the region of Lorraine respectively. By investigating the witch-hunt at the local level based on records of persecution and information on the main features of the judiciary system, a better sense of the relationship at the level of higher authority or whole society in which the accusations of witchcraft took place is attained, argues Briggs, as well as making it easier to generalize across much of Europe (Briggs 1996, p. 10). As Briggs states, "Lorraine material fits remarkably well with the vast majority of detailed studies on the other regions, so that one is recognizably dealing with very similar phenomena" (Briggs 1996, p. 11). This approach differs from Roper in that her study centres on 16th century German culture. Still, since Roper utilizes sources from towns and villages around Augsburg to draw out differences and similarities characterizing her main study in comparison to other ones, the approaches of Roper and Briggs are similar though differing in geographical range.

Roper and Briggs reached different conclusions about how witchcraft developed in early modern Europe. From the Augsburg material, Roper draws out how women borrowed stereotypical witchcraft images to deal with their own psychic conflicts which centred on motherhood (Roper 1994, p. 271). Briggs, on the other hand, offers a "wide range of analyses and explanations" for his investigations on the European witchcraft phenomenon. Although he does not provide a single clear explanation, one of Briggs's arguments is that the phenomenon of witchcraft was culturally constructed; that is, witchcraft "was about envy, ill-will, and the power to harm others, exercised in small face-to-face communities" (Briggs 1996, p. 398). From a psychological perspective, Briggs argues that the propensity to detect witches tended to increase and was more frequent especially during periods of conflict, hostility, and stress, and this was usually coupled with splitting and projection (Briggs 1996, p. 393). In an investigation of the demonic possessions at Loudun in the 1630s, Craig Stephenson (2009) presents an analytical psychology perspective on the phenomenon connecting the possessions with collective factors. The demonological neurosis of the possessed infected others in her convent, polarized the town, and as Stephenson states, "drew crowds from across Europe because her possession articulated both a personal repressed conflict and a collective dilemma in which the collective unconscious was active" (Stephenson 2009, p. 32).

An interesting aspect of Roper's and Briggs's works is that both authors address the issue of the historical account of subjectivity and the criticisms of the application of psychoanalytic theory in studying pre-modern societies. For historians, states Roper, "the concept of subjectivity with which we are presented is often a determinedly collective one. This collective subjectivity is then inscribed on the individual. Consequently, the dimension of the psychic is missing here" (Roper 1994, p. 9). This approach, according to Roper, has evolved a little with the influence of the works of Max Weber, Norbert Elias, and Michel Foucault by connecting social transformations with the individual; however, the "conviction that psychoanalyses could not therefore have anything to say about a pre-Freudian world has been very strong in early modern history" (Roper 1994, pp. 10–11). One of the historians who have taken such a stance is Stephen Greenblatt (1990). Essentially, Greenblatt argues that the concept of the self is the creation of psychoanalysis which was foreign to Renaissance culture, and therefore psychoanalysis attests to the distance that separates early moderns from our understanding of the self (Roper 1994, p. 11; Briggs 1996, p. 374).

By contrast, Roper and Briggs argue that psychoanalytic interpretations could be used as an approach to understand early modern people, "which does more than treat them as colourful p[sy]chic primitives from a carnival world; which takes individual subjectivity seriously" (Roper 1994, p. 12); and as Briggs questions, "how far have familial and peer group pressures at this stage really changed?" (Briggs 1996, p. 374). Based on their archival work, I agree with Roper and Briggs that pre-modern people had conflicts that are very familiar to modern people, as pre-modern people were not, as a whole, just driven by sensory perception and instincts, and, most importantly, that the irrational and fantasy exist now in individuals as they did then. At any rate, Roper and Briggs investigated subjects from the 16th century when discussing the question of whether historians could use psychoanalysis to study early modern societies, whereas my study investigates 20th century mentalities, making questions about the applicability of psychoanalytic and depth-psychological interpretations less pressing. In fact, 1960s Egyptian society was an interesting mix of worldviews, including both religious and secular. For example, one sociologist from an Egyptian university was disturbed by the number of intellectuals who witnessed the apparitions: it might have been understandable "if such a thing had occurred in Upper Egypt, where it is known that the peasants are great believers in supernatural phenomena like this – but physicians, scientists, and professors – *these people are more rational*!" (Nelson 1973, p. 11, italics in original). Moreover, as Cynthia Nelson (1973), a social scientist teaching in Cairo and a prime investigator of the apparitions while they were in progress, noted in the context of her observations of the Zeitoun phenomenon,

> The most important issue to grasp here is that the apparition of the Virgin symbolizes the conditions of modern pluralism in Egyptian society. By pluralism I mean a situation in which there is more than one worldview available to the members of society, a situation in which there is competition between worldviews.
>
> (Nelson 1973, p. 11)

This pluralist society was fostered by Egyptian politics, and in particular, Egyptian President Nasser's vision of a Pan-Arabic region, rather than an Islamist vision, and his push for a separation of religious ideals in political structures. This, however, was a policy that would change, ex-post the Zeitoun apparitions.

The data show that people from diverse backgrounds witnessed the Zeitoun apparitions, intellectuals and peasants, young and old, Muslims and Christians, Egyptians and foreigners. Finally, many people who witnessed the Marian apparitions are still alive today, ergo the conviction of the need of the death of the subject to guarantee historicity should not be relevant for the case under study as the period under consideration would fall under the category of contemporary history.

## Conclusion

This chapter began with an introduction to Jung's epistemological approach and contribution to the study of spiritualistic, supernatural, and collective phenomena. Jung not only approached this topic late in his life, but, as discussed, this undertaking stems from early in his professional career. Jung's interest and focus in investigating the psychological meaning behind a phenomenon was as present in 1902 (when he wrote his doctoral dissertation) as it was in 1959. By 1959, Jung had already developed key concepts and theories such as the archetypes, the collective unconscious, and compensation theory which, I think, help yield a better understanding of the UFO phenomena, without, at the same time, neglecting its supernatural aspects. Given Jung's documented openness to investigating such phenomenon, I argue that a Jungian hermeneutic can be a very useful approach to use to study apparitions of the Virgin Mary, for example by applying the amplification method to extracted symbols and common themes from eyewitnesses via a database. Specifically, I adopt and incorporate aspects of Jung's approach to studying UFOs in *Flying Saucers*, while at the same time, pointing out what are, in my opinion, the weaknesses found in his paper. I lay out ways to overcome these weaknesses with the hope of expanding on the existing theoretical approach and introducing a method in investigating mass visions of the Virgin Mary within their historical context. The chapter ends with a brief discussion on criticisms of the application of psychological principles to historical apparitions, specifically in early modern societies, and point out why these objections do not apply to the case under study, given the 20th century mentalities of the people involved.

## Notes

1 See Kevin Lu's (2013) "*Can individual psychology explain social phenomena? An appraisal of the theory of cultural complexes*" for a comprehensive critical analysis on this topic.

2 I adopt aspects of structuralism and rational choice theory: Joel S. Migdal (2001) argues that social scientists need a method "that looks carefully at its different parts (just as anthropology often focuses on small portions of the society)" (Migdal 2001, p. 116). Seyyed Vali Reza Nasr (2001) used rational choice theory to determine the motives of state actors to consolidate democracy under the guise of Islamization. In the final analysis of this case (see Chapter 6), the two approaches allow for an evaluation of Egyptian society, for example, the various interests within Egyptian society and Nasser as a state actor/leader.

3 The term "collective anxiety" will be used to denote anxiety stemming from a large group which may or may not be attributed to a specific cultural group.

4 Marie-Louise von Franz discusses Adolf Bastian's theory of "elementary thoughts", according to which one never sees the elementary thought but national thoughts point to their existence. Von Franz's critique of Bastian's theory is that archetypes are not only "elementary thoughts", but also elementary emotions (von Franz 1996, p. 8).

# Chapter 3

# Historical events surrounding the apparitions

## Introduction

This chapter is divided into two main parts. After presenting a short overview of the history of Marian apparitions throughout the centuries in the previous chapter, the first part of the present chapter provides an introduction to the Marian apparitions of Zeitoun. Here, the narrative of the Zeitoun apparitions is presented as eyewitnesses and bystanders experienced the Marian phenomenon, based on the existing literature of this event which I have been able to access. The second part of the chapter provides a discussion of key aspects of Egyptian life prior to and during the apparitions at Zeitoun. Specifically, it focuses on the period of Egyptian history under President Nasser between the early 1960s until his death in 1970. Various aspects of Egyptian society will be addressed, particularly key political and ideological decisions taken by the government of President Nasser, its economic policy and stability, the June 1967 War and its impact on Egyptian society, and finally, the social unrest which ensued post-1967 War.

## Zeitoun apparitions: an introduction

### *Descriptions and accounts of the Zeitoun apparitions*

Most reported cases of the visions of the Virgin Mary involved an individual seer or a small group of visionaries. What is interesting about this case is that thousands of people claimed to have seen the apparition of the Virgin Mary. However, there have been other cases of mass visions of the Virgin Mary involving thousands of seers.[1] What is extraordinary is that recent mass apparitions of the Virgin Mary have taken place in Egypt which seem to be close in nature to the Zeitoun phenomenon in terms of the Virgin's form and appearance: Shoubra (1986), Our Lady of Assiut (2000), and Warraq-al Hadar (2009). The apparition at Zeitoun was the first of these modern-era Egyptian apparitions. Although the present study does not investigate these more recent Egyptian apparitions, what makes the case of the late 1960s

Zeitoun apparitions fascinating is, in my opinion, the international historical factors surrounding the event, such as the June 1967 War, as well as the fact that the Zeitoun apparitions anticipated these other more recent ones, thereby representing a type of model or prototype. Moreover, the Virgin Mary of Zeitoun falls under the "legendary" category in that it is connected with a 40-year-old legend (see Chapter 6, which also provides a psychoanalytic interpretation of these events).

The Virgin Mary appeared for the first time on top of the Coptic Orthodox Church of St Mary's in Zeitoun, Egypt on April 2, 1968 at 8:30 p.m. (Johnston 1980, p. 3). Opposite the church of St Mary was a city garage. Two mechanics of Muslim faith had finished their shift and, as they were leaving the garage, one of the men, Farouk Mohammed Atwa, pointed up with his finger towards the church of St Mary and cried out, "Lady, don't jump! Don't jump!" (Johnston 1980, p. 4). As this man later reported, he saw

> a figure dressed in white on top of the dome of the Church. I thought she was going to commit suicide and shouted to her to be careful. My friend called the police and I woke up the doorkeeper. He comes out and cries 'It is the Virgin' and runs to call the priest.
>
> (Nelson 1973, p. 5)

Along with the two workmen were "several women pedestrians in the lamplit street" who also noticed the woman on top of the church, and when she "rose to her feet revealing herself as a luminous being dressed in shimmering robes of light" one of the women cried out, "'*Settena Mar iam!' (Our lady Mary!)*" (Johnston 1980, p. 4). Then, suddenly, glowing white doves appeared out of nowhere and hovered round the luminous figure (Johnston 1980, p. 4). The apparition remained for several minutes and slowly faded away.

The next apparition took place exactly one week later and from then on similar apparitions were repeated regularly, always taking place at night (Johnston 1980, p. 4). As the news spread of the apparitions of the Virgin Mary, people from throughout Egypt would come to get a glimpse of the Virgin. The crowds numbered 1–2000 the first two weeks following the first apparition. Cynthia Nelson (1973), a professor at the American University in Cairo, was teaching in Egypt at the time of the first apparition. After hearing about the apparition from students, Nelson went to Zeitoun and interviewed some of the people in the crowd. Nelson's field notes are an invaluable contribution to the study of this phenomenon because they capture the mood of Egyptians at that time as well as the emotional intensity of the crowds during the apparitions, witnessed by the author herself. One of Nelson's eyewitnesses was a Coptic woman in her fifties who was at the site of the apparitions along with her two teenage daughters. The woman reported seeing the *ma'amur* or police chief who was attempting to disperse the crowds because he thought the apparition was a reflection from the street lights. The police began to break the lights, and as reported by the eyewitness,

> [t]he light of the dome remained, and the vision of the Virgin became even clearer. The *ma'amur* became frightened and said that he wanted nothing more to do with this; while others came closer to be sure of what they saw.
>
> (Nelson 1973, p. 5)

The crowds were very diverse. They represented people from the countryside as well as urban areas, from the middle and upper classes to the working class, from local Muslims and Christians to foreigners, and from believers to nonbelievers (Nelson 1973, p. 6; Johnston 1980, p. 5). The duration of the apparitions was unpredictable, but when the apparition took place it would normally begin between the hours of 9 p.m. to 5 a.m. (Nelson, p. 6; Johnston, p. 5; DeVicenzo, p. 7). In the beginning, the apparitions of the Virgin Mary would take place almost every night, but as time went by they began to decrease to two to three times per week. Often the apparitions would be perceived for a few minutes throughout the night. However, on the nights May 4–5 and June 8–9, the Virgin Mary remained visible continuously through the night (Johnston, p. 5; Palmer, p. 15). This gave people in the crowds enough time to hurry home and return with friends and family members.

By the end of April 1968, the crowds had increased to an estimated 250,000 nightly (Johnston, p. 5). After authorities had made a 15-mile radius search of any sign of the apparition being a hoax, they ordered the garage (which covered a block next to the south side of the church) to be removed to accommodate the large crowds as well as removing the trees around the church so that people could not climb on them (Zaki, p. 22). There were many people who witnessed the event and were keen to provide detailed descriptions of the apparition (Palmer 1969, p. 15). According to the booklet *Our Lady Returns to Egypt* by Jerome Palmer (1969), the Coptic religious weekly *Watani* had "carried from the beginning of the apparitions a spread of two pages each week describing the phenomena at Zeitoun" (Palmer, p. 15). The weekly Watani represents one of the sources from which Palmer has collected his testimonial accounts, complemented by other sources found with the assistance of Father Joseph Mazloum, editor of *Le Mesager*, a Catholic newspaper in Cairo (Palmer 1969, pp. 15–16).

Palmer obtained eyewitness accounts from bishops and priests in addition to ordinary Egyptians. One of the accounts was taken from Bishop Gregorius, prelate for Higher Studies, Coptic Culture, and Scientific Research. Bishop Gregorius said that before the apparitions actually took place, some birds which resembled pigeons appeared and took on different formations.

Sometimes these birds were seen flying eastward and at other times towards the west, and at times they would suddenly disappear. Bishop Gregorius remembers observing the birds on June 9, 1968, the birthday of the Virgin Mary according to the Coptic calendar, as he reported to Palmer,

> I saw two pigeons very white, very bright, luminous, radiating light. I was determined to watch them. They became tiny flakes of cloud and seemed to enter heaven. They did not flap their wings; they glide. In a flash they appeared; and disappeared the same way. . . . Whatever formation they take, they keep. Sometimes as many as seven of them fly in the formation of a cross.
>
> (Palmer 1969, pp. 25–26)

Another Bishop, Athanasius, saw the apparition of the Virgin Mary, having been sent personally by Coptic Pope Kyrillos to prepare a detailed report. Bishop Athanasius visited the church on April 29 and 30, 1968. Upon arrival at 11 p.m., he first sees a silhouette, not very bright in colour. It lasted 20 minutes and then disappeared. He told the people around him that he could not report what he had seen. However, at dawn, the companions he was with said to him, "The Lady is over the middle dome". Bishop Athanasius also witnessed seeing bright pigeons flying quickly over him as well as being able to see the eyes and mouth of the apparition (Palmer 1969, p. 22).

Mr Wadie Tadros Shumbo, a Protestant and employee at the Mobil Oil Company, also experienced seeing the apparition along with his wife. At first, they did not see anything, but after returning back to Zeitoun several times their persistence paid off. As Mr Shumbo reports,

> At about 9:50 we saw lightning over the church, much stronger than one could make with a flashlight. I had a feeling that something was about to happen. A thin line or edge of light appeared like the light you see when you open the door to a lighted room. Within seconds it formed itself into the shape of the Virgin. I could not speak. All who were with me said, 'It is impossible!' The Moslems all started to cry. This sight lasted for five minutes, when the figure rose and vanished. I could distinguish only a difference in color between the skin in the face and hands. It was evident when St Mary walked back and forth. When she disappeared from our side of the church, the people from the other side shouted they were seeing her. Then she returned to our side for five minutes.
>
> (Palmer 1969, p. 33)

Mr Shumbo also includes in his account having seen six or seven pigeons flying over the church.

### *Official reports*

The Coptic Church's Commission of Bishops and the Egyptian Government's Department of General Information and Complaints conducted two official investigative reports on the Zeitoun apparitions (DeVincenzo 1988, p. 4). For this purpose, the Commission of Bishops formed a committee of Coptic clergymen, which were appointed by Pope Kyrillos VI (Johnston 1980, p. 11). The members of the committee of clergymen personally went to the church site to witness the apparition as well as to interview eyewitnesses. In their report, they claimed to have gotten in touch with the garage workmen who first perceived the initial apparition and who confirmed to them that they had seen the apparition of the Virgin Mary. The committee also reported that several people from throughout the country claimed to had seen the Blessed Virgin, attaching in the report written testimonies by those who saw the apparition certifying "the certainty of the appearances" (Johnston 1980, p. 11). The committee of clergymen then remained near the apparition site, specifically staying across the domes until, after a few nights, she finally appeared. This report was submitted to Pope Kyrillos VI on May 5, 1968. An official statement from Pope Kyrillos VI followed that same day. This official statement is well-documented as well as being easily available to obtain. It was reported by six Egyptian newspapers (Al-Ahram, Al Goumhouryia, Al-Akhbar, Wantani, The Egyptian Gazette, and Progres Dimanche) as well as a few overseas newspapers, such as The New York Times, Le Figaro of Paris, and The Times (Johnston 1980, p. 12). In this statement, Pope Kyrillos VI declared "with full faith and great joy and humility of a thankful heart, that the Holy Virgin Mary, Mother of Light, appeared in clear forms on many different nights" (Johnston 1980, pp. 12–13; zeitun-eg.org).

In addition to the Coptic Church's official investigative report, a governmental report was conducted by the Egyptian Government's Department of General Information and Complaints (Johnston, p. 14; Brady 1968; Watani 1968; DeVincenzo 1988, pp. 3–4; Nelson 1973, p. 7). Palmer (1969) reported that the Director of the General Information and Complaints Department submitted a documental report to the Minister, Mr Hafez Ghanem (Palmer 1969, p. 42). Quoting from this investigative report, Palmer (1969) says, "The investigations have proved twenty-seven appearances (to that date) of the Blessed Virgin in various luminous forms. At certain times mysterious doves either preceded, accompanied, or followed the apparitions" (Palmer 1969, p. 42). The following quote slightly differs from quotes reported in DeVincenzo (1988), Johnston (1980), and as posted on zeitun-eg.org, a website dedicated to spreading the message of the Virgin of Zeitoun:

> The official investigations have been carried out with the result that it had been considered an undeniable fact that the Blessed Virgin Mary has

> been appearing at the Coptic Orthodox Church at Zeitoun in a clear and bright luminous body, seen by all present in front of the church, whether Christian or Moslem.
>
> (DeVincenzo 1988, p. 8; Johnston 1980, p. 14; zeitun-eg.org)

Whether these quotes are from the same Egyptian investigative report still remains unclear.[2] An Egyptian daily newspaper reported that a committee was ordered to collect all documents on the Zeitoun apparitions. This committee included the Governor of Cairo, Colonel Saad Zayed, the Director of Internal Security, Mahmoud el Sebai, as well as a number of engineers and some authorities of the Church (Al Ahram 1968).

### *Photos/videos*

In addition to investigative reports conducted by the Coptic Church and the Egyptian government, there are many photographs that were taken by eyewitnesses. One of these photographs which came from Mr Wagih Rizk, a professional photographer from Cairo, Egypt and who took several photographs of the apparition of the Virgin Mary, was published by the Al-Ahram Egyptian daily newspaper (Al-Ahram 1968). Beneath Mr Wagih Rizk's photograph it read, "The photography department at Al-Ahram has inspected the original film and found no traces of photo-montage" (Al-Ahram 1968). Also, in a U.S. documentary film on the apparition of Zeitoun, Dr John Jackson – physicist and author of "Our Lady of Light Comes to Egypt", claims to have examined several photos and verified them as authentic. In this short film, Jackson states, "What you look for in a scientific evaluation of these photographs are internal consistencies or inconsistencies. I spent a lot of time studying those photographs and I can't see any inconsistencies" (www.stmaryztn.org). Despite verification of the authenticity of apparition photos taken at Zeitoun, sceptics of the Zeitoun apparitions argue that Marian observers, predisposed by religious background and social expectation, were interpreting "light displays" stemming from seismic activity in the region from 1958 to 1979 with "an unprecedented peak in earthquakes during 1969" (Bartholomew and Goode 2000, p. 7). Neuropsychologist Michael Persinger and John Derr, who analyzed this seismic activity stated, "The narrow window of significant temporal relationship between luminous phenomena and earthquakes is within the classic time frame of more acceptable antecedents (e.g., microseismic activity) of imminent earthquake activity" (quoted in Bartholomew and Goode 2000, p. 7). These considerations aim at providing a *physical* explanation for the visions seen at Zeitoun; however, the aim of this study is to gain a psychological understanding of the phenomenon and not to explore whether the visions were "real".

## Egypt under Nasser

### *Nasser, Pan-Arabism, and his social contract*

The apparitions at Zeitoun became such a major point of interest and discussion that many Egyptians showed more excitement over the Zeitoun phenomenon than the government's plans toward liberalization policies (Nelson 1973, p. 8). In fact, the Zeitoun phenomenon came to change Egyptian society in the late 1960s and early 1970s, as later argued in Chapter 6. Before discussing how this phenomenon affected Egyptian society, it is necessary to look into the major social and political events which may have contributed to collective anxiety experienced by Egyptians, in particular, prior to the Zeitoun apparitions.

President Gamal Abd al-Nasir, known to many as Nasser, came into power shortly after July 1952, when the "Free Officers", a conspiratorial cabal within the Egyptian army, deposed and exiled King Faruq (Goldschmidt 2004, p. 109). Nasser was the leader of the Free Officers, and his rule was a dictatorship that spanned from 1954 until his death in September 1970. The old regime was accused of being incompetent and by 1952 it was widely felt that

> the landowning elite had become a burden to the peasants, the urban poor suffered from unemployment and low wages, and the foreign businesspeople and technocrats constituted a barrier to the advancement of educated young Egyptians. The level of frustration had become intolerable. The revolution was, if anything, overdue.
>
> (Goldschmidt 2004, p. 108)

Initially in favour of a democracy, two years into office Nasser had full executive control (Goldschmidt 2004, p. 109). Certain political events led Nasser to centralize power in order to maintain full control of Egypt and many spheres of Egyptian society. As argued in the second part of this chapter, some of Nasser's decision-making policies, which includes the centralization of power, may have affected how Egyptians were later to perceive and interpret the visions of the Virgin Mary at Zeitoun.

During the initial months after the July 1952 military coup against the Egyptian King Faruq, the Free Officers did not have a "policy except of opposition to imperialism" (Jillani 1991, p. 77). One of the key aspects of the historical period which was influential in the Zeitoun phenomenon was the ideology of Pan-Arabism popularized by Nasser, becoming a keystone to Nasser's legacy. While Pan-Arabism was an ideology that pre-dated Nasser's rule, Nasser embraced and even championed it. This ideology influenced how Nasser would lead Egypt during the 1950s and 1960s; indeed, these two decades were widely regarded by observers as the era during which secular nationalism was the predominant force in politics in the Middle East, in contrast to the decreasing influence of Islam (Warburg 1982, p. 132).

When Nasser and the Free Officers came to power, the initial aim was to crush imperialism from within Egypt by ending feudalism, establishing social justice, and creating a strong national army (Jillani 1991, p. 77). As time passed, the state ideology focused on Arab unity, specifically Pan-Arabism. One definition of Pan-Arabism is that there exists a connection between Egyptians and their Arab brothers and as long as they had a shared language and shared cultural ties they were united as one (Coury 1982, p. 459). This ideology was evoked in Nasser's speeches (elected prime minister, he became president in 1956 until his death in 1970) shortly after the coup. For example, as he stated in a 1957 speech, "Arab nationalism is a weapon for every Arab state. Arab nationalism is a weapon employed against aggression. It is necessary for the aggressor to know that, if he aggresses against any Arab country, he will endanger his interests" (Danielson 2007, pp. 25–26). Popular Islam was deeply rooted in the country at the time, especially in rural areas, and despite Nasser's natural oratorical ability, he needed more than speeches to get Egyptians behind the idea of Pan-Arabism, which at that time was viewed with caution and even hostility (Jillani 1991, p. 77). In addition to this, Nasser and his regime needed to gain political legitimacy at home as their rise to power was via a military coup and not via a populist revolution. It was after the Nasser regime achieved several political wins that the ideology of Pan-Arabism slowly gained legitimacy – such as the Egyptian-Syrian alliance or military pact in March 1955, the nationalization of the Suez Canal company, and the October 1956 war; in the latter, although Egypt lost the war, it was a political victory for Egypt in that it remained in control of the Suez Canal. The step towards the nationalization of the Suez Canal company was perhaps an attempt by Nasser "to give pride and sense of dignity to the people who had been humiliated by the colonial masters", and consequently, this step "stirred a response in every Arab's heart" and resulted in Nasser's unimaginable popularity (Jillani 1991, p. 80). After the October 1956 war with Israel, the United Kingdom, France, and all Arab states came to the support of Egypt and joined the Egyptian-Syrian alliance in January 1957, creating a treaty of Arab solidarity for ten years.

There was a perception that "Egypt was looked upon as a leader and savior by the Arab world because of its struggle with Western Imperialism" (Danielson 2007, pp. 24–26). The aforementioned political victories and the acts of defiance against the West resulted in Egypt's popularity in the Arab world, especially Nasser's (Jillani 1991, p. 80). Publicly, Nasser said that Egypt should take on a leadership role in the Arab world, but his actions demonstrated that he had exerted himself as leader of the Arab world. It seems that Nasser personally wanted to take on this role, an ambition which could be gleaned from the words of his book, *The Philosophy of the Revolution*,

> history is . . . charged with great heroic roles which do not find actors to play them on the stage. I do not know why I always imagine that in this region in which we live there is a role wandering aimlessly about seeking an actor to play it.
>
> (quoted in Jillani 1991, p. 77)

Egypt's strategic importance also helped to position Nasser to assume the heroic and leadership role, and he used his position in pursuit of his Pan-Arab ideology. Continuous messages to the Arab masses were pushed by the Egyptian propaganda machinery in the pursuit of Arab unity by highlighting commonalities such as the unique peculiarities of Arab civilization, the strategic importance of the Middle East due to its oil wealth, and stressing the homogeneity amongst the Arabs despite ethnic, territorial, and cultural differences (Jillani 1991, p. 79). Arthur Goldschmidt, a scholar of Middle East history, writes, "The idea of uniting all the Arab countries appealed to many citizens, partly because it sounded like a respectable modern version of the older idea of Pan-Islam. Pan-Arabism seemed even better, for it did not exclude Arabic-speaking Christians" (Goldschmidt 2004, p. 129).

Pan-Arabism as the country's uniting force and weapon against the imperialism became the legitimate state ideology; in fact, in January 1956 Pan-Arabism was officially recognized when the first article of the Egyptian Constitution declared that "Egypt is a sovereign, independent ARAB state and the Egyptian people are an integral part of the ARAB nation" (Jillani 1991, p. 79). On the surface, it appeared that Nasser and his regime had solidified the ideology of Pan-Arabism as well as imposing a secularist rule. Nasser's popularity in the region, and, as we will see later, at home gave Nasser the legitimacy needed to move the country in the direction of an ideology that led to a secularist framework, a framework which did not address popular Islam in the country's periphery, and which later contributed to the religious revivalism in the country in the late 1960s.

As Nasser and his regime gained popularity, and consequently, legitimacy in the Arab world, measures were also taken domestically creating the same effect. The policies that Nasser enacted strengthened the economy at home by introducing a wide range of social services which formed part of his social contract. According to Amr Adly, an Egyptian scholar and former diplomat with the Egyptian Ministry of Foreign Affairs, the social contract "was based on a wide social alliance that the state built with mainly public sector workers, university students, state employees, army soldiers, and other members of the national workforce" (Adly 2014). The public services under the social contract included healthcare, education, employment, rent control, low cost housing, subsidized transportation and food, services which were not seen or provided under British Occupation; consequently, the programme was "well-received by the Egyptian population", and it helped to create a modern middle class (Danielson 2007, pp. 31–32; Dargin 2011; Hibbard and Layton 2010, p. 199). Nasser's populist policies, such as free access to public education and healthcare, created a transformation of the social strata (Tonsi 2012), and these policies led to successful results. For example, between 1952 and 1956, the number of registered doctors in Egypt increased from 4470 to 6420 and Egypt saw an increase of 10% of medical facilities (Wheelock 1960, p. 132). Also, on the education side, approximately 4000 primary schools were built between 1955 and 1964, and funding was also increased to universities and secondary schools (Wheelock 1960, p. 112; Danielson 2007, p. 32).

One of Nasser's significant policies was the Agrarian Reform Law of 1952, which was implemented between 1952 and 1961. This measure ensured redistribution of land to the rural poor from large landowners. The Agrarian Reform Law also restricted the amount of land an individual could hold, and in fact, "bonds which had been issued (in the 1950's) to the landowners in payment for their land were declared payable after 40 years, rather than 30, and the interest on these bonds was reduced from 3% to 1.5%" (Kanovsky 1970, p. 210). One-seventh of Egypt's cultivated land was redistributed to the landless and near landless *fellahin*, improving rural incomes and agricultural production (Bush 2011, p. 395). As Robert Eugene Danielson states,

> By enabling more of the population to own land, Nasser allowed the state to not only collect more tax revenue, but it also allowed the population to increase the amount of money they could spend on goods. This increase in income from the harvesting and selling of crops allowed the population of Egypt to participate more in the economy.
>
> (Danielson 2007, p. 32)

Another source of economic development came from the nationalization of the Suez Canal and the building of the Aswan High Dam. The Aswan High Dam was created to make available irrigation to farmers, allowing more crops to grow and be harvested, and the tax revenues from the Suez Canal, which as mentioned above was nationalized in 1956, both paid for the building of the dam and supported public spending of the government (Danielson 2007, p. 34). However, in contrast to expectations, following the Suez Canal crisis, there was hardly any domestic progress in Egypt (Goldschmidt 2004, p. 129).

In 1960, the Five-Year Development Plan was implemented to improve and expand the industrial sector, originally established under British Occupation, and the Egyptian government increased the amount of "public spending of new industries to 1.7 billion Egyptian Lire" (Danielson 2007, p. 34). In comparison, a five-year plan under the monarchy "involved investment of 96 million Egyptian pounds between 1946–47 and 1950–51", although actual investment was lower than expected. In contrast, under the Five-Year Development Plan adopted by Nasser, net investments were to reach 221 billion Egyptian pounds (Kanovsky 1970, p. 209). The rate of economic growth increased significantly between 1956 and 1960: GDP grew at a rate of 4.5–5% annually and this would imply a "per capita increase of about 2.5% annually" (Kanovsky 1970, p. 208). As Eliyahu Kanovsky observes, "the various measures taken by the government to reduce income inequality and various social welfare extensions meant that the rise in average living standards between 1956 and 1960 was enjoyed by a large number of people" (Kanovsky 1970, p. 210). However, in exchange for these services Egyptians had to give up certain rights and freedoms; that is, as "part of an informal social contract where the population accepted constraints on its political freedom in exchange for the promise of higher living standards and a stronger nation" (Hibbard and Layton 2010, pp. 198–199).

Egyptians felt a sense of national pride and dignity as a result of the socio-economic and political changes taking place in their country. Nasser's Pan-Arabism formulae seemed to work. However, Egyptians' high hopes for a bright future were to come crashing down as events in the 1960s began to unfold and Nasser's promise of an Egyptian utopia began to unravel.

### *June 1967 Arab-Israeli War, slow economic growth, and the economic recession*

From an economic standpoint, neither Egypt nor Israel could afford to go to war in 1967 (Goldschmidt 2004, p. 144); however, certain events and miscalculations on the part of Nasser drew Egypt into what turned out to be a humiliating war for Egyptians. Since the early 1960s Egypt had agreed with the U.S. administration to set differences aside with the Israeli state (James 2012, p. 57), and UN peacekeepers on the Sinai border created a buffer between the two countries. According to Goldschmidt (2004), Nasser's pride could not let him remain quiet when leaders from the Arab world taunted him for hiding behind the United Nations Emergency Force (UNEF) while, for instance, the Israeli army shot down Syrian MiGs in April 1967 and an Israeli raid on the Jordanian village of al-Samu took place in November 1966 (Goldschmidt 2004, p. 145; James 2012, p. 57). Border tensions continued throughout the months of April and May 1967 and public criticism of Nasser's lack of action (as the leader of the Arab world) by conservative Arab leaders continued to mount (James 2012, p. 57). On May 14, 1967 Nasser began to send troops into the Sinai after hearing reports from the Soviets that Israeli troops were massing on the Syrian border, and four days later Nasser requested the UNEF to withdraw from its posts in Gaza and the Sinai (Goldschmidt 2004, p. 145; Louis and Shlaim 2012, p. xiii). Another decision made by Nasser which threatened peace and signalled war preparations was blocking the Tiran Straits against Israeli ships and cargo. Both countries did not want a war (Goldschmidt 2004, p. 145). Despite the fact that Egypt and Israel promised to the international community not to fire the first shot and secret meetings were held to avoid a conflict, Nasser's public and radio speeches expressed otherwise, sending doubts about peace to Israel and the world (Goldschmidt 2004, p. 145; James 2012, p. 70). For example, on May 22 Nasser suggested that there could be no peace while ignoring "the rights of the Palestinian people" and said to the Jewish people: "you are welcome, we are ready for war", and Nasser also stated, "the existence of Israel is in itself an aggression" (James 2012, p. 70). According to Middle East analyst Laura M. James (2012), Nasser crossed the lines with Israel when on May 30 he signed a Joint Defence Agreement with Jordan which was the key factor in Israel's decision to act against "the prospect of encirclement" (James 2012, p. 70). Shimon Peres stated: "we were now surrounded by a sort of banana filled with Russian weapons" (James 2012, p. 70).

Nasser's speeches and interviews sparked deep anxiety, and Israel feared that Egypt was preparing a strike at any moment, despite Nasser's insistence that he would not strike first (Goldschmidt 2004, p. 147). Anticipating an imminent attack, on the 5th of June Israeli forces flew below Arab radar and destroyed 80% of the military aircraft of Egypt, Syria, and Iraq. The lack of fighter planes left Egypt vulnerable to Israeli attacks and in just three days Israel captured the Gaza Strip and all of the Sinai along with 5000 prisoners, while 20,000 Egyptian soldiers died due to thirst and exposure (Goldschmidt 2004, p. 147). The surprise attack was devastating to the Nasser regime and Egyptians, and the implications of this war would prove more devastating to the Egyptian economy. As Goldschmidt succinctly states,

> If Nasser had faced acute economic problems before the June 1967 War, he was now confronted by a worse political crisis. He had gambled on challenging Israel, expecting the Americans to restrain the Jewish state and the USSR to back him. He had misled his people and all of the other Arab states to expect that Egypt, despite Israel's preemptive strike, would win the war. His vaunted arsenal of medium and light bombers, MiG-21 fighters, SAM-2 missiles, tanks, artillery, and rifles, for which Egypt had promised to pay billions of dollars in commodities or hard currency, had turned to smoking ruins. His army was battered, tattered, and scattered. He could make neither war nor peace. His wisest course was to resign.
>
> (Goldschmidt 2004, p. 145)

Nasser broadcasted his resignation taking full responsibility for the defeat of the war but, after receiving massive popular support by Egyptians to stay in power, he withdrew his resignation.

Nasser had embroiled Egypt in a war it could not afford, and in addition to the decision to go to war with Israel, Egypt had been experiencing an economic recession just one year prior to the June 1967 War (see Figure 3.1). Before the economic turndown, Egypt saw a period of national economic growth in the early 1960s thanks in part to policies enacted by the authoritarian government. The Five-Year Development Plan was designed to expand the national income by 40% between 1960 and 1965 (Kanovsky 1970, p. 215; Danielson 2007, p. 34). Although the national income did not grow by 40% over this period, the economy under this plan increased by 15–20% (Danielson 2007, p. 35). The gross national product (GNP) increased from LE 1,285 million (in 1959/60) to LE 1,762 million in 1964/65; the annual growth rate of income was 6.5% (compared to a projected rate of 7.0%); the creation of jobs exceeded the original projection of 1 million, reaching 1,327,000 jobs (Kanovsky 1970, p. 217). Although the production and employment figures for the agricultural sector during the plan period were disappointing, official sources showed a growth of production by 8.5% in the industrial sector (Kanovsky 1970, p. 228), a significant increase though less than its ambitious projection of 14.6%. Kanovsky notes that some of the official economic reports from the Five-Year Plan were erroneous, according to some economists, such as the 6–7% growth rate which may have actually been 5.5%, but that the latter estimate was still high (Kanovsky 1970, p. 223).

In addition to national economic growth, monetary input came in the form of foreign aid from the United States and the Soviet Union. Egypt received the highest amount of foreign aid from the United States in the form of development assistance, an economic support fund, and the food for

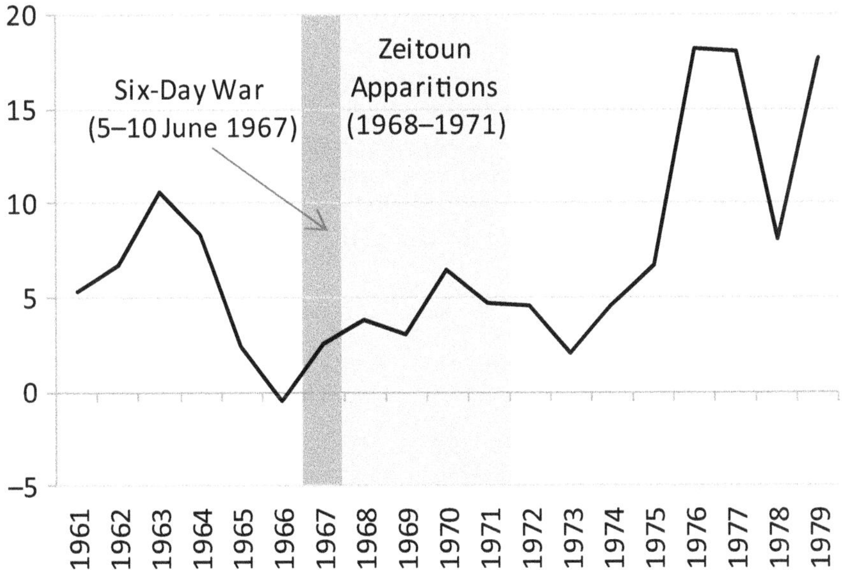


*Figure 3.1* Real GDP growth in Egypt (1961–79)

Source: IMF (IFS Statistics Database).

peace programme (P.L. 480), totalling $200.5 million in 1962 and $146.7 million in 1963 (Sharp 2009, p. 32; Danielson 2007, p. 35); see Table 3.1. The inflow of foreign aid came also from the east, and Kanovsky reports, it "rose from an annual average of $31 million in the five-year period preceding the plan to $262 million during the plan period. By 1964/65 it had reached a peak of $371 million", implying an average of $168 million per year during the plan period (Kanovsky 1970, p. 228).

The Egyptian state had a relatively weak infrastructural capacity economically, being dependent on foreign capital under colonial rule, yet under Nasser's rule the state's infrastructural power increased albeit only modestly (Barnett 1992, p. 213 and 216). However, Nasser's reliance on the Soviets as a benefactor translated into lack of reforms in the domestic and foreign front. As Michael N. Barnett (1992) states, "[Nasser] purposefully avoided placing too great a burden on society because of a combination of the state's limited infrastructural capacities and the perceived political repercussions associated with increased hardship" (Barnett 1992, p. 214); consequently, Egypt's extractive capacity changed little during the period of Nasser rule. Nasser avoided placing any dramatic economic burdens on Egyptians, and "any potential systemic threat to his regime was immediately translated into concentrating more economic power under the state's domain and shifting it away from private economic elites"; and, in fact, the period from 1957–61 was described as "guided capitalism" while 1962–67 was described as the period of "Arab socialism" (Barnett 1992, p. 215). The shift from a capitalist state to a socialist leaning one may have been indicative of Nasser's scepticism of the West's motives. Under the guise of Arab socialism, concentration of economic power continued clamping down on the economic elite of Egypt. By not increasing taxes, thereby limiting the burden on society, the perception of economic stability and of a strong and prosperous Egypt was preserved.

*Table 3.1* U.S. aid to Egypt 1959–1967 [$Mil]

| *Year* | *Direct Assistance Loan* | *Direct Assistance Grant* | *Economic Support Fund* | *P.L. 480 Loan* | *P.L. 480 Grant* | *Total aid* |
|---|---|---|---|---|---|---|
| 1959 | 0 | 2 | 0 | 33.9 | 8.9 | 44.8 |
| 1960 | 15.4 | 5.7 | 0 | 36.6 | 8.2 | 65.9 |
| 1961 | 0 | 2.3 | 0 | 48.6 | 22.6 | 73.5 |
| 1962 | 20 | 2.2 | 20 | 114 | 44.3 | 200.5 |
| 1963 | 36.3 | 2.3 | 10 | 78.5 | 19.6 | 146.7 |
| 1964 | 0 | 1.4 | 0 | 85.2 | 8.9 | 95.5 |
| 1965 | 0 | 2.3 | 0 | 84.9 | 10.4 | 97.6 |
| 1966 | 0 | 1.5 | 0 | 16.4 | 9.7 | 27.6 |
| 1967 | 0 | 0.8 | 0 | 0 | 11.8 | 12.6 |

Sources: Danielson 2007, p. 35; Sharp 2009, p. 32.

Following a period of slowing economic growth, the Egyptian economy had fallen into economic recession (see Figure 3.1). By 1966, not only was real Gross Domestic Product growth negative, but the Egyptian economy was also experiencing high inflation, a decline in productivity, and a drain in its national savings; in fact, defence expenditures doubled to over 10% of GDP during this period (Bayat 1993, p. 72). U.S. economic aid decreased from the early part of the decade to the mid-1960s (see Table 3.1), and aid from the Soviet Union and Eastern Europe was also significantly reduced; additionally, "[p]ublic savings declined and current account deficit rose (to 4.5 percent in 1966 from 1.4 percent of GNP in 1960)" (Bayat 1993, p. 72). The 1967 War exerted additional pressures on the productive sectors of the economy, thereby leading to a sluggish recovery from the recession. Consequently, resources were diverted from public services and allocated to defence spending and the casualties of war (Bayat 1993, p. 72; Danielson 2007, p. 44). Although Nasser supporters were willing to cope with austerity measures – and, in fact, Egyptians had no choice since the country was near bankruptcy – workers and students took to the streets and demonstrated (Goldschmidt 2004, pp. 150–151), as we will see in the next section.

As we have seen, Nasser's "social contract" expanded opportunities to the poor, providing services such as medical care and creating access to education. For the first time, Egyptians began to feel a sense of pride and national identity, and many embraced the ideals of Pan-Arabism. However, socio-political and economic stability came at a cost as Egyptians exchanged certain freedoms for it. Not expecting a humiliating military defeat, Nasser entered a war in the aftermath of an economic recession. Consequently, the June 1967 War had severe consequences to the Egyptian economy, from which Nasser's regime never fully recovered. With the idea of utopia slipping away, Egyptians began to question Nasser's authoritarian regime and his vision of Pan-Arabism along with his policy of a closed socialist economy. What followed was social unrest and upheaval in the form of protests and demonstrations. In the next section, I will analyse the economic implications of the post-war Egyptian economy in relation to the impact it may have had on ordinary Egyptians.

### *Socio-political internal changes*

The economic implications of these events represent only one aspect of the various ripples associated with the June 1967 War as the dire post-war economic situation reached into the social strata of Egyptian society. The unexpected and shocking military defeat in 1967 jolted many Egyptians out of social and political apathy as many took to the streets. The Egyptian economy, battered by the mid-1960s recession, was exacerbated in the aftermath of the war, raising the unemployment rate from pre-war 7.1% to post-war 11.4%, a significant increase. Although it would not be for another ten months after the June 1967 War that the Virgin at Zeitoun would appear, internal changes began to manifest in a few Egyptian cities, and demonstrations which had not been seen since the 1950s began in early 1968. Students and workers gathered to demonstrate in cities like Cairo and Alexandria, leading one observer to write, "Behind the fire of their complaints and demands was the basic question: why after fifteen revolutionary years under Nasser's leadership, is Egypt still scratching its way out of wretched defeat and unchanging poverty?"; the students were "demanding freedom, jobs, a two-party system and butter with their bread" (quoted in Kanovsky 1970, p. 293). Another depiction of the demonstrations by workers and students highlighted the role of the tensions between Israel, which still occupied Egyptian territory, and Egypt, which continued to be high, with the risk of hostilities breaking out again: throughout the winter the Egyptian nation waited but nothing happened, "[t]hen in February there was a sudden and unexpected explosion of feeling in the demonstrations of workers at Helwan and of students in Cairo and Alexandria" (Mansfield 1968, p. 417). The immediate cause of the demonstrations was the lenient sentencing of senior military officers held responsible for the loss of the Egyptian air force during the June 1967 Six-Day War. According to the students, "it seemed that the military caste was closing its ranks in self-protection, and all their frustrations came to the surface" (Mansfield 1968, p. 417). A more detailed account of the demonstrations, described by the author as the "February revolt", is from a 1972 report,

> The reaction broke out first among workers at the military factories of Helwan, the most modern in Egypt and those most intensely under the control of the state bourgeoisie. Workers marched toward the headquarters of the ASU [Arab Socialist Union, the sole legal party] to demonstrate their anger. Police arrived, were quickly overpowered, and the workers occupied the police station. More police were sent in. They fired on the workers, and several were injured. The news came to the University of Cairo, and students decided to march to welcome the workers who were coming to Cairo by train. The government shut down the trains, but the news got around, and more workers went on strike and sent several thousand workers to join the student march. That march had split into various wings that headed for the train station, the offices of *Al-Ahram* (the mouthpiece of the regime), the presidential palace, the National Assembly, and similar places.
>
> (Johnson 1972, p. 11)

Confusion within the police, unaware that the demonstrations were authorized, led to clashes and numerous arrests and injuries (Goldschmidt 2004, p. 151). The student demonstrations also developed

> into a full-force riot in which the police, who had been told to use a minimum of force but were quite inexperienced in handling such a situation (unknown in Egypt for fifteen years), suffered as many casualties as the students.
>
> (Mansfield 1968, p. 417)

Nasser and his regime were frightened by "illegal demonstrations" by students, workers, and the unemployed and acted by banning all protests; however, the next day demonstrations continued and protesters occupied the Poly-technical Institute (Johnson 1972, p. 11). Governmental forces were determined to break the occupation, and for three days a battle of bricks against tear gas ensued, while other protests of solidarity took place throughout the city; at the largest gathering Nasser, a leader who "represented himself as the friend of the people's aspirations" finally called in the army, "symbol of the regime's inadequacy and the focus of the hatred of the people", to break up the protests (Johnson 1972, p. 11). The revolt was broken, and Nasser's regime was now seen as the "agent of repression of political activity" (Johnson 1972, p. 11). As Mohammed Heykal, President Nasser's unofficial spokesman, wrote, "the power groups, including intelligence officers and former members of the armed forces general command, had obtained excessive power" and government promotions were based on personal relationships and not on "efficiency" (quoted in Kanovsky 1970, p. 293).

According to the account of Peter Johnson, a Middle East analyst, Nasser sought to divide the solidarity among various factions of society by isolating them. For example, while meeting with the students he presented himself as understanding their demands and explained that repression had only been directed against trouble-makers (Johnson 1972, p. 11). In addition, added Johnson (1972), he increased the salary of working people in an attempt to separate them from the poor and unemployed (Johnson 1972, p. 11). Moreover, to further placate the people and avoid another revolt Nasser initiated the "30 March Programme", as it came to be known. This was a move towards a liberalization of the economy, from a populist to a capitalist economy. According to Kanovsky (1970), political factors (the February revolt) accounted for this change in government, deemed the most radical change since the 1952 revolution (Kanovsky 1970, p. 293). A new government was formed on March 20, 1968 replacing several ex-military men with civilians such as university professors, scientists, and economists while Nasser remained Premier (Mansfield 1968, p. 417). Nasser addressed the nation on March 30, 1968 and in his speech, he stressed that

> room must be made for the 'more competent' at all levels, but that changes must be accompanied by a radical rethinking of the bureaucratic

> system at all levels. Otherwise it would just mean different individuals sitting in the same offices doing the same work in the same way.
>
> (Kanovsky 1970, p. 293)

The essence of the 30 March Programme, reports Peter Mansfield (1968), was to restore the Revolution and to enact a "clean sweep" of what Nasser called the "centres of power" that

> have stood in the way of reform through fear of losing their influence. . . . The much postponed operation of completing the pyramidal structure of the ASU was to be completed by free and democratic elections from the basic units up to the National Congress.
>
> (Mansfield 1968, p. 417)

When students met with Nasser to air their grievances, they called for an end to the government's secret intelligence apparatus, the "abolition of the system of tutelage and other repressive measures against them, and new laws guaranteeing political freedoms"; however, most of Nasser's promises were never kept, and by the following year new demonstrations had broken out (Goldschmidt 2004, p. 151).

The preceding paragraphs provide an account of the sequence of events which occurred as a consequence of the June 1967 military defeat with Israel. Excluded from this account are the religious implications of the war and the heightened Muslim-Coptic tensions which followed the military defeat. The latter will be included in the section addressing the psychological interpretation of this case study, in Chapter 6.

## Conclusion

The chapter began with an introduction to the events characterizing the mass visions of the Virgin Mary at Zeitoun. More eyewitness accounts will be introduced in Chapter 4 where the accounts are closely examined, and in Chapter 6 as the images are interpreted; however, the accounts in this chapter were selected because they provide a general picture of what people saw at Zeitoun as well as a chronological order of the events.

The second part of the present chapter presented the social and political events that may have been connected to the apparitions at Zeitoun, similar to the approaches used by Blackbourn (1993) and Christian (1987); see Chapter 1. Specifically, four key aspects of Egyptian history under President Nasser's rule were examined, namely: 1) Pan-Arabism, 2) the economic recession, 3) the June 1967 War, and 4) internal socio-political changes. In summary, the 1952 military coup by the Free Officers allowed for national liberation, and Nasser's rise to power ushered in a sense of pride and dignity for many Egyptians during the 1950s and 1960s as they severed ties with their colonial past. Egypt being governed by Egyptians without the interference of Western Imperialists was a pillar of Nasser's Pan-Arabism view. In the Arab world and other Third World states he was respected as a result of the nationalization of the Suez Canal. He "became an instant hero for defying the imperialist West" (Goldschmidt 2004, p. 123). Nasser's social contract raised the economic level of many Egyptians, increasing the middle class. At home, Nasser was also the beloved leader with an 80% approval rating throughout most of his political career (Tonsi 2012). All this changed after the June 1967 Arab-Israeli War, and Egypt entered a phase of reflection and later of defiance and social upheaval.

Chapter 6 provides an examination of how the 1967 military defeat, the economic recession, and social tensions may have contributed to an unusual collective anxiety. In the next chapter, a method is presented allowing the identification of the main common themes and symbols characterizing published accounts of eyewitnesses of the Zeitoun phenomena.

## Notes

1 It should be noticed that among these cases of mass Marian visions, the famous case of Our Lady of Fatima is not included. Although thousands witnessed an apparition, the vision that people saw on October 1917 was not of the Virgin Mary, albeit the Virgin is the reason the crowds gathered at Cova da Iria. In fact, devotees and gatherers at the apparition site claim to have seen mostly visions of the sun, hence this case is now famously known as the *Milagre do Sol*.

2 I made several attempts to obtain this governmental report, but enquiries were never answered or replied to. This may be due to consequences of the Egyptian Spring Revolution.

Chapter 4

# Data sources, description, and elaboration

## The materials

### *The origins of the primary sources of this study*

In order to study the Zeitoun apparitions, I will consider published accounts by eyewitnesses that are available to the best of my knowledge. The material introduced here includes primary sources in the form of both qualitative and quantitative data. These testimonies were taken from six different sources, primarily from the investigation of Father Jerome Palmer who recorded these accounts in his book, *Our Lady Returns to Egypt* (1969). According to Palmer (1969), the testimonies are "brief resumes of taped interviews" of witnesses of the Zeitoun apparition (Palmer 1969, p. 15). In January 1969, Father Jerome Palmer was asked by Sir Emmett J. Culligen of Culligan Book Company in San Bernardino, California to go to Egypt and interview eyewitnesses of the apparition. The material was gathered while the apparition was still taking place and reports were still coming in from Zeitoun (Palmer 1969). The other sources come from booklets and articles from investigators such as Pearl Zaki (1982) and Cynthia Nelson (1973), both of whom claim to have personally witnessed the apparitions and interviewed those around them. According to Bishop Samuel, Zaki is a devout American Christian who after seeing the apparition, "dedicated much of her time and efforts to witness to it by writing articles for periodicals" and daily papers (Zaki 1982, p. iii). Zaki's book documented her experience as well as collected and documented eyewitness testimonies. At the time of her investigation, Nelson was an anthropologist and taught at the American University in Cairo. Nelson researched the apparition while the apparitions were taking place; and she undertook this investigation in order to understand "how Egyptians construct their social world" as well as to examine it in "the context of its broader implications to people's perception of reality" (Nelson 1973, p 3). Other sources stem from investigations which recorded and documented the events as well as collecting a few eyewitness reports, such as from national and international newspapers.

Given the high number of thousands of eyewitnesses (Palmer 1969), the aim is to collect as many testimonials as possible in order to understand what people had seen; therefore, the selection procedure is based on the availability of published testimonial reports.[1] To my knowledge, a systematic collection of eyewitness testimonies in the form of narratives has not been conducted other than the investigation led by the Coptic Church (see Chapter 3). In particular, a committee was appointed by the Coptic Church to examine the apparitions and one of the committee members stated that "a great number of [witnesses] have certified with enthusiastic written messages their testimonies" (Palmer 1969, p. 40). Despite this small sampling pool in relation to the reported number of eyewitnesses, the descriptions of the apparitions are very rich, vivid, and full of emotion on the part of the eyewitnesses. To supplement this small sampling pool, inclusion of quantitative information from a questionnaire of more than 100 respondents[2] who were witnesses to the 1968 apparitions in Zeitoun (see Kamell, Jackson and Jackson 1996, pp. 281–289) also form part of the primary sources of this study. This survey was conducted in 1986, i.e. approximately 18 years after the first reported apparition sighting, and the timing of the questionnaire brings to question the reliability of the recollection of the interviewees. For example, there was a higher percentage of eyewitnesses from the case studies who claimed to have seen the apparition of a dove/bird than from the respondents in the 1986 survey. There are more differences in details of their descriptions than in the main aspects of the descriptions, such as the visions of the Virgin Mary, which hold more weight in importance.

## Organizing published testimonies

The aim of this method is to extract the common themes, images, and symbols which can be associated to, and that therefore characterize, the apparition reportedly seen by eyewitnesses; that is, the purpose of extracting the material is to identify what took place during the apparition as commonly described by eyewitnesses so that it (the material) becomes the core starting point for my analyses of the phenomenon. A database was assembled to include information from the above-mentioned survey and 22 published eyewitness testimonies or case studies. The different sets of information are each summarized by a table. The first information set is based on the 1986 Kamell, Jackson, and Jackson survey, not modified in any form, with all results in their entirety transferred to the database. The second information set is based on data from the 22 published eyewitness testimonies. These two information sets are then combined, as explained later, to derive a set of common themes characterizing the apparitions.

The information set on the case studies includes *44 variables*. It encompasses the information which was extracted from the 22 eyewitness testimonial reports, and the variables represent the key words and phrases which were used to describe the apparition. Most of the 44 variables were coded with either a "1" or a "0" (1 = reported as seen, 0 = reported as not seen). [3] For example, I code a 1 for cases who reported seeing a "pigeon" and code a 0 for those reported not having seen one. Some of the key words include words like "birds", "dove", "walked", "blessing", and "bowing". However, there are some minor groupings within this database due to commonalities of descriptions such as "Christ Child" or "Jesus", "Apparition flamed"/"bright"/"luminous", and "Birds"/"dove"/"pigeons preceded appearance".

The first column of Table 4.1 shows all 44 specific variables. The information, thus organized, can be used to condense some of these specific variables into other, more general, encompassing variables in which I later derived four categorizations (see Table 4.2). The aim of this grouping or general variables, is to identify the common themes by selecting the most frequently used descriptions (i.e. key words or phrases) of the apparition. A necessary step in this process is represented by the identification of the usage of different language to describe the same object. Later, I will explain in more detail how the four general categorizations or common themes were derived.

The specific variables which were not included in a categorization lacked sufficient volume or number of times an individual case made a reference to it and/or there were not any similar descriptions reported with which to pair it. Despite their lack of categorization, I have included them in Table 4.1 since they may reveal some symbolic aspect of the apparition that otherwise may be lacking within the six categorizations.

Some of the information in the 1986 Kamell, Jackson, and Jackson survey is used to determine the common themes as we shall see later. What is of value in this survey and which is otherwise lacking in the 22 case studies are the demographics of eyewitness. Moreover, unlike the 22 case studies, the survey comes closest to any systemic investigation of the 1968 Zeitoun apparitions that I have been able to obtain. As presented next, the descriptions of the apparitions are quite detailed and provide information missing in the 22 case studies.

## Descriptions of sources and what eyewitnesses reported

### *The 22 case studies*

Based on what is gleaned from the testimonial reports, the apparition could be described in three different parts, similar to the beginning, middle, and end of a story or a myth. Therefore, this section is separated into three parts:

*Table 4.1* Specific common themes characterizing the apparitions

| *Key words* | *Number of people* | *Percentage* |
|---|---|---|
| Pigeon | 6 | 27% |
| Birds | 7 | 32% |
| Dove | 2 | 9% |
| Seven fly in formation of a cross | 1 | 5% |
| Saw 2 doves/birds/ pigeons | 1 | 5% |
| Saw 3 or 4 doves/ birds/pigeons | 1 | 5% |
| Saw 6 or 7 doves/ birds/pigeons | 2 | 9% |
| Saw 12 doves/birds/ pigeons | 1 | 5% |
| Birds/dove/pigeons preceded appearance | 3 | 14% |
| Light preceded apparition | 7 | 32% |
| Rays coming from hands | 1 | 5% |
| Blue, bright stars or light around apparel | 3 | 14% |
| Complete luminous body | 4 | 18% |
| Apparition aflamed/ bright/luminous | 8 | 36% |
| Luminous birds | 1 | 5% |
| Radiant phosphorous statue | 3 | 14% |
| Ended with light and faded | 3 | 14% |
| Cross behind apparition illuminated | 2 | 9% |
| Halo | 2 | 9% |
| Standing/knelt/looked before cross | 5 | 23% |
| Blessing | 4 | 18% |
| Palms up | 1 | 5% |
| Olive branch | 1 | 5% |
| Christ Child or Jesus | 3 | 15% |
| Nun-like figure | 1 | 5% |
| Smoke of incense | 2 | 9% |

| *Key words* | *Number of people* | *Percentage* |
|---|---|---|
| Identified as: Blessed Virgin/Virgin | 11 | 50% |
| Identified as: Our Lady | 4 | 18% |
| Identified as: Blessed Mother | 3 | 14% |
| Identified as: St Mary/Mary | 9 | 41% |
| Walked | 2 | 9% |
| Moving/movement of apparition | 5 | 23% |
| Waved | 1 | 5% |
| Veil | 5 | 23% |
| Bowing | 4 | 18% |
| Dressed in white | 3 | 14% |
| Full-figure | 3 | 14% |
| Half-figure or bust | 3 | 14% |
| Features visible | 3 | 14% |
| Larger than natural size | 3 | 14% |
| Crown | 2 | 9% |
| Quiet | 1 | 5% |
| Shawl about her head | 1 | 5% |
| Face of the Virgin on moon | 2 | 9% |

that is, descriptions of reports referring to before, during, and after the phenomenon respectively.

Thirty-two percent of eyewitnesses claimed to have seen birds, while 27% saw pigeons. Only 9% of eyewitnesses claimed to have seen a dove. These bird-like objects are described to have taken different movements and even formations. As Case 7 reports, "They appeared like small planes or gliders. It was impossible to say whence they came and whither they went" (Palmer 1969, p. 32). Case 22 claimed to have seen seven

> pigeon-like birds, flying so swiftly like arrows. They appeared out of nowhere and disappeared suddenly in the sky. The most recognizable thing about them is the fact that they were not flapping their wings, and they moved rapidly like arrows penetrating the darkness of night.
> (Kamell, Jackson and Jackson 1996, p. 79)

Similar to Case 7, Case 3 also reported seeing some birds gliding without flapping their wings as well as seeing "seven of them fly in the formation of the cross" (Palmer 1969, pp. 24–29). Only Case 3 reported having seen birds fly in the formation of a cross. Some eyewitnesses claimed to have seen more than one bird, like Case 11 who saw 12 doves and Case 8 who saw "six or seven pigeons over the church" (Palmer 1969, pp. 32–34, 37). In addition to the birds' movement, formation, and number, some eyewitnesses described them as "very white, very bright, luminous, radiating light" (Palmer 1969, pp. 24–29). One may ask how these birds differ from an ordinary bird or pigeon. Case 22 stated that "[i]t is well known that pigeons can never fly at night", and Case 3 claimed that "[o]ne does not see feathers at all – just something bright" (Kamell, Jackson and Jackson 1996, p. 79; Palmer 1969, pp. 24–29). These birds are described as bright and luminous and just as luminous as the apparition itself. Case 1 and Case 20 describe the light surrounding the apparition as "stars, rather blue in color" and that the apparition was surrounded by bright stars respectively (Palmer 1969, pp. 19–21; Kamell, Jackson and Jackson 1996, p. 67).

Prior to the apparition, 14% of eyewitnesses reported seeing the birds, pigeons, or doves. As Case 20 reports, the apparition "was accompanied by, or preceded by the appearance of white pigeons that encircled the church" (Palmer 1969, pp. 19–21; Kamell, Jackson and Jackson 1996, p. 67). Not only were birds described as preceding the apparition, but 32% reported seeing some form of light. The light is described as blue fluorescent light, "a luminous halo surrounded with a circular frame all ablaze", or fire or flames (Kamell, Jackson and Jackson 1996, p. 79; Palmer 1969, p. 35; Zaki 1982, p. 9). Most of the eyewitnesses who saw some form of light preceding the apparition claimed it transformed into the apparition. As Case 8 described the experience,

> At about 9:50 we saw lightning over the church, much stronger than one could make with a flashlight. I had a feeling that something was about to happen. A thin edge appeared like the light you see when you open the door to a lighted room. Within seconds it formed itself into the shape of the Virgin.
>
> (Palmer 1969, pp. 32–34)

Case 22 also reported a similar description as Case 8, "a thin long stream of blue fluorescent light appeared between the central dome and the northeastern one. This thin long stream of light became wider and wider, developing into the shape of the beloved Virgin Mary" (Kamell, Jackson and Jackson 1996, p. 79). Case 9 reported that "fire, flames, then smoke" could be seen "as it took the form of St. Mary" (Palmer 1969, pp. 32–34). Case 17 was one of the first people to see the apparition, and claims that after the police chief broke the street lights, "[t]he light of the dome remained, and the vision of the Virgin Mary became clearer" (Nelson 1973, p. 5). Case 3 reported,

> a light appeared in the center of the opening beneath the small dome. The light took the shape of a sphere, moving up and down. Then very slowly it moved out through the supporting archway and took the form of St. Mary.
>
> (Palmer 1969, pp. 24–29)

Similar to Case 3's report, Case 14 reported seeing some type of lighted circular form before the appearance of the apparition, and provides the following description:

> The whole scene was bathed with a luminous halo surrounded with a blue circular frame all ablaze. Little by little the vision became more distinct until the figure of Mary became evident to the vast multitudes who filled the space surrounding the church of Zeitun.
>
> (Zaki 1982, p. 9)

The next part of this phenomenon is the appearance of the image as it takes its form from the luminous light described previously. The descriptions of its physical appearance, as reported by eyewitnesses, seem to correspond with one another despite the various usage of language to describe it. Thirty-eight percent of eyewitnesses describe the apparition as either aflame, bright, or luminous. Case 5 described the form of the apparition "full of glory, as if all aflame" (Palmer 1969, p. 29). Case 12 reported that the light cloud of the apparition was so bright it almost blinded his eyes (Johnston 1980, p. 8). In fact, Case 16 described the form "as bright as a millions suns" (Zaki 1982, p. 21). And finally, the descriptions recounted by Cases 18, 19, and 20 of the apparition included the terms "illuminated", "light", and "luminous" respectively (Nelson 1973, p. 9; Kamell, Jackson and Jackson 1996, p. 67).

In addition to references to light in the apparition's descriptions, 18% of eyewitness claimed that its body was completely luminous or made reference to its luminous clothing. Furthermore, 14% reported that the apparition appeared as a radiant figure. For example, Case 1 stated that the apparition appeared "in a complete luminous body as a radiant phosphorescent statue" (Palmer 1969, pp. 19–21). Case 2 reported that even though the apparition was like a phosphorescent statue, it was not as stiff as one (Palmer 1969, pp. 21–24).

Once the apparition had manifested from the luminous light into a form or figure, it appeared as a female. In fact, a strong majority, or 77%, of the people in the sample identify the figure as the religious Mary, mother of Jesus. Fifty percent identified the apparition as either the "Virgin" or the "Blessed Virgin", 41% had identified it as "St Mary" or "Mary" as well as "Our Lady" and "Blessed Mother", with 18% and 14% respectively. Although the remaining 13% did not identify the apparition with the religious Mary, one case had implicitly linked the apparition to her. For example, Case 13 recounts of her experience, "she was standing there on the ground besides St. Mary Church in a position similar as we know her to the Lady of Fatima" (Zaki 1982, p. 8). Another case identified the apparition as female, reporting that "rays [came] down from her hands" (Zaki 1982, p. 18).

There were some eyewitnesses within this sample that reported detailed descriptions of the physical appearance of the image of the Virgin Mary. As Case 8 reports, "I could distinguish only a difference in color between the skin in the face and hands and the veil. There was some color in the face and hands" (Palmer 1969, pp. 32–34). Case 10 stated that the figure was thin and not very tall, and that she could not distinguish its features because "the light was too bright" (Palmer 1969, pp. 36–37). Case 20 recounted seeing it wear "a long robe extending below her feet" (Kamell, Jackson and Jackson 1996, p 67). Case 21 offered more details of the features of the image by giving the following report:

> She looked young and beautiful, thin, tall, dressed in a whitish blue, long dress that covered her feet and a veil of the same color on her head . . . [she] looked very human. Her features were clear and unforgettable. She looked towards the area where I stood, and she smiled. I believe I saw her teeth when she smiled.
>
> (Kamell Jackson and Jackson 1996, pp. 71–73)

Case 21 saw the apparition again later that evening and reported seeing it dressed in red and blue though he could not recall whether the dress was blue and the robe was red or vice versa. Another eyewitness also identified the figure as young and beautiful, and in addition recounted that "she appeared larger than natural size", and moreover, this case claimed to have seen the apparition in another form. As he recalls, "She looked like the Sorrowful Mother. She did not look happy" (Palmer 1969, pp. 24–29). Case 2 claimed to try to distinguish the figure's face and features and added that, "I can say there was something about the eyes and mouth I could see" (Palmer 1969, pp. 21–24).

There are some distinct features that were reportedly associated with the apparition. Twenty-three percent of eyewitnesses reported that the apparition had on a veil while one eyewitness reported seeing a "shawl about her head". As Case 20 reports, "[s]ometimes she was surrounded by bright stars and, other times, she had a shawl about her head; her hands were extended" (Kamell, Jackson and Jackson 1996, p. 67). Nine percent of eyewitness reported to have seen the apparition with a crown, and as Case 6 reports, "[s]he wore a crown that shone like diamonds, all of light" (Palmer 1969, pp. 29–32).

Some eyewitnesses reported on the size of the apparition. Fourteen percent recalled the apparition being either "full-figure" or "half-figure or bust". One eyewitness said, "there she was standing in full figure" and another one reported, "I have seen the Virgin, I tell you. I have seen her in full body" (Palmer 1969, pp. 21–24, 32–34). Case 4 claimed to see the apparition clearly, and he reported the following: "At the time I saw the apparition in the form of a bust or half-figure in one of the openings beneath the dome at the northeast corner" (Palmer 1969, p. 29). And finally in reference to her features, 14% of eyewitnesses reported that the apparition was "larger than natural size". Case 5 described the figure as "twice the natural size and not resting on anything" (Palmer 1969, p 29). Case 21 claimed that the apparition was "almost double the human size" (Kamell, Jackson and Jackson 1996, pp. 71–73).

The details of what occurred during the apparition's manifestation vary case by case. However, there is general agreement on the position or area in which the apparition appeared. According to the testimonies, after the light formed into the image of the Virgin Mary, the position of the figure hovered above one of the domes of the church. In fact, 59% of eyewitnesses reported seeing the figure above the dome, church, or mid-air. Case 2 claimed that the apparition "was five or six meters above the dome" (Palmer 1969, pp. 21–24). Case 5 recounted that the apparition was in "mid-air" and that it remained for about ten minutes (Palmer 1969, p. 29). Case 6 claimed that the apparition was "above the roof [of the church] between two of the domes" (Palmer 1969, pp. 29–32). Case 7 recounted a vivid experience after witnessing the bird phenomenon, and reported "[t]hen a large cloud in the shape of Mary moved across the sky, above the church, entirely apart from the church" (Palmer 1969, p. 32). Case 18 describes her experience in the following way:

> She was like a statue, hands folded in front, head veil and bent. She rose up in the sky completely and was illuminated. I first saw the halo, then

> I saw the Virgin completely. She came down between the palm tree and the dome on the side street.
>
> (Nelson 1973, p. 6)

And finally, Case 21 describes his experience and the moment the apparition appeared

> At 8:30 p.m., a light appeared inside the southwest dome. The light increase immensely, and suddenly, she stood on the roof outside the dome. The crowd cheered and shouted, calling on her in different ways. After a while she began to go to the northern side – where I stood – and, on her way, she knelt in front of the western cross and stood near the north end of the roof just above me, at a distance of about 13 yards.
>
> (Kamell, Jackson and Jackson 1996, p. 67)

As mentioned earlier, there is a general consensus concerning the position of the apparition as it appeared. However, there are variations of what the apparition did while appearing to the crowd. There was a relatively high percentage of eyewitnesses (23%) who claimed the image of the Virgin Mary stood, knelt, or looked at the cross which was on the church. "She looked down towards the cross on the main dome" reported Case 3 (Palmer 1969, pp. 24–29). Case 8 had gone to his car for a moment and found it difficult to return to the church because of the crowd. He then heard people shouting and as he reports, "Above the center dome I saw Mary in full body, standing before the cross. I cannot describe what I felt" (Palmer 1969, pp. 32–34). Case 20 reported that "[t]he Virgin would walk over the church, especially over the middle dome, and bow before the cross that shone" (Kamell, Jackson and Jackson 1996, p. 67). Lastly, Case 22 relayed that as the light developed into the shape of the Virgin Mary, she knelt in front of the cross on top of the central dome (Kamell, Jackson and Jackson 1996, p. 79). Nine percent of the people who reported the apparition near the cross claimed that the cross was illuminated.

Eyewitnesses also reported seeing the apparition expressing itself in different ways such as moving around the church. Moreover, eyewitnesses reported seeing the apparition bowing and blessing the crowd. Twenty-three percent of eyewitnesses reported to have seen and/or associated the apparition with "movement" or "moving" while 18% claimed that the apparition had bowed and blessed the crowd, and only 2% associated the word "walk" to the apparition. Case 6 reported that the apparition "was not stationary. She moved and the people shouted" (Palmer 1969, pp. 29–32). Case 13 reported the apparition was "bowing and moving as a living being" (Zaki 1982 p. 8). Case 1 recounted that "[t]he apparition walked toward the west, sometimes moving its hands in blessing, and sometimes bowing repeatedly" (Palmer 1969, pp. 19–21).

The movement and the apparition's connection with the cross as well as bowing and blessing the crowd were the main actions reported by eyewitnesses. In addition to these actions, 14% of eyewitnesses reported seeing the image of the Virgin Mary with the Christ Child Jesus. As Case 7 reports, "Our Lady appeared in the branches of a tree on the south side of the churchyard, with the infant on her left arm" (Palmer 1969, p. 32). One eyewitness described the apparition with "a babe in her arms" (Kamell, Jackson and Jackson 1996, p. 67). One eyewitness that reported seeing "the Christ Child" also reporting seeing the apparition with an olive branch in her right hand (Palmer 1969, pp. 24–29). Lastly, two eyewitnesses, or 9%, reported the scent of incense. As Case 20 described his experience, "[s]ometimes a numinous mist spread everywhere and gave off the strong pleasant scent of incense that pervaded the whole area" (Kamell, Jackson and Jackson 1996, p. 67).

Fourteen percent of eyewitnesses reported that when the apparition vanished or disappeared, it usually ended with light, and then it faded. Case 7 reports that after five minutes of the appearance of the apparition, it "then began to grow fainter, little by little. The light gave way to a cloud, bright at first, then less and less bright until it disappeared" (Palmer 1969, pp. 21–24). Another eyewitness recounted that after the apparition's appearance "[s]he disappeared in a short time . . . on our way home, we walked around the church where I heard a sound of fire. I looked up and found that the northeast dome of the church was full of orange flames that dissolved and reappeared three times" (Kamell, Jackson and Jackson 1996, pp. 71–73). The figure growing fainter and then disappearing typically marked the end of the apparition. However, sometimes the apparition would reappear again. The general scene of the apparition at Zeitoun can be summed up with an excerpt from Case 3's testimonial report:

> The most wonderful scene I experienced was one under the northeast dome, above the icon of Our Lady. It occurred on the feast of the Flight of the Holy Family, June 1. About nine or nine-thirty at night a light appeared in the center of the opening beneath the small dome. The light took the shape of a sphere, moving up and down. Then very slowly it moved out through the supporting archway and took the form of St. Mary. It lasted two or three minutes, and as usual the people shouted to her. She usually acknowledges their greeting with both hands, or with one, if she should be holding the olive branch or the Christ Child. She looks somewhat happy and smiling, but somewhat sad, always kindly. She then returned to the dome and the figure became a round ball of light and gradually faded into darkness.
>
> (Palmer 1969, pp. 24–29)

This was the typical scene of the apparitional event at Zeitoun as described by eyewitness testimonies from the first set of information or case studies.

The material from the case studies sets itself apart from the questionnaire because they are interview extracts which "paint a picture" of the phenomenon. However, the interviewers framed the questions to the interviewees, and possibly the selection of the material to be included in their respective documentation influences the narrative presented in the accounts.

## The 1986 survey

In this section, I will present the results of a survey of the 1968 Zeitoun apparition eyewitnesses that was conducted in 1986 (Kamell, Jackson and Jackson 1996, pp. 281–286). The questionnaire includes 43 questions, and many of these are not reflected in the qualitative data. Therefore, some data found in the questionnaire allow overcoming some of the shortcomings of an analysis based purely on the published eyewitness testimonies; for example, by providing a broader picture of the types of eyewitnesses present. Nevertheless, the descriptions of the apparitions from the questionnaire are very similar to the ones given by the 22 published reports, and therefore, it can be argued that the qualitative and quantitative data are consistent with, and complement, each other.

As stated earlier, this survey is the only systematic collection of eyewitness testimonies from the Zeitoun apparition in 1968 that I have been able to obtain. Unlike the 22 case studies compiled from various sources,[4] this survey provides information on the demographics of eyewitnesses. Unfortunately, the interviewees of this questionnaire are either Coptic Orthodox or belong to other Christian faiths and neither includes Muslims nor people from non-religious persuasions. However, question 3 of the questionnaire points to a diverse demographic breakdown of the interviewees' residences, ranging from Cairo, Egypt to California, United States. Out of the 111 respondents, 76 were residents of the United States, 32 were from Egypt, and 3 came from England. Forty-two of the 93 respondents were female, and out of 84 respondents, 37% fell into the 31–40 age group, 19% into the 18–30 age bracket, both the 41–50 and the 51–60 age groups included 17% of respondents, and lastly, 10% of respondents were 61-years-old or older. As regards the occupation of the respondents, many of the eyewitnesses interviewed for this survey were white-collar workers. Indeed, while out of 86 respondents, there were 2 seamstress, 9 homemakers, 4 students, and 2 retirees, the remainder of professions reportedly held by respondents were professional careers ranging from businessperson (9 respondents), engineer (8 respondents), professor (7 respondents), physician (6 respondents), to name a few.

This survey also provides a perspective of what people reported experiencing during the manifestation of the Virgin Mary. While it has been claimed that thousands, even hundreds of thousands, of eyewitnesses were at attendance at any given manifestation, over 100 people were interviewed for this survey, and within this sample size, similarities and differences can be found between the two set of sources (case studies and survey).

There are many similarities between the survey and the reports of the eyewitness testimonies from the 22 case studies. First, respondents overwhelmingly agreed that the vision seen was the image of the Virgin Mary. The survey study shows that in 65% of interviews, either the answer by the respondent or the terminology used by the interviewee to describe the event referred to the Virgin Mary. Fourteen percent described the vision as the "Apparition of the Virgin", while another 14% described it as just "Apparition" and 4% described it as "The light". By contrast, only 3% of the 78 respondents of this question reported seeing doves, and furthermore, there is only one other mention of eyewitnesses seeing any type of bird. While the image of birds is significantly pronounced in the testimonies of case studies as well as appearing in photographic images, references to birds are mostly absent in the survey questions.

Another feature of the survey that is also reflected in the case studies is the appearance of the vision; that is, reporting of both case studies and questionnaire respondents bear a similarity in the same descriptions of the image of the apparition. In describing the "brightness" of the apparition, 46% out of 78 survey respondents reported that the brightness of the event or apparition was lighter than the other objects in the surrounding environment, while 53% claimed that it was similar to a full moon. The colour of the apparition was also described and reported by survey respondents. Fifty-seven percent of respondents claimed that the apparition was "bright white". These responses, as regards to the apparition seen as "bright", support the claims as reported by the case studies. When asked about the appearance of the apparition, 90% of 83 respondents reported that the apparition looked like "Human with a definite shape". Indeed, 92% of 48 respondents claimed that human features were discernible in the apparition, with 49% out of 61 respondents reportedly seeing its hands, while 10% saw its feet. Only 4% of the 83 respondents described the apparition as "Dove-like". Although a few eyewitnesses of the case studies described seeing the apparition's human-like features, the survey respondent's reports corroborate with the reports of the case studies.

The church's dome appears to be a prominent aspect in respect to the apparition's location during its manifestation. This aspect is also reflected in the case studies testimonials. In fact, out of 90 survey respondents, 74% claimed that the event or manifestation occurred either, "In the dome", "On the dome", or "Over the dome hovering". Eighty percent claimed that the manifestation occurred in the sky and 2% claimed that it was on the ground. "Movement" was also another aspect of the apparition that was reflected in the survey as well as the case studies. In answer to the question, "Did the apparition move?", 81% out of 81 respondents answered positively. In addition, when asked how the apparition moved, 31% responded with

"Blessing"; that is, respondents identified certain movements of the hands as blessing the crowd. The results of the case studies revealed that 18% of eyewitnesses associated the apparition with blessing. Kneeling was also a theme with the case studies, but the responses associated the act of kneeling with the cross which lay on top of the church. While 31% of respondents reported seeing the apparition walking, only 5% of the case studies eyewitnesses reported seeing the apparition walking. Another similarity that can be drawn is that 2% of respondents claim that the apparition was smiling. Only two of the 22 cases reported that the apparition smiled. In fact, Case 21 claimed to have seen the apparition's teeth while it smiled.

Finally, the last common feature with the case studies that can be noticed in the survey is the appearance and disappearance of the apparition. Sixty-nine percent of 83 respondents reported that the apparition "Suddenly appeared/disappeared", while 17% reported that it "emerged gradually/lingered a while". The eyewitnesses from the case studies which report whether the apparition appeared/disappeared suddenly or gradually associated the apparition's appearance/disappearance with "light"; that is, light preceded or ended with the appearance and disappearance of the apparition (see the excerpts for Cases 3 and 21 earlier). As mentioned, the light formed part of the apparition prior to transforming into the image of the Virgin Mary. More precisely, the light is the apparition, whatever form it takes, as can be inferred from the eyewitness testimonials as well as the description of it as bright in colour by the above-mentioned survey respondents. Therefore, the references to the apparition appearing and disappearing can be considered equivalent to the references to the apparition being preceded by a light and ending with light and fading, as reported in Table 4.1.

The material in this survey reflects many of the descriptions that were extracted from the descriptions found in the case studies. However, there are some differences in the survey which provide another perspective into this phenomenon. Consequently, the authors of the survey included in the questionnaire the experiences of the eyewitnesses and the reactions of people nearby. Unfortunately, their demographics were not provided in the survey. When comparing this information with the case studies, it can be noticed that reactions from eyewitnesses were rarely recorded. The experiences of the survey interviewees were mixed; that is, there were variations in the way they experienced seeing the apparition. Out of 36 respondents, 31% experienced the event in prayerful devotion, while 19% of respondents described the event as "joyous", and 14% referred to being "excited". Eleven percent described the experience with the term "amazed", and the same percentage referred to the term "contentment". By contrast, 8% of respondents who experienced the apparition felt "fearful", and 3% characterized the event with the expression "hysteria and frantic behaviour". However, when asked how other eyewitnesses around them reacted, 31% out of 109 survey respondents reacted with "hysteria and frantic behaviour". By contrast, none of the eyewitnesses from the case studies reported feelings of hysteria and frantic behaviour nor did they report seeing anyone express these feelings. When asked if others saw the event, 98% of 87 respondents said yes. Lastly, 94% out of 71 survey respondents knew someone who experienced the same event. By contrast, in the testimonials from the case studies, few eyewitnesses report that they knew someone who had seen the same apparition. For example, some report a friend, colleague, or family member accompanying them to the church, while others describe separating from their party due to the large crowds. In two of the case studies (Cases 6 and 7) two male friends and two sisters are interviewed at the same time making it difficult to distinguish who reported what; therefore, their testimonials accounts were counted as one. Nevertheless, these data reveal that the eyewitnesses were not alone and this experience was a shared and collective one.

There are questions related to the aspect of the appearance that were not documented in the case studies. For example, 89% of the 80 people surveyed reported that the visual appearance of the apparition was "sharp", while 11% stated that it was "blurred". Therefore, it seems that most people present during the manifestations could clearly see the physical details of the apparition. Accordingly, 99% out of 81 respondents reported the apparitions as "life-like", in contrast to 1% claiming that it looked "artificial". This piece of information is relevant because it questions the theory presented in Chapter 1 referring to light displays from seismic activity during the period the apparition took place (Bartholomew and Goode 2000, p 7). How can the image of the Virgin Mary be sharp, as eyewitnesses claimed, if they supposedly were witnessing the light displays from seismic activity? If it was a seismic activity, the images should have been overwhelming reported as "blurred".

Lastly, one of the noteworthy differences between this survey and the case studies is represented by the physical phenomenon experienced by eyewitnesses. Of the 65 people interviewed, 60% claimed to have experienced a physical phenomenon. Unfortunately, there was not a follow-up question to this. Respondents did not report what kind of physical phenomenon they had experienced. However, I found several instances where eyewitnesses claimed to have been cured by the apparition of the Virgin Mary. These were reported in newspapers, articles, and eyewitnesses interviewed by Palmer (1969).

Not all of the 43 questions from the survey have been included in this discussion. For example, I did not include the proximity of the eyewitness to the apparition. Though these aspects may be instrumental in characterizing more comprehensively the experience of the event, they are of secondary importance in the process of extracting key and common themes, which is the main purpose of this chapter.

## Criteria for the derivation of the common themes

The objective of this section is to derive a set of common themes characterizing the apparitions from both the case studies and the 1986 survey. Accordingly, the analysis of these two sets of information will include the description of the criteria for the derivation of common themes as well as the application of these criteria. A preliminary step in this context is represented by the organization of what the eyewitnesses reported. The common themes will then be interpreted in the next chapter.

As a first step in the derivation of the common themes, I have categorized the descriptions of the apparition as reported by eyewitnesses in both sets of information. More precisely, when specific variables can be seen as belonging to the same category (such as "bird", "pigeon", and "dove"), they are joined in a common grouping (such as "Reference to seeing birds"). The categorization of the descriptions not only allows for a clearer understanding of this collective vision, but also leads to a database which gathers and organizes these descriptions allowing one to obtain common themes by way of statistical methods. The second step is represented by defining a set of criteria to be applied to each set of information, case studies and survey, based on their sample size. The crowds at St Mary's Church in Zeitoun during the period of the apparitions were reportedly in the hundreds of thousands. The sample size of our reference information sets ranges from 82 to 131 eyewitnesses, depending on the number of survey respondents for each question. Due to the relatively small sample size, I have set as threshold for inclusion in the common themes the value of a statistical bar of 25%. More precisely, a category of description of the apparition is included in the common themes set if it is mentioned by 25% or more of the case studies witnesses, or if it is referred to by at least 25% of the survey respondents. Summarizing, the criteria for inclusion into the common theme set of specific categories from survey and case studies are:

- I If case studies category is mention by at least 25% of witnesses, it will be included in the common theme set.
- II If case studies results are less than 25% but a similar category in the survey is referred to by at least 25% of survey respondents, it will be included in the common theme set.

## List of common themes

The above-mentioned criteria applied to both information sets give rise to seven common themes. The fourth column in Table 4.1 shows the list of the common themes that was extracted from the case studies. As briefly mentioned earlier, four categorizations were derived from the *44* specific variables as shown in Table 4.2. In creating these categorizations, I grouped specific variables with similar descriptions, though these descriptions were expressed in different words or phrases.

In the first categorization, *Reference to Birds*, I included variables such as "pigeons", "birds", "dove", and "saw 12 doves"/"birds"/"pigeons". This category represents all individual cases which reported seeing, or describing all or part of the apparition with a reference to, a bird. Ten people, or 45%

*Table 4.2* Categorization of common themes characterizing the apparitions

| *Key words* | *Number of people* | *Percentage* | *Grouping* | *Number of people* | *Percentage* |
|---|---|---|---|---|---|
| Pigeon | 6 | 27% | | | |
| Birds | 7 | 32% | | | |
| Dove | 2 | 9% | | | |
| Seven fly in formation of a cross | 1 | 5% | Reference to birds | 10 | 45% |
| Saw 2 doves/birds/pigeons | 1 | 5% | | | |
| Saw 3 or 4 doves/birds/pigeons | 1 | 5% | | | |
| Saw 6 or 7 doves/birds/pigeons | 2 | 9% | | | |
| Saw 12 doves/birds/pigeons | 1 | 5% | | | |
| Birds/dove/pigeons preceded appearance | 3 | 14% | | | |
| Light preceded apparition | 7 | 32% | | | |
| Rays coming from hands | 1 | 5% | | | |
| Blue, bright stars or light around apparition | 3 | 14% | | | |
| Complete luminous body | 4 | 18% | | | |
| Apparition aflamed/bright/luminous | 8 | 36% | Reference to light | 19 | 86% |
| Luminous birds | 1 | 5% | | | |
| Radiant phosphorous statue | 3 | 14% | | | |
| Ended with light and faded | 3 | 14% | | | |
| Cross behind apparition illuminated | 2 | 9% | | | |
| Halo | 2 | 9% | | | |
| Standing/knelt/looked before cross | 5 | 23% | | | |
| Blessing | 4 | 18% | | | |
| Palms up | 1 | 5% | Reference to religious symbol | 11 | 50% |
| Olive branch | 1 | 5% | | | |
| Christ Child or Jesus | 3 | 14% | | | |
| Nun-like figure | 1 | 5% | | | |
| Smoke of incense | 2 | 9% | | | |

(*Continued*)

*Table 4.2* (Continued)

| *Key words* | *Number of people* | *Percentage* | *Grouping* | *Number of people* | *Percentage* |
|---|---|---|---|---|---|
| Identified as: Blessed Virgin/Virgin | 11 | 50% | | | |
| Identified as: Our Lady | 4 | 18% | Reference to Mary | 17 | 77% |
| Identified as: Blessed Mother | 3 | 14% | | | |
| Identified as: St Mary/Mary | 9 | 41% | | | |
| Walked | 2 | 9% | | | |
| Moving/movement of apparition | 5 | 23% | | | |
| Waved | 1 | 5% | | | |
| Veil | 5 | 23% | | | |
| Bowing | 4 | 18% | | | |
| Dressed in white | 3 | 14% | | | |
| Full-figure | 3 | 14% | | | |
| Half-figure or bust | 3 | 14% | | | |
| Features visible | 3 | 14% | | | |
| Larger than natural size | 3 | 14% | | | |
| Crown | 2 | 9% | | | |
| Quiet | 1 | 5% | | | |
| Shawl about her head | 1 | 5% | | | |
| Face of Virgin on moon | 2 | 9% | | | |

of eyewitnesses, fall into the category of *Reference to Birds*. In the second category, there is a high number of eyewitnesses who made a reference to light, representing 86% of the total. There is also an overlap of this categorization between *Reference to Light* and *Reference to Religious Symbol*. In the latter category, which is the third category, 50% of eyewitnesses belong to this grouping. In the fourth category derived from the case studies, 77% of eyewitnesses can be classified as making a *Reference to Mary*.

There are a few specific variables which meet the 25% criterion which are not categorized as a common theme. For example, 27% of eyewitnesses reported seeing "*Pigeons*" during the apparition and 50% identified the apparition as "*Blessed Virgin/Virgin*". The high frequency to these themes warrants a specific discussion of these references in the interpretation; however, given the close association of these variables with other ones, for the purpose of the derivation of the common themes they are not included separately but only as part of the corresponding grouping.

The next set of categories comes from the 1986 survey in which three common themes are derived. The first common theme derived is the dress or colour of the apparition, or what I categorized as "*Dressed in White*". In the case studies, 14% of eyewitnesses reported that the apparition was white. However, 57% survey respondents stated that the apparition was white or dressed in white. The next common theme is categorized as "*Hands*" since 49% of 61 survey respondents claimed to have discerned hands from the apparition. By contrast, there was no mention of hands in the case studies. Third, I categorized "*Blessing*" as a common theme due to the 31% of survey respondents who described that specific movement of the apparition. In the case studies, 18% described the image of the Virgin Mary blessing the crowd.

## Conclusion

In this chapter, the primary sources of the present case are introduced which were derived from authors who collected eyewitness testimonies while investigating the Zeitoun apparitional phenomenon. I explain how the published accounts are used to extract common themes and symbols; specifically, a database is created in order to identify the most described aspect of the apparition by eyewitnesses. Included in the primary materials for the present study is a survey of eyewitnesses conducted in 1986, the number of respondents averaging around 65. Though the contents of the 1986 Survey were not altered in any form, aspects of the apparitional event missing from published accounts from the 22 case studies are presented, such as demographic background. As mentioned previously, the question of reliability of the questionnaires' memory and recollection of events was raised. Should the survey material be included? I chose to include it because, after assessing the questionnaire responses, the contents in the survey complement the material found in the case studies, as many of the descriptions found in the survey were already identified in the case studies.

In all, seven common themes were extracted from the primary sources, and as shown in Table 4.2, within each of the four groupings or categorizations are subcategories revealing colourful descriptions of the apparitions and of which many will be amplified in the next chapter. For example, in the category *Reference to Religious Symbol*, the symbol of the cross, olive branch, and Christ Child are amplified in the interpretation chapter. Moreover, some of the outliers or those descriptions which were not grouped into a category in Table 4.2 will be included in the interpretation as some of them come out of the amplification of other symbols such as the crown and moon. As stated earlier, "*Blessed Virgin/Virgin*" meets the 25% criterion, but I did not separate it with its own category, and left it under the *Reference to Mary* category to show the high percentage of eyewitnesses claiming the apparitions as the Virgin Mary. In Chapter 5, however, the virgin aspect of the Virgin Mary is amplified, marking its own section. Consequently, the *Reference to Mary* category appears as two separate parts as it is structured, but as you will see in the next chapter, the virgin and mother aspect of the image, symbolically at least, later unite as one.

## Notes

1 There may be other published eyewitness testimonies available in Arabic newspapers (although the published reports from translated newspaper clippings are not as long and descriptive as the ones I have collected), but it is likely that some testimonies may have already been documented in the five sources mentioned earlier since it seems that some testimonies have been recycled from one investigation to another.
2 This number varies from question to question. In this questionnaire, the average number of respondents is 65, 19 being the lowest number of respondents and 111 being the highest. This data for this questionnaire was collected in 1986.
3 There is one exception to this coding procedure, which relates to one witness who explicitly stated not having seen any bird. This was coded as -1, a choice made for purposes of completeness, in particular to record that a case had mentioned the key word "bird" although the subject had not actually seen it.
4 Although the survey provides the largest number of eyewitnesses, the first 11 eyewitnesses of the case studies come directly from Father Jerome Palmer's book, *Our Lady Returns to Egypt*.

Chapter 5

# Symbol interpretation

## Introduction

In the previous chapter, I presented a method allowing the identification of the main common themes and symbols characterizing published accounts of eyewitnesses of the Zeitoun phenomena. In the present chapter, the amplification method is applied to these symbols and common themes. The interpretation begins with the amplification of the Virgin Mary, carried out in two sections. This first section analyses the virgin aspect of the Virgin Mary, while the second concentrates on the mother aspect. Following the interpretation of the main figure mentioned in accounts of the Zeitoun apparitions, other identified symbols are amplified, including light, the Christ Child, and birds. The amplification method will also examine aspects of the historical Mary and the cult surrounding her in order to gain a broader understanding of her impact in both the Western and Eastern worlds. It should be mentioned that the main aim in this undertaking is to understand the Marian myth and not to pursue and present an extensive dissection of the historical figure of Mary, which belongs more to the realm of the work of theologians and scholars of Christianity and Mariology. Along with other works, I shall draw largely on Marina Warner's (1976) book *Alone of All Her Sex*, which presents a thorough account tracing the cult of Mary from the time of the gospels onwards and analyses many aspects and layers of the Virgin Mary; Warner, more importantly, devotes a chapter on Mary's virginity.

## Mary as Virgin

As reported in Chapter 4, 77% of eyewitnesses from the case studies and 79% of survey respondents described the main image of the Zeitoun apparitions as the Virgin Mary or Mary. While some eyewitnesses reported that the image they saw was represented by Mary, Our Lady, or St Mary, 50% of eyewitnesses from the case studies and 79% of survey respondents distinctly labelled the apparition as the Virgin Mary. There are several different titles (i.e. Queen of Heaven, Our Lady of Peace, Holy Mother of God, Holy Virgin, Saint Mary, etc.) attached to Mary and some vary from culture to culture and throughout time. These titles refer to the same person, and it is clear from the primary sources that the central image seen at the church in Zeitoun was the apparition of Mary, but it might be worth researching the frequently mentioned virginity of Mary and the meaning it might reveal. In this section, this aspect of the Mary is amplified – that is, her virginity.

Today Mary is a recognizable global figure venerated by her followers despite little mention of her in the canonical gospels. Mary is also a historical figure; hence her origins should be examined (despite the scarce amount of information documenting her life). Since the time of her life over 2000 years ago, the Catholic Church declared four dogmas about the Virgin Mary: her divine motherhood, virginity, Immaculate Conception, and her Assumption into heaven. The title of "virgin" is largely inseparable to her identity, along with her identification as "mother", and for the purpose of understanding the concept of "virginity", tracing its origins and its connection to Mary may prove that underlying this concept is the archetype of the virgin. As regards the dogma of the virginity, states Warner, "the evangelists, far from asserting it, raise a number of doubts" (Warner 1976, p. 19). Matthew is the only evangelist to clearly state a virgin birth as he asserts in Matthew 7:20, "that which is conceived in her is of the Holy Ghost" and he states that Jesus was unequivocally "conceived by the power of the Holy Ghost, *before* Mary and Joseph 'came together'" (Warner 1976, p. 19, italics in original). Matthew strengthens his statement by suggesting that Isaiah's prophecy in the Old Testament applies to Mary in the New Testament – "Behold a virgin shall be with child, and bring forth a son, and they shall call his name Emmanuel, which being interpreted is, God with us" (Isaiah 7:14; Matthew 1:23) – and as Warner asserts from these passages,

> They form the lynch pin of the Christian argument for the virgin birth of Christ, which almost all Christians hold, and the virginity of his mother Mary, which Catholics and some reformed Churches believe to have continued all her life.
>
> (Warner 1976, p. 19)

The insistence on the virginity of the mother of Jesus was important for Matthew because it was an "essential precondition of Christ's divinity" (Warner 1976, p. 21). Luke also borrows from the Old Testament in accounting for the origins of Jesus and "had established that he [Jesus] had entered the world as the messianic hero should" (Warner 1976, p. 22). As will be explained later, the insistence on Mary's virginity was influenced by culture and tradition, and out of this insistence sprang the concept of virginity to include an ascetic philosophy. Nonetheless, the virgin birth was "a necessary precondition" of Jesus's divinity which may have stemmed from a mythological tradition which pre-dated the Gospels (Warner 1976, p. 24).

The myth of the virginity of Mary may stem from the pagan gods of antiquity, and the resemblance of this "exposed a Christian nerve" (Warner 1976, p. 35). Although differences were stressed between Christ's birth and the birth of pagan gods by early Christian writers, Warner argues,

> [t]he historical fact remains that the virgin birth of heroes and sages was a widespread formula in the Hellenistic world: Pythagoras, Plato, Alexander were all believed to be born of woman by the power of the hold of a holy spirit.
>
> (Warner 1976, p. 35)

Andrew Greeley (1977), Catholic writer and author of *The Mary Myth*, in referring to the pagan influence on the Marian cult, argues that,

> [i]t would be wrong . . . to think that there was no anticipation in the pagan worship of the Queen of Heaven to the Christianization of that cult in the honoring of Mary . . . if Mary had not come along, the pagans might have had to invent her.
>
> (Greeley 1977, p. 77)

There were many aspects of pagan cults that were infused and removed from the Mary of Christianity, and as Marion Woodman (1985) in *The Pregnant Virgin: A Psychological Transformation* states,

> If we can tear off the old glasses and look at the symbolic meaning of the Virgin Mary, without prejudices put upon her through centuries of church history, we can begin to see the significance of the virgin archetype. . . . We have also to remember that the symbolic content of myth, including Christian myth . . . has its roots in the human psyche.
>
> (Woodman 1985, pp. 80–81)

If elements of paganism and myths of antiquity were infused into the Virgin Mary, what significance and meaning could be gleaned from the virgin archetype?

There seems to be a prevailing interpretation of the virginity of goddesses found in the ancient myths of the pre-Christian era. Lesley Hazelton's (2004) biography of Mary draws on historical and ancient texts to recreate the life of the Virgin. Hazelton states that *Maryam*, Mary in Aramaic, was born in a world full of goddesses that had been worshipped for hundreds and even thousands of years. They were virgin goddesses and

> [f]ew were remotely virginal in the modern sense of the word. They had . . . active sex lives. But their virginity was never defined in terms

> of the existence of a hymen . . . virginity becomes something infinitely grander and more mysterious than the presence of a membrane.
>
> (Hazelton 2004, p. 113)

To be virginal or a virgin did not mean to be chaste. The word chaste in Latin stems from the word *castus* which means "clean, pure, morally pure" (The American Heritage Dictionary). The virginity aspect of Cybele, Diana, Athena, etc. has little to do with abstinence but more with, as Hazelton puts it, something grander and more mysterious. The goddesses of the Hellenistic world represented virginity unlike the concept which was later developed in the medieval world.

In *The Virgin Archetype*, John Layard says, "the word 'virgin' does not mean chastity but the reverse, the pregnancy of nature, free and uncontrolled" (Layard 1972, p. 291). The virgin is free and unchained and answers to no one, especially to human laws. Similarly, Nor Hall (1980), in her study of the moon goddesses, describes the *virgin* as

> 'belonging-to-no-man' . . . one-in-herself; not maiden inviolate, but maiden alone . . . to be virginal does not mean to be chaste, but rather to be true to nature and instinct. . . . The virgin acts according to her own nature; she may give herself to many lovers but, like the moon, she can never be possessed. . . . She is the goddess of childbirth and the womb opener.
>
> (Hall 1980, p. 11)

The virgin is "latent and unrevealed" (Chevalier and Gheerbrant 1994, p. 1070), pure potentiality waiting to be expressed and manifest, become fruitful and eventually, born. Virginity is also connected with the soul, and it is called virgin when it is emptied and "ready to receive [the] divine seed" (Chevalier and Gheerbrant 1994, p. 1070). Master Eckhart describes the virgin soul as "free from all external impressions and as malleable as before it was born", and this virgin soul is likened to a bride who receives the "enlightening influx" of the Bridegroom (as quoted in Chevalier and Gheerbrant 1994, p. 1070). Consequently, as this influx takes shape in man (or the individual)

> and reaches its fullness, the soul is raised to that highest level which denotes the state of the Mother of God. . . . The symbol of the Virgin, in her aspect of Mother of God or Theotokos, denotes the soul which God himself inhabits, self-conceiving within himself. . . . The Virgin Mary stands for the soul made perfectly one.
>
> (Chevalier and Gheerbrant 1994, p. 1070)

If we take a closer look at Eckhart's description of the symbolic meaning of virginity, a similarity between this and the myths of antiquity is found. In many myths, mortal women were conceived by gods like the story of Danae and Perseus, Semele and Dionysus, Alcmene and Heracles, to name a few. Zeus, who impregnated many women, "transformed himself into a variety of species" including various bird forms (Warner 1976, p. 38), and in Christianity the dove is associated with the Holy Ghost. Zeus could be associated with the Christian Holy Ghost. Virginity could be described as the mating or fertility dance between the Bride (maiden) and the Groom (god, Zeus, Holy Ghost). The Bride, who is a mortal, represents Earth, while the Groom being celestial represents Heaven, and this union, as stated above represents the symbolic meaning of the Virgin and the unity of these two aspects. Consequently, this union results in the miraculous birth of the hero or divine child.

Considering the above-mentioned interpretation of virginity, a different understanding of the symbolic meaning of the Virgin emerges, which stands in contrast to the Church's definition. Marina Warner (1976) argues that some of the ideas of the pagan's conception of virginity influenced Christian asceticism and the celibacy of the priesthood (Warner 1976, p. 48). In the world of gods and goddesses, "virginity was powerful and magic and conferred strength and ritual purity"; the goddess Hera, for example, was annually dipped by nymphs in a spring in order to renew her maidenhead and "celebrants of sacred mysteries in the ancient world often prepared themselves by abstaining from food and drink as well as from sexual intercourse in order to acquire the condition of strength and purity appropriate to serving the gods" (Warner 1976, p. 35). As the layers of religious interpretation of the Virgin Mary are stripped away, not only do we find the pre-Christian meaning of the Virgin archetype, but we may begin to piece together a psychological understanding. The rituals of the ascetic or the pagan strive to achieve spiritual union with God. In the Greek Demeter and Persephone myth, we also find the archetypal image of the virgin. Persephone or Kore, depicts the maiden, and the maiden is sometimes personified as the whore – one who takes on many lovers representing a vital and sexual yet latent energy waiting to become expressed, manifest, one. When she is personified, she entices the individual in order for him to impregnate her with the "divine seed". As the maiden, she represents one aspect of the anima as Jung states that,

> [i]n the products of the unconscious, the anima appears equally as maiden and mother, . . . the anima is bipolar and can therefore appear positive one moment and negative the next; now young, now old; now mother, now maiden; now a good fairy, now a witch; now a saint, now a whore.
>
> (Jung 1951a, para. 356)

The practices of the ascetics and pagans perhaps derive from the psychological need of the individual to become renewed, pure, and reborn again.

The incest-taboo is yet another example of how the individual's desire is not to impregnate the mother, but rather to seek rebirth through her (Jung 1952a, para. 332; Layard 1972, p. 295). This is reminiscent of the sun myths and they served the function of "incest prohibition" as Jung argues:

> the sun myths and rebirth myths devise every conceivable kind of mother-analogy for the purpose of canalizing the libido into new forms and effectively preventing it from regressing to actual incest. For instance, the mother is transformed into an animal, or is made young again [maiden], and then disappears after giving birth, i.e., is changed back into her old shape [mother].
>
> (Jung 1951a, para. 332)

The initial desire is bad or evil, but this desire becomes powerful when spiritualized (Jung 1951a, para. 332). The bad or evil desire is like an *anima* figure such as a mermaid or nixie who initiates contact and allures and enchants men, and if the men are not careful the anima sucks the life out of them (Jung 1954a, paras. 52–53) or otherwise the libido is regressed.

The bad or evil desire is a necessary component of the renewal process. The *anima* is the "chaotic urge to life" (Jung 1954a, paras. 64) and without her intervention an individual's life can remain stagnant, lifeless, without meaning, or lack creativity. It is a daeomic power like a beautiful woman who seduces men who cannot resist her animal-like instinctive nature. In *Women's Mysteries* (1971), Esther Harding, a former student of Jung, examines religions based on the moon and the virgin goddess of ancient cultures through the lens of Jungian psychological principles. Harding compares the animal-like nature of a woman to the dark moon or the early phase of the new moon. She states, "[w]hen a woman lives in this phase of her nature only, she is not individual, not human. She is, instead, the personification of a nature force" (Harding 1971, p. 121). This "nature force" can be personified in the mermaid mentioned earlier; that is, the cold and fishy tail represents her dark and sinister aspect all the while charming men with the top half of her beauty. The ancient cultures acknowledged the dark aspect of the goddess (Harding 1971, p. 111). The dark aspect of the goddess is associated with magic, which is connected "with love, metamorphosis, and *pharmaka*, medicine in the primitive sense of 'magic', potent healing or destructive powers" (Harding 1971, p. 114). The dark aspect of the virgin or the Black Virgin, for instance, is known for her healing works and powers throughout Europe (Harding 1971, p. 115). Indeed, the *anima* can act as the trickster by bringing happiness one moment and misery the next. Like a man who has fallen in love with a beautiful, young maiden, she snaps him out of the banality of civilized life urging him to live and fully embrace life. The bewitched man is made to believe "incredible things, that life may be lived" (Jung 1954a, paras. 56); she is passionate towards her lover one moment, cold and heartless the next. However, Harding suggests that the *anima* or feminine instinctiveness is not necessarily destructive, as she argues:

> If it is made to serve the ends of human love and cultural development, it is a force of great value. It is not evil in itself; but neither is it good in itself. It is energy, which can be used for either good or evil. Energy, if left to itself, however, produces nonhuman effects. . . . Human intervention is needed to convert energy into work through which something of value can be achieved.
>
> (Harding 1971, pp. 122–123)

A man could be possessed by and fall victim to his *anima* or he can acknowledge and integrate it. The negative aspect of the *anima* may lead some to conclude that it has a meaningless function or even one which should be avoided, for what good can come from an encounter with it? On the contrary, her function is essential, one that awakens an individual from periods of stagnation or times when a renewal or healing is much needed.

As mentioned previously, the Kore-Demeter myth exemplifies the dark aspect of *anima*, but the myth also illustrates the unity of both positive and negative aspects. In the myth, Kore is gathering flowers and as she reaches for a beautiful flower the earth opens up with Hades flying in his chariot seizing the girl. She is taken by her uncle without notifying her mother Demeter. The grief-stricken Demeter roams the earth looking for Kore, and Helios and Hecate tell her that she has been taken to the Underworld. Demeter lives among the mortals mourning the loss of her daughter for a year, and still despairing Kore's loss, the crops begin to die. Zeus intervenes and persuades Hades to allow Demeter to see her daughter. Before Kore leaves to see her mother, Hades offers her a pomegranate which she eats, ensuring that she will return to the Underworld one-third of the year. Delighted to see her daughter, Demeter allows the crops to grow (Martin 2003, pp. 77–83). Demeter and Kore are reunited, and in this Eleusinian mystery it is possible to uncover the motif of *heuresis* or "finding again", "the reunion of mother and daughter" (Neumann 1963, pp. 307–308). When represented in images, often Kore and Demeter appear to be almost identical, but there is a distinction between maiden and mother; the maiden bears the flower while the mature goddess bears the fruit (Neumann 1963, p. 307). In other images, the maiden "remains the young and seductive goddess . . . she represents not so much the transformative anima character of the Feminine as the world-governing unindividual love principle and sexual principle of life" (Neumann 1963, p. 307).

Kore's sojourn in Hades signifies her journey into the unconscious. She is not only fascinated "by the male earth aspect[,]by sexuality" (Neumann 1963, p. 307), but this descent may also represent dark aspects "of ourselves that we find hard to face" and which we must confront and incorporate

(Carter 1979, p. 328). The *heuresis* signifies the annulment of the male rape-Hades abduction of Kore – and reestablishes the "primordial relation of daughter to mother . . . and is renewed and secured" in the matriarchal mystery (Neumann 1963, p. 308). The annulment of the rape could be interpreted as Kore's desire to no longer remain in the dominion of Hades, the Underworld, or the unconscious. A woman, for instance, who is animus-ridden, tries to have control over her animus by protecting herself (Fritz 1980, p. 175), but the wish not to be under anyone's dominion prevents the *hieros gamos* or sacred marriage and the integration of the animus. If an individual does not confront the dark aspects of his or her unconscious, these aspects will not be integrated. Nevertheless, Neumann argues that the true mystery is this:

> the daughter becomes identical with the mother; she becomes the mother and so is transformed into Demeter. Precisely because Demeter and Kore are archetypal poles of the Eternal Womanly, the mature woman and the virgin, the mystery of the Feminine is susceptible of endless renewal.
> (Neumann 1963, p. 309)

As Kore-Demeter she is whole and "one-in-herself" and she is part of the cycle of life-death-rebirth like a seed that decays in the earth in order to grow into a fruit. This concept is also found in Christian texts: "unless a grain of wheat falls into the earth and dies, it remains alone; but if it dies, it bears much fruit" (John 12:24). The idea of being one-in-herself is similar to the primordial divinities (e.g. Chaos, Nyx, and Ge/Gaia) of ancient Greek's parthenogenetic (self-generated) ability. The beings Chaos, Eros, Ge/Gaia, and Tartarus were first *autogenetic* beings; "that is, they were self-generated, having been created out of themselves/the void/nothingness/the All" (Rigoglioso 2010, pp. 15–16). Ge/Gaia, for example, is credited for "parthenogenetically producing all life on earth, including human beings" (Rigoglioso 2010, p. 15).

To remain in the Kore state, the individual remains child-like and enslaved to his unconscious femininity and left to the fate of the possessive *anima*. Yet, at the same time, the individual like Kore needs to descend into the Underworld or unconscious. According to Harding (1971), the Underworld in myths is the psychological language that ancient cultures used to describe the unconscious, as she posits, "[t]he ancients knew no inner or psychological realm, to them the inner-world was conceived of as the underworld, the spirit realm, the place where all spirit things dwelt" (Harding 1971, p. 114). In Hades, Kore is Queen of the Underworld; that is, she has confronted the dark aspects of her unconscious. When the individual "comes to grip with the anima", the individual senses that behind her chaos lies a deeper meaning (Jung 1954a, paras. 64 and 66). The integrated individual has new meaning in life and the creative energy renews the stagnant life. Kore-Demeter then brings fertility to the barren, and the individual who has integrated the animus is able to give birth to herself.

Although Kore-Demeter is a matriarchal myth and is seen to represent the archetypal mother-daughter relationship, its symbols reflect a psychological process in which an individual, whether male or female, can maintain cyclical renewal (of libido energy) akin to the death-birth-rebirth cycle of the harvest. In fact, in ancient cultures rituals of the virgin goddesses demanded a *hieros gamos* or sacred marriage. The virgin priestesses who served the goddess temples were hierodules or sacred prostitutes; some had sexual intercourse with male worshippers or initiates who sought union with the goddess which formed part of the initiation into the mysteries of the goddess (Harding 1971, p. 134–135). They were also one-in-themselves, and as Harding states,

> these women were pledged to the service of the Goddess, their sex, their attraction, their love, were not to be used for their own satisfaction. . . . They could not unite themselves to a husband, for their woman's nature was dedicated to a higher purpose, that of bringing the fertilizing power of the Goddess into effective contact with the lives of human beings.
>
> (Harding 1971, p. 132)

The priestess could not act on her feelings of love aroused during the sacred marriage. She would become virgin or one-in-herself in the recognition that the arousal is a manifestation of the goddess of love and part of this experience is the recognition that her own love is not returned on the human plane; this is the nature of the *hieros gamos* or the marriage with the god which makes women virgin (Harding 1971, p. 145–146). Consequently, Harding suggests that psychological virginity could be attained through "ravishment of a god" or *hieros gamos* (Harding 1971, p. 146). Furthermore, she argues that sacred prostitution reflected a psychological need of renewal met through an external action (Harding 1971, p. 144–145). In the temples of Ishtar and Aphrodite, for example, ordinary men took part in the *hieros gamos* once in their life, and it "was a sacrament of union with the divine feminine nature and was also a ritual for the renewal of his powers of fertility" (Harding 1971, p. 141). Ordinary women also partook of the *hieros gamos* once in their life and the significance for them was submission to their instinct (Harding 1971, pp. 144–145).

The ritual of the *hieros gamos* was an act which reflected a psychological need of ancient cultures to establish true polarity between the masculine and feminine principle. This external act of the sacred marriage performed by the worshippers was similar to the alchemist's transmutation of base materials into gold; the aim was to achieve transformation from the concrete and material world to the spiritual and psychological realm. The result of this inner experience is that the initiate is transformed. As a Gnostic text states, "only as a pure virgin can the spirit of man achieve union with God" (Harding 1971, p. 152).

When the initiate of the virgin goddess passes the test (achieves transformation), the goddess grants him immortality. Not the immortality of constant perfection, but rather "an ever-renewed life like the moon's own, in which diminishing and dying are as essential as becoming" (Harding 1971, p. 212). Some symbols of the moon cycle are represented by the two crescents and a circle. The Triple Goddess is also a representation of this concept, and in fact, the Greek goddess Hecate forms part of the Hecateia along with Kore and Demeter representing the Underworld, Heaven, and Earth (Carter 1979, p. 328) where these goddesses had dominion. Other representations of the triad are the Greek Moirai or goddesses of Fate, the Nordic Norns, and the Celtic Bridgets. This triad also represents the life-death-rebirth cycle. The idea of the triad also represents the past, present, and future, as Harding suggests,

> In psychological terms, he who has attained to the realm of the full, or complete, moon has gained knowledge of the unconscious, as past, source, origin; he has power in this present world; and has insight into the realm of the future. He has become in a certain sense timeless, he transcends the limitations of time. He has gained immortality.
>
> (Harding 1971, p. 212)

The concept of virginity is the cyclical renewal process like the phases of the moon, and the individual who attains it succeeds in overcoming his sterile life. An individual, for example, who has repressed his emotions by maintaining perhaps a one-sided rational attitude, may find these emotions erupting in the form of dreams, visions, or fantasies. Worshippers of the virgin goddesses may have been able to, through rituals, integrate the feminine principle and to help restore life.

In summary, the amplification reveals that the Virgin Mary, like the Virgin Goddesses of the ancient world, contains a dual aspect of maiden and mother, and these aspects manifest themselves in negative and positive forms. In this section, the virgin aspect of Mary is amplified, and from the angle of the maiden aspect, she is seen as an instinctive and natural force and possesses the ability of renewal and fertility. This aspect also represents the negative side of the *anima*, which manifests itself in forms like the mermaid and nymph and, if an individual fails to integrate it, he not only remains anima-possessed, but also fails to attain the wisdom of self-renewal or immortality. In essence, the virgin archetype, though potentially dark and negative in its manifested forms, represents the capacity to fertilize barren lands, renew or rejuvenate the sterile and banal life, and especially during times of crisis, bring forth a rebirth. The activation of this aspect of the Marian image may point to the psychological need of the Egyptian psyche to seek a social and political change and renewal away from Nasser's regime. In the Kore-Demeter myth daughter (maiden) and mother are reunited, and the unity of the dual image may signify becoming "one-in-herself". In the next section, the mother aspect of the image will be analysed in depth.

## Mary as Mother

Based on the sources, Mary was the primary image seen at Zeitoun. The amplification of the virgin aspect of Mary revealed the significance of the virgin archetype. The obvious next step is to amplify the mother aspect of the Virgin Mary who is known as well as identified by eyewitnesses as the Blessed Mother. To Anne Baring and Jules Cashford, Mary is the "unrecognized Mother Goddess" of the Christian church, bearing a similar pattern or script to goddesses who existed before her – Cybele, Demeter, Isis, Ishar, Aphrodite, among others – by giving birth to a divine child who dies and is reborn (Baring and Cashford 1993, p. 547). In order to understand this symbolic pattern, it can be useful to unpack some of the imagery embedded in the mythological stories of Mary's predecessors: the virgin mother goddesses who are one-in-themselves. The common thread holding these goddesses together is that they give birth to a child, from whom they are separated by death or in other ways, followed by a rebirth or union, as was seen in the unity of Demeter and Persephone earlier. This pattern is, as discussed previously, the process of transformation and one of the main characters of the Archetypal Feminine. In his analysis of the structure of the Archetypal Feminine, Erich Neumann (1963) posits that two characters may be distinguished: the elementary and the transformative. These characters, "in their interpenetration, coexistence, and antagonism, are essential parts of the Feminine as a whole" (Neumann 1963, p. 24). The elementary character is described as the Great Container holding close to it everything which springs from it. In a sense, it is very maternal like the relationship between mother and infant; the baby is undeveloped and dependent on the mother for survival. From a depth-psychological perspective, it is "a tendency of the ego to return to its original unconscious state" (Neumann 1963, p. 26).

The transformative character, on the other hand, drives towards motion, change, and transformation; it compels tension, development, and movement (Neumann 1963, pp. 29–34). Gradually, the personality moves away from the dominance of the elementary character towards development and independence. It is a movement from one place or situation to another. The emphasis of *movement* plays an important role in the transformative character, and I would argue that the Virgin Mary represents this character in its projective form. Subsequently, another form of transformation could be expressed as the Mediator or Mediatrix. Taking Neumann's definition of the transformative character as movement, or moving from one state to another, the meaning of a mediator falls into this definition. A mediator is one who intercedes and brings about a truce between two parties towards reconciliation; they are moved from a state of dispute, anxiety, or crisis to one of agreement, relief, or peace. Therefore, the Virgin Mary may be a symbol of transformation, but more specifically, she may symbolize the intervener, protectress, and mediator of the worldly affairs of human beings. This is similar to the way the positive anima intervenes and acts as guide to the individual on his path towards individuation, e.g. Athena in the Odyssey.

The Great Mother is also the goddess of time and of fate; the changes of the day and night as well as "the changes of the months, seasons, and years are subordinated to the all-powerful will of the Great Mother" (Neumann 1963, p. 226). The Great Mother also appears as the Great Spinstress who "weaves the web of life and spins the thread of fate"; the Great Mother also represents the lunar triad (Neumann 1963, pp. 227–228). This archetypal character is projected in fairy tales, for example with the appearance of the witch as the spinner of destiny, such as the Wicked Fairy in Sleeping Beauty – a fairy tale whose origin comes from Hera and Zeus's wedding feast – where the life of the princess is suspended (Baring and Cashford 1993, p. 559). As Baring and Cashford point out,

> As eternity spinning time, growth and destiny, [the Great Mother] weaves the great web of life in the image of a mother with a child in her womb. . . . The *Moirae*, the Greek goddess of fate, [such as Eileithyia, Athena, and Penelope] were all spinners and weavers of the threads of destiny, and Mary stands as the last link in this chain of transmission.
>
> (Baring and Cashford 1993, p. 559)

In an early Catalan painting of the Christian Madonna, the Virgin Mary, as the Goddess of Fate who spins destiny, is seen with a long thread in both hands signifying, Neumann argues, the redemption of the world; the uplifted hands announcing the angel and the lowered hands onlooking mankind (Neumann 1963, p. 233).

Some Mother Goddesses went beyond the role of the intervener and were warriors themselves. In Celtic religion, the virgin aspect of the Virgin Mother Goddess was a prerequisite for her supremacy as a warrior; furthermore, Celtic women took on the role as messengers from the Otherworld as well as war-goddesses (Chevalier and Gheerbrant 1994, p. 678, 1071). Goddesses of fate appear in Germanic mythology as the Valkyries, who as "the weaving goddesses of fate merge with the bloody goddess of war and death" (Neumann 1963, p. 232). The Greek Virgin Mother Goddess Athena was bestowed heavenly powers as the daughter of Zeus; she was

> a protectress into whose care one could commend oneself with pious trust in those peaceless, war-filled times. . . . The strong, the valiant, the

> defender, she protects cities and fortresses from hostile invasions. . . . She holds her hand outstretched over cities and covers them with her golden shield.
>
> (Kerényi 1978, p. 14)

Athena was not only a protectress, but she was also the Goddess of War:

> Then from his head, by himself,
> He produced Athene of the gray eyes,
> great goddess, weariless,
> waker of battle noise, leader of armies
> a goddess queen who delights in war cries,
> onslaughts and battles.
>
> (quoted from Kerényi 1978, p. 30)

In Revelation John describes his vision of a Mary different from modest Mary of the Gospels, taking up the role of hero by battling the dragon, a "role of the old Virgin Goddess who was co-opted into war" (Baring and Cashford 1993, p. 570). The Archetypal Feminine manifests in the form of the Virgin Mary, and in this differentiated form, she personifies a specific role e.g. intervener, protectress, warrior, mediatrix, etc., depending on the circumstances and events for which the individual or society is compensating. For an individual, the projection may be one precise role and may be experienced in a vision, fantasy, dream, etc. as the positive loving mother. The collective, on the other hand, may experience overlaps in the projected role and associate, for instance, the Virgin Mary as intervener and warrior at the same time; as discussed in the next chapter, the apparitions personify one aspect to one group while differing to another group.

In the last thousand years, there have been 21,000 visions of the Virgin Mary and, of those, 210 were reported between 1928 and 1971 (Baring and Cashford 1993, p. 557). The worldwide phenomena of the visions and apparitions play a significant role in understanding the symbol of the image of the Virgin Mary, as Baring and Cashford argue:

> even when the 'status' of an image is archetypal . . . the image itself needs to be understood in its local historical context. The two dimensions of such an image, the archetypal and the historical, do *not* exclude each other, but are both required for an estimation of its meaning and implications.
>
> (Baring and Cashford 1993, p. 555; italics in original)

The reported material by individuals or groups experiencing a vision or apparition, whether partaking of the event directly or not, may be useful information in understanding the narrative or myth developed around respective apparitional phenomena, and in ascertaining the specific role or roles associated with the Virgin Mother. This historical material on previous Marian apparitions as well as non-apparitional historical references to the Virgin Mary enhances an understanding of the symbolism of this image, which in my opinion forms part the amplification or comparative material. The next few paragraphs include such material.

In 1311, Italian painter Duccio di Buoninsegna completed the Maestà, the largest painting at the time, with the Passion of the Christ on one side and the Virgin enthroned on the other. An inscription on the base of the throne where the Virgin sits reads as a prayer: "Holy Mother of God, be thou the cause of peace for Siena and, because he painted thee thus, of life for Duccio" (Dougherty 1998, p. 479). M. Dougherty posits that when Duccio prays these words, the Virgin is acknowledged as the "political and religious protectress of Siena . . . and that She could bring peace to the Sienese after years of war with the Florentines" (Dougherty 1998, p. 480). Duccio's painting may have represented his unconscious contents, and it may be an example of how the painting reflected the collective attitude and concerns of the Sienese as can be exemplified by the shutdown of the city for a devotional procession of Duccio's masterpiece (Dougherty 1998, p. 479). In this example, the Virgin Mary is obviously projected as the protectress against the warring Florentine neighbours through the medium of the image of the painting.

Visions of the Virgin Mary may also manifest themselves as a backlash against secularization and not only during times of war. In April 1948, Italians headed to the polls to vote for their first parliament after two years of fascist dictatorship with the choice of two main contenders: the Christian Democrats or the Popular Front – a coalition of Italian Communist and revolutionary Socialists. Before the election, Pope Pius XII spoke to the Italians regarding the political decision that they faced by reducing their decision to two choices: "*essere con Cristo o contro Cristo: è tutta la questione*", to be either with Christ or against Christ (Ventresca 2003, p. 439). This statement came against the backdrop of "the grand Marian pilgrimages of 1947–1948" followed by the wave of apparitions of the Virgin Mary throughout the country. The most famous of the apparitions was in Assisi, the birthplace of Saint Francis, where a woman claimed to see a statue of the Virgin Mary move her head and chest "as if the Virgin was breathing heavily, as if she were sighing" (Ventresca 2003, p. 444). News of the woman's vision spread quickly through the towns and villages, and a local radio station announced without scepticism that the Madonna sighed heavily "as if She was in deep pain"; Ventresca comments that the suffering and weeping Madonna "was presumed to represent celestial displeasure at the course of events on Earth" (Ventresca 2003, p. 445). The description of the apparitions from the 1947–48 Italian era appear to be of a suffering, mournful, and pained Virgin Mary. For example, a 43-year-old woman named Annunziata Gentili from the village of San Giovannone claimed that the Virgin appeared to her in a series of dreams. In the dreams the image appeared on the walls of the grotto of San Giovannone with a sad expression "covered in rivulets of water, and surrounded by small rocks and patches of wild grass", and in another dream the Virgin appeared dressed in black with the look of pain (Ventresca 2003, p. 445).

A mournful image of the Virgin that is well-known is of the statue of Michelangelo's *Pietà*. In this image, she is the Mater Dolorosa, lamenting the crucifixion and death of her son in the same way Isis lamented for Osiris, Aphrodite for Adonis, Demeter for Persephone, and Cybele for Attis (Baring and Cashford 1993, p. 584). In Zeitoun, one of the eyewitness said the Virgin looked like the Sorrowful Mother (Palmer 1969, pp. 24–29). Baring and Cashford (1993) state that the mourning of "the mother for her son can be felt [as] the universal human loss of all that is finest in life, even finally that life itself" (Baring and Cashford 1993, p. 584). The loss of a son, or Christ, may represent the loss of one's Self, the divine and unity in oneself (see Mary with Child). The rivulets of water in Gentili's dream are like the tears of the weeping Madonna, similar to the symbolic dew emitting from the Moon Goddess. In Greece and Babylon, the moon goddess was called the All-Dewy-One and dew is the symbol of fertility; furthermore, in these hot regions where moon goddesses were worshipped, "rain and dew cause the earth to bring forth the green things" (Harding 1971, pp. 110–111). The bringing forth of "green things" and the "patches of wild grass" from Gentili's dream are symbolized in the unity of Demeter and Persephone: "Demeter is seen as the ripe grain, Persephone as the tender shoots; together they are invoked as the 'two goddesses'" (Carter 1979, p. 327). As virgin and mother, according to Neumann, the "two goddesses" belong together in their transformation of one another (Neumann 1963, p. 307).

Gentili, in her dreams, is urged by Mary to look for her, and once the townsfolk were informed of her dream a dig was organized. Following the instructions of Mary in the dream, a stone carving of a woman holding something was found. A similar event took place in a town near Naples where a woman dreamed of something buried, and like the dig in Gentili's town, a dig was also organized and a 14th-century statue of Mary was discovered. In both dreams the women were moved or urged to dig for a buried object deep in the earth. Earth is the representation of the Mother Goddess, but within the context of the dream, digging into the earth could symbolize the psychological need of the dreamers and their townsfolk to have an encounter with the unconscious. In the Demeter-Kore myth, the earth opens up and Persephone is taken deep into the earth, into the Underworld. In fairy tales, a door or well is the gate to the underworld, and according to Neumann (1963), "these motifs are 'the domain of the earth mother' and the rising water of the spring is the erupting motif of 'being born' and of the creative movement, which strongly accented than that of being contained" (Neumann 1963, p. 48).

In one of Gentili's dreams, Mary urges Gentili to find her and says, "the water is deep". Again, the water motif appears in the dream, but this time the water seems to be engulfing the Virgin as she implores the dreamer to hurry, "before extraordinary events occur. The water is deep and I have been sleeping here for centuries!" (Ventresca 2003, p. 445). The level of urgency in this dream prompts Gentili to inform the people in her town of Mary's message, and in effect, the dig is organized. If the dreamer does not hurry and find the Virgin, "extraordinary events" may occur and the Virgin may not intervene or protect the dreamer and townsfolk from these events. The urgency of the dream may also reflect the unconscious psychological need of the dreamer to seek out the Virgin Mary, which in its differentiated form represents the Archetypal Feminine's elements of transformation and rebirth, in the hope of ushering in a new era of politics in Italy. That the Virgin has been "sleeping here for centuries" may be hyperbolic language manifested in Gentili's dream to express the anxiety created by the rise of Communism and the fear of the fate of the Catholic Church if communists seized power, including any one-sided material which may have been constellated in the cultural unconscious due to secularism under fascism.[1] Water brings forth fertility and growth, but an engulfment of water or a flood causes destruction. The message of Mary in Gentili's dream heeds a warning if the Virgin is not found. An aspect of the archetypal Terrible Mother manifests as the Goddess of Floods such as Dhari Devi, a form of the Goddess Kali, who supposedly caused a destructive flood killing hundreds of people after her statue was removed from its ancient temple. One believer of the goddess stated, "Dhari Devi wanted to teach the atheists ruling this country a lesson" (Gusain 2013). Had the dreamer and the townsfolk not dug out and found the statue of Mother and Child, it could not be known for certain if an extraordinary event or destruction would follow to either the dreamer or townsfolk. Nonetheless, the urgency of the dream warns of negative consequences if believers do not answer her call. The 1947–48 Italian Marian apparitions seem to be an adumbration of the apocalyptic Mary described in the Book of Revelation as well as apparitions taking place in the mid to late 20th century.

Against the backdrop of "widespread societal anxiety, foreign war [World War I], and conflicts over church-state issues", three shepherd children reported seeing visions of the Virgin Mary beginning in May 1917 at Fátima, Portugal (Manuel 2003 p. 4). After having had lunch and praying the rosary, as was their habitual routine, the children reported hearing "lighting in a clear sky" and decide to head home for fear of an approaching storm (Manuel 2003, p. 7). They claimed that a strange light in the sky moved towards them and then a beautiful lady appeared before them, and

> above the holm oak tree, wearing a pure white mantle, which was edged with gold, which went to her feet. In her hands the beads of a rosary shone like stars, with its crucifix the most radiant gem of all.
>
> (Manuel 2003 p. 7)

Some of the imagery used to describe the Virgin Mary in Fatima by the young seers overlaps with the imagery described by seers in Zeitoun. For example, several reports from the Zeitoun case studies reported seeing the image of the Virgin Mary manifesting near a tree. In some Marian apparition cases, the image of the Virgin is projected inside or near a chthonic or mother symbol like a grotto, e.g. the apparitions in Italy and Lourdes. However, in both Fatima and Zeitoun the tree forms part of the narrative, albeit it is not an actual apparition like the Virgin Mary or the doves flying in the sky. Case 5 reported seeing the image of the Virgin "high in the air" between the space of "two tall trees" (Palmer 1969, p. 29). Case 7 claimed that "Our Lady appeared in the branches of a tree", while Case 18 reported that the Virgin "came down between the palm tree and the dome" (Palmer 1969, p. 32; Nelson 1973, p. 6). And finally, Case 8, who later witnessed the apparition on a separate occasion, recounted the experience of other seers, stating that "The beam of light came to rest on a tree and the people said they could see St. Mary visible on the tree" (Palmer 1969, pp. 32–34). The symbol of the tree is another representation of the Great Mother as Neumann posits:

> The Great Earth Mother who brings forth all life from herself is eminently the mother of all vegetation. The fertility rituals and myths of the whole world are based upon this archetypal context. The center of this vegetative symbolism is the tree. As fruit-bearing tree of life it is female: it bears, transforms, nourishes; its leaves, branches, twigs are "contained" in it and dependent on it. The protective character is evident in the treetop that shelters nests and birds. But in addition the tree trunk is a container, 'in' which dwells its spirit, as the soul dwells in the body. The female nature of the tree is demonstrated in the fact that treetops and trunk can give birth.
>
> (Neumann 1963, pp. 48–49)

Neumann goes on to explain that the tree is also an earth phallus symbol, and the accent of the symbol depends on whether the tree symbol is embedded in a matriarchal or patriarchal culture (Neumann 1963, p. 49). Nonetheless, the accent Neumann refers to is not pertinent to this discussion;[2] however, what is pertinent is that the feminine aspect lies hidden in the phallic-masculine tree. As Jung states, the feminine quality of the tree is contaminated with phallic symbolism (Jung 1952a, para. 324). According to Jung, the tree-soul is divided into a masculine and feminine figure which corresponds to the "alchemical Mercurius as the life principle of the tree, for as a hermaphrodite he is duplex" (Jung 1954b, para. 420). One of the primary images of the Mother Goddess was the Tree of Life and within it "all pairs of opposite are reconciled" (Baring and Cashford 1993, p. 496).

Neumann associates the Great Mother to the Great World Tree which in her positive aspect shelters, protects, and nourishes the vegetative and animal world, to which man also belongs (Neumann 1963, p. 49). In this respect, she is the protectress and good mother. As a mother symbol the tree is associated with the tree of life, and Jung argues that it may have been "in the first instance, a fruit-bearing genealogical tree" (Jung 1952a, para. 321). Some myths recount the way humans came from trees, especially how heroes were enclosed in the "maternal tree-trunk" like Osiris and Adonis (Jung 1952a, para. 321). In some moon religions, the cutting of trees and lopping off the branches were rituals which portrayed castration and death before the mother, such as the enclosure of the bodies of Osiris and Attis in the trunk of a tree. The tree symbolizes the mother who embraces and encloses the son (Harding 1971, p. 45). According to Baring and Cashford (1993), "[t]he ritual cutting down of the tree signified the dying phase of the totality of being, seasonally celebrated as the 'fall', which, far from preventing rebirth, acknowledged its perennial possibility" (Baring and Cashford 1993, p. 584).

In her analysis of stone carving of early representations of the moon deity, Harding (1971) posits that the tree images were frequently found to be an emblem of the moon, and that the sacred Moon Tree appears over and over in religious art of ancient times (Harding 1971, p. 42). In some pictures of stone carvings, the moon tree is often covered with fruits and lights similar to the Christmas tree as well as the ribbons on the Maypole, and as Harding states,

> Perhaps a dance may have taken place around the tree in those faraway days, like the dance which is still performed round the Maypole on May Day. In such a dance the ribbons would be interwoven, as in our own dance, to represent the decking of the bare tree with bright-colored leaves and flowers and fruits, all gifts of the moon goddess, giver of fertility.
>
> (Harding 1971, p. 45)

The fruits of the tree also had special meaning in that the fruit "is the source of that drink of immortality, of secret knowledge, and of inspiration"; the belief in the power of the tree predates Genesis story, the garden of Eden's fruit of knowledge (Harding 1971, p. 45). One of the earliest religious poems known is the Hymn of Eridu which commemorates the moon tree and its fruit:

> Its root (or fruit) of white crystal stretched toward the deep.
> Its seat was the central place of the earth;
> Its foliage was the couch of Zikum, the (primeval) mother.
> Into the heart of the holy house which spreads its shade like a
> Forest
> Hath no man entered,
> There (is the house of) the mighty mother, who passes across the
> Sky
> (In) the midst of it was Tammuz.
>
> (Harding 1971, pp. 46–48)

Tammuz, or the Green One, is the son of the Moon Mother, or Ishtar, and represents "the divine fruit of the sacred moon tree" (Harding 1971, p. 48). Harding argues that the reference in the first line of this poem to the root stretching towards the deep signifies the moon tree's connection with the underworld. Indeed, the roots of a tree symbolize its chthonic aspect in its connection and entrance to the underworld, like the doors on trees found in fairy tales. The line "into the heart of the house . . . hath no man entered" may signify that the meaning of the Moon Goddess and her moon tree is a mystery, as Harding posits; however, in addition to this interpretation it can also be associated to the meaning of forest as virgin. That is, man cannot trample on the virgin forest or the moon tree: it will remain free from the laws of civilized man.

In *The Philosophical Tree* (1954b) Jung posits that the tree is the seat of transformation and renewal and that it has feminine and maternal significance (Jung 1954b, para. 418). Case 18 had reported that the apparition of the Virgin Mary came down between the dome and a palm tree. The palm tree plays a significant part in the story of the Holy Family in Egypt. According to local tradition, Mary nursed infant Jesus under the tree in Giza, and the palm tree was the only tree in the region bearing fruit (Perry 2003, pp. 131–133).[3] In Matareyah, Egypt stands the Tree of the Holy Virgin where the Holy Family was believed to have rested under its shade. Jesus then caused water to flow from a spring and after Mary poured water on the ground from his washed clothes a balsam plant began to blossom. In many Eastern countries, such as Egypt, Crete, and Greece, a tree was planted in the middle of the temple of the Mother Goddess (Baring and Cashford 1993, p. 496). It was also under the palm tree that Mary[4] and the Goddess Leto gave birth; Maya gave birth to Buddha under the shade of a holy tree; Adam was said to have been created out of the "earth of the tree of life" (Jung 1954b, para. 418).

Jung states also that the feminine-maternal aspect of the tree is associated to Sapientia; the tree of knowledge is in Genesis and the tree of wisdom in the Book of Enoch (Jung 1954b, para. 419). Similar older references to the tree as wisdom and gnosis is found in the *Acta Archelai*: "But that tree which is in paradise, whereby the good is known, is Jesus and the knowledge of him which is in the world"; and, says the Allegoriae sapientum: "For thence [i.e. from the tree] cometh wisdom" (Jung 1954b, para. 419).

The tree is also a libido symbol or psychic energy and, as stated previously, the incest-taboo is not the desire to engage in actual incest, but rather the libido's aim for renewal and rebirth (Jung 1952a, paras. 329, 332). As the seat of transformation, Jung states that the tree "symbolizes the opus and the transformation process . . . it also signifies the life process in general. . . . Since the opus is a life, death, and rebirth mystery, the tree as well acquires this significance" (Jung 1954b, paras. 418, 459). The literature on tree-symbolism in relation to the Great Mother image is vast and complex,[5]

> Selene (the moon) becomes that heavenly star which hangs as an intermediary between the sublime light of Helios (the sun) and the earth, the great mediator between the world of pure spirit of the fixed stars and the dark sensuality of earthly elements.
>
> (Warner 1976, pp. 257–258)

The symbolic imagery of these lines reflect the function of the Virgin, a function as well as a representation previously attributed to the Church, and the intermediary role played between believer and God.

As the *Stella Maris* the Virgin acts as the mariner's guiding light, and in Paris around 1300 a song was composed for Mary in honour of her birthday: *Stella maris hodie processit ad ortum* (The star of the sea moves today to its rising) (Warner 1976, p. 263). In the 7th- or 8th-century antiphon *Ave Maris Stella*, the Virgin appears as the ocean's guide and pole star and is evoked as the fate of heaven and light-bearer who purifies sinners with fire; and St Bernard associated the symbol of the star to Mary's incorrupt virginity because a star burns and is never consumed (in Warner 1976, p. 263). As St Bernard states in ones of his sermons,

> If the winds of temptation arise, if you are diving upon the rocks of tribulation, look to the star, invoke Mary. If you are tossed upon the waves of pride, of ambition, or envy, or rivalry, look to the star, invoke Mary.
>
> (Warner 1976, p. 264)

In medieval times, the night star's function was navigation, and the association given to Mary endowed her with earthly powers, i.e. the stillness and calming of waves similar to her goddesses' predecessors before her; for example, a storm subsided when the abbot Elsinus "promised he would institute the feast of the Immaculate Conception on his safe return to England" (Warner 1976, pp. 265–266).

The Virgin Mary was also associated with the *stella matutina* or the morning star. The ancients called the morning star Phosphorus by day and Hesperus by night, "the first star of evening and the last star of morning, so dazzling that it casts a shadow in the darkness" (Warner 1976, pp. 263–264). Interestingly, the visions of Mary in Zeitoun appeared from late evening to the early morning hour. Case 1 reports that, "At 2:45 in the morning the Blessed Virgin appeared. . . . After a short while the apparition vanished. It appeared at four o'clock and remained until five o'clock – dawn" (Palmer 1969, pp. 19–21). One eyewitness reported that on May 4, 1968 the Virgin's apparition remained from 9 p.m. until 5 a.m. the next morning (Palmer 1969, pp. 24–29). On May 6, 1968, the Virgin appeared around 3:30 a.m. for two hours (Palmer 1969, p. 32). According to the 1986 survey (see Chapter 3), 54% of respondents claimed that the apparition appeared "At night", 23% said "During the evening", 10% reported "Early morning/before dawn", and 9% reported "In the middle of the night". In other apparition cases, the Virgin Mary is seen typically during the day, e.g. Lourdes, Fatima etc., while in Zeitoun only 3% reported seeing the Virgin during the day. Although stars were described surrounding the Virgin like a crown, the time that the apparition appeared is also relevant; and the morning, for instance, has its own symbolic meaning. Morning symbolizes "the time when light is fresh, of beginnings when all is still uncorrupted, pure and uncompromised"; it is a symbol of purity and promise, "it is the time of Edenic existence"; and in the Bible, it "denotes the time of God's blessings" (Chevalier and Gheerbrant 1994, p. 675). Our concept of time correlates to the day equating with the sun, says Neumann (1963), and according to him, early mankind had a different conception of time (Neumann 1963, p. 223). In the patriarchal solar world the morning represents the time of the sun's birth; however, in lunar mythology "the reckoning of time begins and ends with nightfall" (Neumann 1963, p. 224). For example, in ancient Egypt the evening brought the appearance of the stars and the moon and it was the visible "birth" while the morning was a time of the "death" as the luminaries of the sky vanished, being devoured by the daytime sky (Neumann 1963, p. 224). The matriarchal perspective seems to give importance to the evening and night sky as the representation of birth and the morning as the representation of death. This perspective may explain the meaning of the Virgin of Zeitoun appearing from evening until dawn as a birth-symbol. On the other hand, the meaning of morning is changed in the patriarchal perspective as the sun becomes the centre of importance seen in the sun and rebirth myths (see as follows Christ Child).

The Virgin Mary is not only depicted with stars, whether in the form of a rosary, as in the Fatima children's description, or stars above her head in paintings. Mary is also depicted with a crown. Case 6 reported that the Virgin "wore a crown that shone like diamonds, all of light", and Case 21 reported, "she appeared as a queen with a big crown of light over her head" (Palmer 1969, pp. 29–32; Kamell, Jackson and Jackson 1996, pp. 71–73). The structure of a crown as a circle (see later Birds) is associated with the symbol of the infinite, and rulers who wore them were understood to be representatives of a solar cosmology (Biedermann 1992, pp. 84–85). The circular shape of the crown symbolizes perfection, eternal life, and the feminine principle (Vries 1974, p. 121). The Virtues Faith and Hope, Wisdom (Sophia), and the Church (Ecclesia) were portrayed as wearing crowns in medieval sculpture (Biedermann 1992, p. 85). The crown surrounded or related to the head symbolizes wisdom, insight, and elevated thought (Vries 1974, p. 121). Originally, crowns were made out of the limbs of trees and therefore connected to the symbolism of trees. The crown of rays of light, similar to the description given by Case 21, "are symbols of light and spiritual enlightenment"; and in alchemy, planetary spirits are depicted in books receiving their crown or light from their king (Cirlot 1971, p. 72). A crown of light represents glory, beauty, and honour (Vries 1974, p. 121) which reflect the description of the Virgin of Zeitoun as "beautiful", as Case 3 recounts: "But she is always like a queen, very beautiful, very healthy, standing upright" (Palmer 1969, pp. 24–29). Also in alchemy transmutation or achieving the crown is a symbol of spiritual evolution by way of "victory of the higher principle over the base principle of the instincts" (Cirlot 1971, p. 72). It is a symbol of immortality: "Be thou faithful unto death, and I will give thee a crown of life" (Rev. 2, 10). As defenders of cities especially during times of war and crisis, the great mother goddess, Cybele, Diana of Ephese, Rhea, etc. wore crowns.

The coronation of Mary must have been a need that was previously missing, argues Baring and Cashford (1993):

> as Christ places the crown reverently upon Mary's head, it is though once again there is a celebration of the Hieros Gamos, or Sacred Marriage, of the sun and moon, which was the supreme moment of the Mysteries of pre-Christian cultures.
>
> (Baring and Cashford 1993, pp. 604–606)

The union of Mary and Jesus represents the union of masculine and feminine principles; *zoe* (Mary) and *bios* (Jesus) become one and the duality (male-female, life-death, time-eternity) is transcended (Baring and Cashford 1993, pp. 604–607). In alchemical studies a legend in Cantilena Riplaei tells of a noble king who laments his sterility, and in order to be born anew, he "wished to return to his mother's womb and to dissolve himself in the *prima materia*" (Jung 1952b, para. 491). The mother became pregnant with him again, and when he was born he resembled the moon and then changed into the sun. The mother or Crowned Maid (*Virgo redimita*) was crowned and "set as a star in the highest heaven" (Jung 1952b, para. 491).

The *prima materia* is the basis of the alchemical *opus*, and though the alchemists had several names to represent it, including "mother", Jung stated that, "it represents the unknown substance that carries the projection of the autonomous psychic content" (Jung 1952b, para. 425). The *prima materia* may be similar to the latent energy contained within the concept of virginity, as explained previously. The coronation of Mary may also be a psychological representation of the need for the inclusion of the fourth element of the Trinity. In *Psychology and Religion*, Jung argues that the Christian formula of the Trinity is not complete because "the dogmatic aspect of the evil principle is absent" (Jung 1940, para. 103). With regards to evil, it represents the dark element in man, the earth, and feminine quality; and the fourth element is earth or body and the inclusion of this is symbolized outwardly by the glorification of the body in the form of the Assumption of the Virgin (Jung 1940, para. 107, p. 63n). When the philosophers of antiquity added the fourth element to the Trinity, it produced the quaternity or *circulus quadratus*, "whose symbol was the hermaphroditic *rebis*, the *filius sapientiae*": the *rebis*, meaning "made of two", is the philosopher's stone, and in it, masculine and feminine nature are united (Jung 1940, para. 107, p. 63n). The return of the feminine in the Trinity denotes a return to the inner source of psychic libido or vitality, and "thus withdrawing the projection from a 'God outside' to the numinous and overwhelming experience of the 'God within'" (Adler 1961, p. 32n; para. 102); the experience of the archetypal God-image takes on the quality of numinosity, and in one which Jung categorized as a religious experience.

The crowning of the Virgin in the legend of the noble king symbolizes the importance attributed to the Virgin Mother as she is given a place in heaven. The Assumption of the Virgin Mary is the recognition that her body is reunited again with her soul after death and taken up to heaven. Mary is referred to "Mater" or Queen of Heaven and beside her sits the King, Jesus; "for in her the earth substance, becoming transfigured in her resurrected body, is absorbed in the Godhead" (Jung 1952b, para. 500). In a 1457 painting by the French School the Virgin is being crowned by representations of the Father, Son, and Holy Spirit (Jung 1952c, fig. 233, p. 422). In Christianity, the crown is associated with the majesty of the Lord and the highest attainable level of human existence (Biedermann 1992, p. 85). The crown symbolizes the achievement of the highest goal of evolution, and Jung suggests that in the Christian idea "those who have conquered [themselves] win the crown of eternal life" (Jung 1952a, para. 397). The coronation of Mary is a myth which represents a step in the path towards the psychological process Jung called individuation. Since there are various definitions of individuation presented by Jung in his writings as well as by the post-Jungians,[6] an explanation is presented to include the "religious overtones" of the individuation process. As Jung posits in *Aion*, "It is . . . well to examine carefully the psychological aspects of the individuation process in light of the Christian tradition" (Jung 1951c, para. 79).

The role that the Virgin Mary plays in the individuation process is reflected in the symbol of the *hieros gamos* or sacred marriage, the marriage of the son with the mother-bride or in the depth-psychological concept, the *coniunctio oppositorum*. The marriage takes place in heaven free from impurities and above the devastated world, and as Jung asserts, this is the Christian programme which must be fulfilled before the Incarnation of God (Jung 1958a, para. 743). The incarnation of God through man is a psychological metaphor to explain the individual's encounter with the Self, which coincides with the God-image (Jung 1951c, paras. 71–75). The implications of the individuation process are reflected in individuals as well as in the collective; that is, the implication being the response in the form of renewal or a new concept. The implication for the individual being that he moves past his neurosis by integrating unconscious contents that had earlier possessed him, i.e. integration of the anima. The implication for the collective is a less observable phenomenon due to its abstract nature; it is also difficult to pinpoint because of its temporal constraints, as in the case of the Zeitoun apparitions. In addition, the challenge is in controlling for several environmental variables such as social and political reactions affecting the individuals involved. Despite these challenges, a picture can be painted with information gathered from environmental variables and statements from a group of individuals involved once the dust falls, so to speak. Baring and Cashford seem to suggest that a transformation is observable in the collective:

> A new 'incarnation' of the myth of the goddess and her son-lover seems to manifest when human consciousness is ready to deepen its understanding by searching for a new revelation of life's meaning. It is as though the numinosity of the images gives birth to a new moment of consciousness, which helps to bring about a transformation of the image of the deity in a particular culture at a particular time. The new revelation that allows humanity's values to evolve emerges from the depths of the human soul, whose most ancient image of itself is the goddess.
>
> (Baring and Cashford 1993, p. 607)

A more detailed explanation of this idea is discussed in Chapter 6, but it is pertinent here to introduce the meaning of the *coniunctio* and the significant role played by the Virgin in bringing forth a new incarnation of meaning, concepts, and revelations to a culture. The psychological mechanism behind the dogma of Assumption of Mary forms part of the individuation process (Jung 1958a para.755), and the historical events of the collective are an indication of this process. Subsequently, Jung argues that the popular movement of the Virgin Mary fuelled by the increase of apparitions in the early 20th century as well as the psychological need behind it was the most powerful motive for the dogma of the Assumption (Jung 1958a, para.748). As Jung states,

> [t]he impelling motive behind [the proclamation of the Assumption of Mary] did not come from the ecclesiastical authorities . . . but from the Catholic masses, who have insisted more and more vehemently on this development. Their insistence is, at bottom, the urge of the archetype to realize itself.
>
> (Jung 1951e, para. 142)

Overall, in the first part of this section, after an examination of historical material relating to the Virgin as well as material from previous Marian apparitions, I posit that the mother aspect of the image of the Virgin Mary symbolizes the intervener, protectress, and mediator of the worldly affairs of human beings. Moreover, I argue that aspects of the virgin archetype could be found in the mother archetype, specifically, the theme of rebirth and renewal. The tree symbolizes libido or psychic energy, and it is also a life-giving symbol that transforms stagnant psychic energy into vital energy. The stars and crown also represent birth and renewal. As the morning star, it represents the time of the sun's birth, and it is a symbol of purity and promise. The amplification of the crown revealed the Virgin Mary's association with the *hieros gamos* or *coniunctio*. The union of Mary and Jesus represents the union of masculine and feminine principles with the possibility of creating a third or the future birth of the divine child. In depth-psychological language, this represents a move from the old prevailing attitude to a new attitude, as the Virgin Mary also symbolizes transformation.

## The Christ Child and Jesus

Although only 14% of eyewitnesses from the case studies claimed to have seen the Christ Child or Jesus, as opposed to over 75% of those who referenced the Virgin Mary in both the case studies and survey, the image is a significant religious symbol and forms part of the Marian myth. We need only analyse other popular apparitions of the Virgin Mary to find that Jesus is oftentimes part of the seer's narrative. The Virgin Mary may represent rebirth and the possibility of renewal, but Jesus and the Christ Child is the manifestation of this potentiality as well; and, within the scheme of the individuation process these symbols represent the religious experience with the God-image, an encounter with the self.

In the case studies, eyewitnesses claimed that Mary carries an "infant on her left arm" and "a babe in her arms". As one eyewitness recounts, "Our Lord has also been seen as an Infant. She holds him to identify herself. Jesus is always on her left arm" (Palmer 1969, pp. 24–29). The image of Jesus typically manifested itself in the form of a child, according to these accounts, and even though this symbol appears during the individuation process (Jung 1951b, para. 270), the child archetype has several representations. For example, the child motif appears in fairy tales and often takes on leading roles such as Hänsel and Gretel and symbolizes the "undeveloped facets of one's individuality"; children are undifferentiated sexually and psychically and closer to the hermaphroditic state (von Franz 1996, p. 192). Child motifs also present themselves in folklore such as the elf or dwarf personifying the hidden forces of nature (Jung 1951b, para. 268).

The child or the result of the sacred marriage is sometimes associated with the fruit of the (hermaphroditic) tree of life. Sinn, the moon god of Babylonia and before the moon lost its male sex and became feminine, is shown to be the fruit of the sacred moon tree, "the hero who overcomes the enemy of his father. He is the fruit of the tree. The soma drink, pressed from this fruit, bestows upon the participant divine gifts which he, the divine fruit, possessed" (Harding 1971, pp. 88 and 240). Other divine gods were associated with fruit, such as Adonis, who represented the fruit of the tree, and Dionysus, often associated with grapes or the fruit of the wine. Dionysus represents the god of wine whose blood was wine drunken by his followers, and this mystery was assimilated in Christianity in which the cup of sacrament held the wine that represented the blood of Christ. As Harding concludes, "[i]t was the blood or juice of the fruit of the tree, that fruit which represented the highest development of the tree, which is the tree of life, and whose essence gives immortality" (Harding 1971, p. 240). There are also parallels to the blood of Christ in alchemy in which the water of the philosophers was named *spiritualis sanguis*, and this water was of the Holy Ghost, the *aqua permanens*, which symbolized the spirit assimilated to matter (Jung 1940, para. 151). What *sanguis* and *aqua* symbolized to the alchemists was the spirit (*pneuma*) and coming from God, it "is also the cause of the 'greenness', the *benedicta viriditas*" (Jung 1940, para. 151). God blesses the vegetation and breathes into created things, and as is written in Hildegard of Bingen's Hymn to the Holy Ghost: "From you the clouds rain down, the heavens move, the stones have their moisture, the waters give forth streams, and the earth sweats out greenness" (quoted in Jung 1940, para. 151). The divine *pneuma* is an incorruptible force present in every person, and it is a force "that generates itself, that causes itself to grow; it is its own mother, sister, bride, daughter; its own son, mother, father; a unity of the whole"; its fiery origin has the procreative urge and its fire is related to blood (Jung 1954c, para. 359). The spirit was known as Mercurius and it is referenced in alchemical arcanum: "Whatever the wise seeks is in mercury" (Jung 1940, para. 151). Mercurius was a god of revelation (like Hermes) disclosing the secret of art to the adept; he was also the "soul of the bodies" and "anima vitalis" and "a spirit that penetrates into the depths of the material world and transforms it" (Jung 1954c, para. 356). The spirit appears to possess a life force which nourishes all matter, and psychologically may be analogous to psychic or libido energy.

The Virgin is seen blessing the crowds in Zeitoun as reported by eyewitnesses from both the survey and case studies, 31% and 18% respectively. One eyewitness reported that she lifted "both hands in blessing", and another said that the apparition moved "its hands in blessing". According to Chevalier and Gheerbrant's (1994) definition of blessing, it symbolizes the transfer of power, and to "bless really means to sanctify, to make holy through the WORD, that is to say, to approach holiness, the highest form of cosmic energy" (Chevalier and Gheerbrant 1994, p. 99). The symbols of the child archetype, e.g. fruit, blood, spirit, etc., representing psychic and libido energy, may signify blessing in a form of reinvigorating a languishing individual or populace.

The futurity aspect of the child archetype is another representation appearing in dreams, fantasies, and visions in addition to those found in religion and ancient mythology. Jung categorizes the several psychological aspects of the child archetype in *The Psychology of the Child Archetype* (1951b). The appearance of the child motif signifies "an anticipation of future development" (Jung 1951b, para.278). The seers of the Fatima apparition in 1917 were children themselves, and they claimed that the Virgin had given them three secrets. The first and second of the secrets were revealed to the public, but the third was sent to the Vatican in Rome. The third secret was not revealed until the 2000s; however, during the Cold War believers felt that the secrets directly concerned 20th-century events, and they understood the first two secrets as prophecies to the ending of World War I and II; and if people did not stop offending God, another war would break out (Zimdars-Swartz 1991, p. 206). There are other apparitions similar to the events at Fatima, such as San Sebastian of Garabandal (1961) and La Salette (1846) which seem to be embedded with a prophetic script or pattern. In these cases, the seers were children who also reported seeing Jesus with the Virgin Mary. As anxieties increased during the Cold War period, so did the number of reported apparitions (see Chapter 1, Figure 1.1). With so much anxiety and fear of a possible third world war during this period, it is not surprising that people may have looked to children as in ancient times as saviour child-gods. As Jung posits, the child is a "symbol which unites the opposites [unconscious and conscious elements]; a mediator, bringer of healing, that is, one who makes whole" (Jung 1951b, para.278).

Another aspect of the child archetype is the child hero, often associated with the supernatural or perceived as semi-divine (Jung 1951b, para.281). The child hero can be identified by portentous circumstances and his conception and birth is a miraculous one linked to the intervention of gods and goddesses or celestial beings (Jung 1951b, para.282). Many heroic myths are solar in design, unlike their predecessor lunar myths common in ancient matriarchal societies observing the phases of the moon which represent chaos and death (in Baring and Cashford 1993, p. 290). As Mircea Eliade posits,

> [t]he moon confers a religious valorization on cosmic becoming and reconciles man to death. The sun, on the contrary, reveals a different mode of existence. The sun does not share in becoming; although always in motion, the sun remains unchangeable; its form always the same.
>
> (quoted in Baring and Cashford 1993, p. 290)

There was a change in consciousness when societies transitioned to a solar-centric mythology from a lunar-centric one (Baring and Cashford 1993; Harding 1971). As the hero transitioned from moon to the sun, like the sun, Eliade continues,

> he fights darkness, descends into the realm of death and emerges victorious. Here darkness is no longer, as it is in lunar mythologies. . . . Darkness is no longer valorized as a necessary phase in cosmic life. . . . In the end *sun* and *intelligence* will be assimilated to such a degree that the solar

> and syncretistic theologies of the end of antiquity become rationalistic philosophies; the sun is proclaimed to be the intelligence of the world.
>
> (quoted in Baring and Cashford 1993, p. 290, italics in original)

This transition meant a shift from the worship of the moon's "creative and fecund powers of nature and of the wisdom that lies inherent in instinct and in the at-one-ness with natural law" to the worship of the sun god via the sun hero attributing powers of order, formulation, and discrimination, and by slaying the dragon "of ignorance and sloth, thus acquiring consciousness, a spiritual value of a different order" (Harding 1971, p. 31). Subsequently, the solar gods must confront and kill a dragon, serpent, or another representation of evil and death such as the famous Egyptian Ra who defeated the huge serpent-demon Apophis who threatened to swallow up the sun or the Canaanite Baal who descended into the underworld and upon rescuing his sister-wife Anat defeated Mot (which in Hebrew means death) (Baring and Cashford 1993, p. 291). The transition to sun worship and solar-based myths subjugated chaos and death which had earlier formed part of the totality of the moon represented in her phases. These parts represent the feminine aspect of the moon, and embedded in the structure of sun myths is a solar god of war destined to slay the demon, another representation of the feminine. According to Baring and Cashford (1993), this representation does not exclusively lend itself to an interpretation of the sun hero defeating the mother goddess culture in which it is in contrast to the dominance of the masculine principle or Logos, but may also symbolize the individual gaining control over his instinctual powers (Baring and Cashford 1993, p. 294).

The hero's journey represents the process of individuation, and as Jung states, the various "fates may be regarded as illustrating the kind of psychic events that occur in the entelechy or genesis of the 'self'" (Jung 1951b, para. 282). The achievement of psychic wholeness is met with enormous obstacles, such as the appearance of the Minotaur or the dragon which led mythic heroes such as Jason, Theseus, Hercules, etc. to set out on a quest, achieving it after the defeat of their respective monsters. The slaying of the dragon by the sun hero, as the tale typically goes, symbolizes the mastery of his inner darkness – the darkness representing the unconscious. The darkness may also symbolize fear, ignorance, or collective beliefs or values. Moreover, the defeat of the dragon is mastery over instinctual and unconscious behavioural patterns and limitations of the hero's knowledge (Baring and Cashford 1993, p. 294). The threat of the obstacles, if not overcome or defeated, signifies the new consciousness acquired slipping back into the instinctive or unconscious psyche (Jung 1951b, para. 282).

The myth of Christ fits into the pattern of the hero's myth as his birth was both prophesized and miraculous, and consequently he was deemed the messiah and saviour.[7] The mother of Jesus is also "special" or selected in some way as she, like many mothers of semi-divine men, also conceived miraculously, in Mary's case through the assistance and intervention of the Holy Spirit. Jesus's name is followed by Christ; "Christ our saviour", "Christ our Lord". Jung presented an explanation of the meaning of Christ in *Aion* and *Psychology and Religion*. On the real Christ, Jung postulates,

> At a very early stage . . . the real Christ vanished behind the emotions and projections that swarmed about him . . . he was absorbed into the surrounding religious systems and moulded into their archetypal exponent. He became the collective figure whom the unconscious of his contemporaries expected to appear, and for this reason it is pointless to ask who he "really" was. He opened men's eyes to revelation precisely because he was, from everlasting, God, and therefore unhistorical; and he functioned as such only by virtue of the consensus of unconscious expectation.
>
> (Jung 1948a, para. 228)

Psychologically, it may be fruitless to ask who the real historical Jesus Christ was, while mythically his tale reveals, similar to the case of Mary via the virgin archetype, a pre-Christian and archaic meaning. Similar to the meaning of the Christ Child, Jesus Christ symbolizes the vine and those that hang on him are his branches; his body represents bread to be eaten and his blood wine to be drunk; and in human personification he is the hero and God-man "born without sin, more complete and more perfect than the natural man" (Jung 1948a, para. 229). According to a Jungian perspective, when an individual's unconscious produces symbols of the Christ in dreams, fantasy, and visions, they are typically represented by a man of heroic proportions, a treasure hard to find, a crown, or circle; this archetype is a "reflection of the individual's wholeness, i.e., of the self" (Jung 1948a, para. 230). Christ is the representation of the Self (Jung 1948a, para. 230), and this is what the concept of Christ represents. The images of the Self –produced by the unconscious – occur during the course of the individuation process. Self-realization or individuation is not the alteration of consciousness, but rather "the restoration of an original condition, an apocatastasis" (Jung 1951c, para. 73). The restoration is the original state of oneness with the God-image which brings about an integration bridging a split in the personality "caused by the instincts striving apart in different and mutually contradictory directions" (Jung 1951c, para. 73).

The motif of suffering and sacrifice is found in myths like that of Mithras who took his bull on his back for the love of Mater Natura and carried this burden on the *via dolorosa* of the Transitus (Jung 1952a, para. 460). Christ, too, bore his cross, and the motif of the Cross is found in the Zeitoun apparitions with 9% of testimonies claiming to have seen it: "The Virgin would walk over the church . . . and bow before the cross [on top of the dome] that shone" (Kamell, Jackson and Jackson 1996, p. 67). According to Jung's interpretation of the symbol of the cross,

> The cross, or whatever other heavy burden the hero carries, is *himself*, or rather *the* self, his wholeness, which is both God and animal – not merely the empirical man, but the totality of his being, which is rooted in his animal nature and reaches out beyond the merely human towards the divine. His wholeness implies a tremendous tension of opposites paradoxically at one with themselves, as in the cross, their most perfect symbol.
>
> (Jung 1952a, para. 460, italics in original)

The motif of suffering is also associated with the feminine aspect of the psyche. In its projected form the images are more in line with the Terrible Devouring Mother, but they can also represent the unconscious, i.e. the descent into the underworld. The suffering and sacrifice have their function, as Neumann states, "[b]ut even where the transformative character of the Feminine appears as a negative, hostile, and provocative element, it compels tension, change, and an intensification of the personality. In this way an extreme exertion of the ego is provoked and its capacity for creative transformation is directly and indirectly 'stimulated'" (Neumann 1963, p. 34). The suffering or sacrifice element is another form of the anima which, unlike the Great Mother who has no interest in the "independence of the individual and the ego", may be a vehicle of the transformational character of the hero, or the individual (Neumann 1963, p. 35). When the hero in fairy tales or myths answers a riddle, the princess willingly gives herself to the victor; that is, the anima is integrated by the individual (Neumann 1963, p. 35). The Devil or Satan is another transformational instigator such as Mephistopheles in Goethe's Faust. Jung's interpretation of Job in regards to the relationship between Yahweh and Satan is as follows: "Yahweh allows himself to be fooled by Satan, deals faithlessly with Job, misjudges the situation, and then has to admit his error. But although Job is obliged to bow to brute force he carries off the moral victory" (Jung 1952a, para. 398).

In many apparitions, including those at Zeitoun, the theme of suffering is prevalent, albeit one needs to closely analyse historical material by drawing out the contributing factors that lead to the suffering of the community affected, and consequently, how this suffering leads to collective anxiety. When the historical material of apparitional phenomena is analysed, whether relating to apparitions in La Salette, Marpingen, or Zeitoun, what we find are monsters, dragons, and devils in the form of economic depression, religious repression, and political tyranny. Under such conditions, the usual steps towards a revolt against depressive conditions take place through underground organizing, typically in support of a leader with messianic qualities, but in cases of apparitions they find their strength in the metaphysical. Yet through this religious imagery the victims of those oppressing conditions are brought together, and somehow in unity change is not only possible, but inevitable. It is in their suffering that they are brought together, and through a united front against their oppressors (whether real or perceived) the realization of a transformation of their community or state is achieved. Whether their end goal is met or not, the experience of unity in forms of camaraderie and story-telling amongst neighbours, acquaintances, and strangers has transformed them – as in Zeitoun where Muslims and Christians joined in peace and brotherhood – and during the course of this period of time they had a religious experience, or to put it in Jung's words, an encounter with the Self.

## The symbol of light

The most statistically significant aspect featuring in the descriptions of the apparition reported by the case studies is the presence of *light*, with 86% of eyewitnesses claiming to have seen it. This percentage is even higher than that relating to references to visions of the Virgin Mary (at 77%). There were various types of descriptions of the light seen by eyewitnesses, grouped into a category called Reference to Light in the last chapter (see Chapter 4, Table 4.1 for the complete group list). Some of these descriptions of light overlapped with other features or symbols mentioned, such as stars (14%), birds (5%), and cross (9%). Despite overlapping with references to other aspects, the symbol of light clearly stands out from the material, and the imagery of light seems to permeate through almost every case study collected for this project. By contrast, only about 3% of respondents from the 1986 survey described the event or apparition as including some type of light. It is curious that such a small percentage of respondents reported using light as a term to describe the apparition when light was a prevalent description in the case studies. Could the 18-year time gap between the apparitional event and the time the survey was conducted have impacted the recollection of the seers? After such a time lapse, could it be that the image of the Virgin Mary was more of a powerful imagery than the images of light? The low percentage in the 1986 survey may be also linked to the phrasing of questions asked in the survey. These two diverse sample materials (the case studies and the survey) may signal the importance of the timing of data collection during or immediately after an event or phenomena such as this one. The timing may ensure a recording of details that may otherwise be lost due to the failure of the seer's recollection of specific aspects of events ex-post. Fortunately, the timely collection of data characterizing the case studies, despite a relatively small sample size as presented in the previous chapter, implies that this material reveals what seems a strong emotional reaction from the seers, such that the details of their accounts reflect this emotion. The image of light is a key detail of the apparition, and I think its significance warrants an analysis of its possible meaning.

The symbol of light is a universal symbol "of divinity and the spiritual" (Biedermann 1992, p. 204). For example, in the Book of Genesis, God hovers over the waters of the formless earth, and says "Let there be light" on the first day of creation, and with this declaration God separates the light from the darkness (1: 2–4). Light is manifested in the formless, dark world, and this becomes the primal symbol of duality. God, performing a function similar to that of the moon and sun, gives birth to life and life forms. God hovers over the waters, a feminine symbol as well as the symbol of the unconscious, and out of this union the creative process is initiated and the concept of an earth is created. In patriarchal societies light is typically associated to the sun, and conversely the moon is symbolized by darkness (Biedermann 1992, p. 204). To understand the symbol of light, we must understand its counterpart, darkness. Also in patriarchal societies, light is the symbol of masculinity whereas darkness is feminine. In Christianity, the Saviour is called "the light of the world" (Biedermann 1992, p. 204; Vries 1974, p. 297); Jesus the Saviour was born to save man from his sins (darkness), and later in the Book of Revelation, Jesus, portrayed as a Holy Warrior, engages in war against sinners. The Christian battle against evil is similarly found in a late Babylonian hymn to the sun god Shamash (9th century B.C.):

> Thou who dost illumine darkness and the sky, destroyer of evil above and below, god Shamash. . . . All princes rejoice to gaze upon thee; all the gods of heaven exult in thee. In thy brilliance do they see even that which is hidden, and thus do they walk secure in thy [?] light. . . . All the gates of heaven are open wide, and all the gods of heaven do sacrifice unto thee!
>
> (Quoted in Biedermann 1992, p. 204)

The light force does not only try to destroy darkness, but they can also complement each other, e.g. Yin and Yang (Biedermann 1992, p. 204). When masculine and feminine energies are synthesized, a transformation occurs and a new energy is created, for instance. Viewed from this perspective, light and dark aspects work together rather than conflict or clash. The light embraces and engulfs the darkness, creating something new. Even though heroes and divine beings are portrayed as warriors and destroyers, I agree (with Jung and Neumann) that the symbolic meaning behind their respective mythical stories, such as the slaying of a dragon, may reflect the unity of light and darkness.

This unity is transformed into *grace*, or at least grace is a representation of this union. In ancient times, we have The Graces and they represented the division into three of the Great Goddess of Fertility; they are the same as the Three Fates brought out in Spring by Hermes-Mercury (Vries 1974, p. 223). In classical Greek mythology Aglaia represented "brightness", Eurphrosyne "joyfulness", and Thalia represented "bloom" (Vries 1974, p. 223). The archaic idea of grace represented in The Graces as defined in Vries (1974) is one of fertility, growth, and change. In Christianity grace represents a similar function. Santhosh Thomas Karingadayil (2011), a scholar in comparative theology, examines the concept of salvation comparing the theological and soteriological position of Thomas Aquinas, and through this examination the meaning of grace is explained. According to Karingadayil, the term grace stands for the symbol of salvation, and goes on to present grace as

> a free gift of God's good pleasure in acts designed to assist and bless human beings. Human beings are called to a supernatural goal, the union with the triune God, which goes beyond the capacities and actions of any created nature. When sin and its punishment stood as a permanent block between God and human beings, there arose the need for divine intervention. A person needed a special gift of God, grace, to supply a new supernatural nature equipped with new powers of faith, hope, and love that elevate, empower, and incline him to enter eternity. This empowerment and elevation speaks of the necessity of grace as the attainment of salvation. Grace thus becomes the chief element in our redemption.
>
> (Karingadayil 2011, pp. 119–120)

In this case, grace is not God, but it is a gift from him. And the function of grace is similar to the meaning of grace associated with The Graces. Sinners are blocked from the gates of heaven, so to speak, and grace functions as a guide towards balance, renewal, and rebirth. According to Aquinas, "grace brings not only forgiveness but transformation of the person as well. Grace can overcome the obstacles that separate people from the transcendence of God and it equips them for their encounter with God" (Karingadayil 2011, p. 121). Grace also has a transformational element to it. In the *Archetypes and the Collective Unconscious (1954a)*, Jung presents five forms of rebirth. The last one is called "participation in the process of transformation", and here the initiate participates in a rite of transformation such as the ceremony of the Mass or initiations into the Eleusinian mysteries. During these rites, the initiate participates in divine grace; one initiate of the Eleusinian mysteries praised the grace conferred through the certainty of immortality: "Truly the blessed gods have proclaimed a most beautiful secret: Death comes not as a curse, but as a blessing to men". (quoted in Jung 1950a, para. 205). Later in the chapter, Jung explains that individuals attending a ceremony such as the Mass are participants in a ritual or in the "sacral action by their mere presence in this place where grace abounds" (Jung 1950a, para. 209). In the same paragraph he goes on to say,

> The Mass is an extramundane and extratemporal act in which Christ is sacrificed and then resurrected in the transformed substances; and this

> rite of his sacrificial death is not a repetition of the historical event but the original, unique, and external act. The experience of the Mass is therefore a participation in the transcendence of life, which overcomes all bounds of space and time. It is a moment of eternity in time.
>
> (Jung 1950a, para. 209)

The state of grace or to be full of grace is similar to the act of blessing or being blessed, and as I briefly explained earlier, blessing may be a religious representation of psychic energy and libido, and grace seems to also fit this description.

The representation of psychic energy and libido is expressed and symbolized in many religious texts. Mircea Eliade (1965), in *The Two and the One*, devoted a chapter to the experience of "light". In his study, Eliade brings together several religious perspectives on the meaning of light in Buddhism, Hinduism, and Christianity, to name a few. I will extract and present here some of Eliade's findings since they are rich in descriptions and pertinent to the universal symbolic meaning of light. Similar to the symbolic experience of individuals during the ceremony of the Mass, grace and blessing may be felt by the believer and she or he may experience transcendence or illumination. Among the Esquimos, "lightning" or "illumination" is a mystical experience, and one cannot become a shaman without the experience of *quamaneq* or illumination (Eliade 1965, p. 22). Case 20 reported seeing "a lightning-like light" appear (Kamell, Jackson and Jackson 1996, p. 67). Before the image of the Virgin Mary took form, 32% of eyewitness reported that a light preceded the apparition, and in the example of Case 8 lightning preceded the formation: "At about 9:50 p.m. we saw lightning over the church, much stronger than one could make with a flashlight. I had the feeling something was about to happen. A thin line or edge of light appeared like the light you see when you open the door of a lighted room. Within seconds it formed itself into the shape of the Virgin" (Palmer 1969, pp. 32–34). The lightning flash has been compared by many religions to the rapidity of spiritual illumination, and surviving a lightning strike changes a person and begins a new existence. According to Eliade, this is how a Yakout survivor explained his experience: "God had come down from heaven, broken his body into pieces and then brought him back to life – but after his initiatory death and resurrection he became a shaman" (Eliade 1965, p. 22).

The imagery of a thin line seen similar to opening the door of a lighted room by Case 8 can be analogous to a door or gateway to another world or dimension or perhaps heaven. According to the Upanishads, followers of Hinduism believed that "being manifests itself by the pure Light and that man receives knowledge of being by an experience of supernatural Light", and at the moment of death the soul rises towards the Sun, the Gate of the World, and only those who know how can enter (Eliade 1965, p. 26). Moreover, Eliade posits that, "he who gains it not only gains knowledge but also, and principally, a new and superior way of being" (Eliade 1965, p. 26). He goes on to argue that this revelation is sudden like the lightning discussed previously, and that Buddha himself received this "instantaneous illumination" in a moment outside time (Eliade 1965, p. 26). In *The Tibetan Book of the Dead*, the light – appearing as sparkling, bright, and radiantly awesome – is referred to as "Pure Truth", and as a dead character in the text says: "Be not daunted thereby, nor terrified, nor awed. This is the radiance of thine own true nature. Recognise it!" (Eliade 1965, p. 38).

In India, religions and philosophies have a basic idea of the mystique of the Light, observes Eliade, which is that light is creative and procreative; in addition, the *atman* is an immortal and fearless entity found at the heart of man in the form of a light in the heart (Eliade 1965, p. 26). The idea that the cosmos and man were born of the light in Christianity is also found in Tibetan myths. However, primordial men were asexual and without sexual drive and the light radiated within them. According to the myth, the sun and moon did not exist until the sexual instinct was awoke, and this when the light was extinguished from men; as a Tibetan monk explains:

> At the beginning men multiplied in the following way – the light emanating from the body of the male penetrated, lit and impregnated the womb of the female. The sexual instinct was satisfied by sight alone. But men degenerated and began to touch one another with their hands, and finally they discovered sexual union.
>
> (Eliade 1965, p. 42)

Losing the light, or it becoming extinguished from man, represents a degenerated state, according to this Tibetan myth. Primordial man seems to have lost his connection to his Self, the light, and descended into a physical and instinctual state. Interestingly, the above Tibetan's monk story reminds me of the 1993 film, *Demolition Man*, with Sandra Bullock and Sylvester Stallone where Stallone plays a police officer who is cryogenically frozen and is reawakened in 2032 (Brambilla 1993). The character of Bullock offers the cop coitus, but he is shocked by the technological method used to engage in sexual intercourse by 21st-century people: electrical helmets are worn by the couple while sitting across from each other. When the cop protests against the strange and artificial method and suggests the "natural" way, Bullock is disgusted by his suggestion and assures the cop that this way prevents transmission of sexual diseases and bacteria. Physical sexual union in both the myth and the movie suggests a descent from man's higher state of being in which one has access to knowledge and a "superior way of being". Elements of the idea of procreation by using the light to impregnate a female womb can be also linked to Greek mythology; recall earlier Zeus's ability to transform himself into various animals, including birds, to impregnate moral women and its similarity of the Virgin Mary's conception by the Holy Ghost.

## Symbol of birds

The final symbol to be amplified is the grouping labelled as *Reference to Birds* from Chapter 4. The interpretation of light is still incomplete since descriptions of light by eyewitnesses were also associated to the apparition of birds. Only two eyewitnesses, or 9% of the case studies, describe the birds as luminous, but the report from Case 3 is one of the most detailed explanations documenting the experience of the so-called apparition of the birds. As Case 3 recounts:

> Before the apparitions took place some birds that look like pigeons – I don't know what they are – appear in different formations. Sometimes two appear on the dome just as if they had come out of it. However, the dome is closed; the windows do not open. Everyone watches to see where they come from. They might be flying eastward, then wheeling about and flying to the west, and while one watches them, they suddenly disappear.
>
> I remember particularly on June 9, the birthday of Our Lady (in Coptic calendars) I was in Zeitoun when I saw two pigeons very white, very bright, luminous, radiating light. I was determined to watch them. They became tiny flakes of cloud and seemed to enter heaven. They do not flap their wings; they glide. In a flash they appeared; and disappear in the same way. They do not fly away but [stay] above and around the center dome. . . . They fly very swiftly. They are not light on one side only, but are completely lighted. One does not see feather at all – just something bright. They are radiating creature[s], larger in size than a dove or a pigeon. Sometimes as one of them flies lower, it gets larger and larger. People realize these are not pigeons. They are there to honor St. Mary, and usually appear some time before an apparition.
>
> (Palmer 1969, pp. 24–29)

The Holy Ghost/Spirit is associated with light, and similar to Zeus, manifests itself in the form of a bird. In Christianity, it is the Holy Spirit which impregnates Mary: "This is how the birth of Jesus Christ came to be . . . she was found to be with child through the Holy Spirit . . . what is conceived in her is through the Holy Spirit" (Matthew 1:18). In Christian art, the Holy Spirit is depicted as a dove surrounded by light rays ("The Holy Spirit as a dove in Annunciation", by Philippe de Champaigne, 1644; "Annunciation" by Bartolomé Esteban Murillo 1677; "The Annunciation" by Paolo de Matteis, 1712; "The Annunciation" by Peter Paul Rubens, btw. 1608 and 1628). In the Lutheran service book, the title of hymn 496 is "Holy Spirit, Light Divine", and the first stanza reads as follows: "Holy Spirit, Light Divine, Shine upon this heart of mine, Chase the shades of night away, Turn the darkness into day". The Holy Spirit may encompass elements of the symbol of the dove and light, and as the meaning of light it represents creation and procreation. As the manifestation of the dove, the Holy Spirit may present itself to the collective as a symbol of hope and peace.

In the case studies, 2% of eyewitnesses reported seeing a dove, while 3% of survey respondents also reported seeing a flying object described as a dove. The majority of eyewitnesses from the case studies, 32%, described the flying objects as birds. Within the pagan context, the dove was associated with physical love; for example, Aphrodite's bird "represented the pledge of love which the lover offered the object of his desire" (Chevalier and Gheerbrant 1994, p. 306) and her sacred doves, which were associated with her lover Adonis and with Cupid, were kept in her shrines, Cythera and Paphos (Biedermann 1992, p. 101). In the ancient world, the dove represented "erotic terms of affection for a woman with whom one was intimate", and the love-goddess Astarte was associated with this idea of the bird before the Greeks took over this concept from Semitic traditions in the 4th century B.C. (Biedermann 1992, p. 101). The dove is a universal metaphor for woman (Chevalier and Gheerbrant 1994, p. 307), and in ancient traditions it was associated with the Great Mother or mother, e.g. the All-Mother as a dove lays the Universal Egg. The fertility statue of Demeter holds a dove in one hand, related with the Moirai (life-destiny-death) and the moon phases. Two of the doves of snow-white were the daughters of Anius who can make every land fertile and "they were changed into doves by Bacchus" god of wine and fertility (Vries 1974, p. 144). Therefore, the symbol of the dove also contains a feminine and fertility element to it. In ancient Rome, the dove was sacred to Venus and its eggs were thought to have aphrodisiac powers, and in China they appeared in the headdress of the fertility goddess (Biedermann 1992, pp. 101–102).

Christianity, on the other hand, adopted a slightly different take on the meaning of the dove such as one of purity, innocence, and peace in contrast to the pagan representation of physical love. In fact, winged creatures are thought to represent the sublimation of instincts, and a flying dove represents the Holy Spirit and peace (Chevalier and Gheerbrant 1994, p. 306). Doves are thought to embody the virtues of moderation and many are depicted in Christian art with saints, the Evangelists, Thomas Aquinas, Theresa of Avila, etc. (Biedermann 1992, pp. 101; Vries 1974, p. 144). In Christian tradition, the dove is a symbol of faithful marriage, and St Basil said, "Let women imitate the turtle dove, keeping their marriage vows sacred" (Chevalier and Gheerbrant 1994, p. 307; Biedermann 1992, p. 101). The idea that the dove represents these virtues is connected to the Christian meaning of the Holy Spirit which is of divine inspiration, wisdom, and guidance; Mohammed (Islam) was inspired by the dove of the Holy Spirit, Noah sends out a dove (Vries 1974, p. 144).

Jung offers an interpretation of the Holy Spirit. More precisely, Jung speculates why the Holy Trinity was not a more reasonable and natural "Father, Mother, and Son" combination. He argues,

> it is not a question of a natural situation, but of a product of human reflection added on to the sequence of father and son. Through reflection, 'life' and its 'soul' are abstracted from Nature and endowed with a separate existence.
>
> (Jung 1948a, para. 235)

The definition of reflection is not of thought, Jung explains, but it is "a spiritual act that runs counter to the natural process. . . . It should, therefore, be understood as an act of *becoming conscious*" (Jung 1948a, p. 158n, italics in original). Similar to the ancient Egyptian view, argues Jung, "father and son are united in the same procreative force embodied in Ka-mutef as the breath or 'spiration' of the Godhead"[8] (Jung 1948a, para. 235). Also, the dove as the symbol of the Holy Spirit "expresses the non-human character of the totality or self" (Jung 1948a, para. 276). The Holy Spirit usually has a neuter designation, but sometimes exchanges it for a feminine one especially from the perspective of Gnosticism: they viewed the Holy Spirit as the mother, as one who enlightens, influences, and inspires (Jung 1948a, para. 240). The Holy Spirit is personified by Sophia who is symbolized by a dove, the bird belonging to the love-goddess of the Spirit of Wisdom (Jung 1948a, para. 646; Vries 1974, p. 144).

Whether the Holy Spirit expresses itself as a dove or a feminine or anima personification such as Sophia, I think the underlying psychological reasoning for these manifestations could be explained as the activation of the archetype of the Self. If the Holy Spirit expresses the non-human character of the Self as the symbol of the dove, as Jung suggests earlier, then more evidence is needed to justify this argument in the case of the Zeitoun apparition. In *Flying Saucers (1959)* (and elsewhere), Jung interprets circular objects such as the spherical objects of UFOs as symbols of the Self. In addition to seeing a large strange pigeon, Case 2 reported to have seen "[s]everal bright spotlights" move quickly over him and the people around him, Case 3 claimed the Virgin became "a round ball of light and gradually faded into darkness", and Case 7 even reported seeing birds which "appeared like small planes or gliders" (Palmer 1969, pp. 21–24, 24–29, and 32 respectively). One eyewitness not only describes the experience, but offers an explanation of the experience:

> The whole scene was bathed with a luminous halo surrounded with a blue circular frame all ablaze. Little by little the vision become more distinct until the figure of Mary became more evident to the vast multitudes who filled the space surrounding the church of Zeitun. The luminous circle seemed to symbolize to me the perfection of eternity in contradistinction to the fragmentary limitations of our seemingly dreary mechanical measure of time.
>
> (Zaki 1982, p. 9)

The apparitions of the birds also seem to take on metaphysical feats of movement and transfiguration similar to the descriptions of circular forms of UFOs reported in *Flying Saucers*. With such descriptions of the circular phenomenon at Zeitoun, the same interpretation presented by Jung in *Flying Saucers* may also be applied here; that is, the circular visions of Zeitoun were manifestations of totality "whose simple, round form portrays the archetype of the self, which . . . play the chief role in uniting apparently irreconcilable opposites and is therefore best suited to compensate" split-mindedness (Jung 1959, p. 17).

Given the state of social and economic problems at the time of the apparitions in Egypt, the symbol of the dove may have represented a psychological need for Egyptians who sought unity and wholeness. The dove appears as a symbol of peace when the Egyptian people most needed it, and it is not surprising that the image of the Virgin Mary coincidently appears holding an olive branch in her right hand (Palmer 1969, pp. 24–29).

## Conclusion

The chapter began with amplification of the image of the Virgin Mary which is divided into two sections. First, the virginity aspect of Mary is interpreted, revealing associations with the virgin archetype. Similar to the ancient virgin goddesses of antiquity, the Virgin is free and uncontrolled, and "belonging-to-no-man", the symbol of the virgin archetype represents her loyalty to instinct and nature. This aspect of Mary also represents the negative side of the anima manifesting as a witch or some type of enchantress, and if this aspect is not integrated, she can possess or devour man. The other side of the anima is the ability to bring forth fertility and renewal. In the second part of the amplification of the Virgin Mary, the mother aspect of the image is interpreted, and aspects of the virgin archetype could be found in the mother archetype, especially in the symbolic meaning of the tree, stars, and crown. The differentiating factor of the mother archetype from the virgin archetype can be found in its mediating and intervening role. As the Great Mother, she is the goddess of time and faith, and similar to the Great Spinstress she spins the thread of fate. Moreover, the mother archetype could also represent the goddess of war such as the Greek Virgin Mother Goddess Athena, an image of strength and protector of cities in times of war. The crowning of the Virgin is associated with the *hieros gamos* or *coniunctio*, representing the union of masculine and feminine principles with the possibility of the birth of the third or symbolically the child, and in this form the Virgin Mary symbolizes transformation.

The process of interpretation through amplification continued with a focus on the three other main common themes identified in Chapter 4: *Reference to Religious Symbols*, *Reference to Light*, and *Reference to Birds*. The other three categories derived from the 1986 survey, *Dressed in White*,

*Hands*, and *Blessing* are interweaved with the amplification of the other symbols. Some of the latter symbols, such as the Christ Child and Jesus, olive branch, and blessing, emerged more prominently in the amplification than other ones, including the image of the hands and the image dressed in white. This difference in prominence could have occurred because of the close connection that the latter specific images have with the main symbols. For example, the image of the Virgin Mary dressed in white is connected with the image "bathed in light", and the hands with the movement of blessing. Nevertheless, the amplification of all of the symbols seems to point to one common theme: rebirth and transformation.

In the final chapter of this study, the material from this chapter will be merged with the historical material surrounding the Zeitoun apparitions. The material discussed in the present and the previous chapters represents the internal, or "inner-world" factors, while the historical material represents the external, or "outer-world" factors. The aim in the next chapter will be to develop further the interpretation proposed in this chapter, by jointly analysing the main "outer-world" factors represented by the socio-economic and political aspects with the above-mentioned "inner-world" factors.

## Notes

1 Although after the Unification of Italy in the late 19th century the newly unified state fell under the control of the secularists, religious persecution at the level seen during other apparitions such as in Spain and Germany is mostly absent. During the Italian Fascist regime (1923–43), its leader Benito Mussolini had an erratic relationship with the Catholic Church; in some periods during his rule he supported the Vatican, while at other times he harshly condemned it. Subsequently, the main anxiety that seems to plague the Italians during the period of the 1947–48 apparitions was the threat of Communism.

2 See Neumann's *The Great Mother* and his discussion on "matter" accentuated in matriarchal and patriarchal societies and their respective meanings, pp. 49–50.

3 The author of this book travelled to Egypt and interviewed several Coptic priests and locals, collecting stories and traditions in his investigation on the Holy Family trail.

4 Koran 19: 22–26.

5 See Jung's *The Philosophical Tree.*

6 See *Individuation* in "A Critical Dictionary of Jungian Analysis" by Andrew Samuels, Bani Shorter, and Fred Plaut.

7 There are different stories of the historical Jesus's life stemming also from the Synoptic Gospels and Q.

8 In *Psychology and Religion*, Jung devotes a section to the Holy Spirit. He describes the function of the Holy Spirit linking its existence with the autonomous functioning of the unconscious or archetypes.

Chapter 6

# Analysis and interpretation

## Introduction

In Chapter 3, the historical context of the present study was introduced and focused on key aspects of the life of Egyptians prior to and during the apparitions at Zeitoun as well as on events which had taken place under the rule of President Nasser. Various aspects of Egyptian society were addressed, particularly, the 1967 Arab-Israeli War, economic policy and stability, and key political decisions taken by the government of President Nasser. As discussed in Chapter 1, historical material has been used by investigators of apparitions to explain and connect external factors, and I argued that it is an essential component to the study of mass vision of Marian apparitions. Moreover, Jung's study of *visionary rumours* in *Flying Saucers* (1959) was discussed in Chapter 2, where he points out the connection between worldly events and the collective psyche, specifically the effects of worldly event on collective distress and anxiety. Against this background, the aim of this chapter is to elaborate on the interpretation proposed in general terms in Chapter 5, by merging the socio-economic and political aspects of this case with the "inner-world" factors. The "inner-world" factors specific to this case are represented by the common themes and symbols that were extracted from primary sources in Chapter 4. Before presenting my interpretation, I examine explanations proposed by eyewitnesses and bystanders and the underlying anxieties associated with the explanation. Subsequently, in the second part of the chapter both the "inner-world" and the external factors will function as the main material used to translate into psychological language the application of depth-psychological concepts, most prominently the application of compensation theory for the interpretation of this case.

## Interpretations and psychological analysis

This part of the chapter is devoted to interpreting the historical material and the common themes and symbols relating to the Zeitoun apparitions and comprises three parts. First, the evidence pointing to the existence of cultural anxiety will be examined through the narrative associated to the distress and psychic cause of the phenomenon. Second, three main explanations of the apparitions given by eyewitnesses and bystanders will be identified and analysed. Third, I lay out my interpretation of the Zeitoun phenomenon taking into account the historical material, common themes and symbols identified in Chapter 5, and the three set of explanations. I conclude with a short analysis on synthesis and integration.

### *The psychic cause of the Zeitoun phenomenon*

The main objective of this section is to determine whether there is a *psychological* case for a "causal basis", or *emotional tension*, as regards the Zeitoun visions "having its cause in a situation of collective distress or danger, or a vital psychic need" (Jung 1959, p. 7); that is, the aim is to determine whether an *unusual emotion or tension* existed prior to the appearances of the Zeitoun visions. The psychological projection or visions of the Virgin Mary must have a psychic cause behind them. Existing studies of Marian apparitions examine them mostly from a socio-economic and political perspective, sometimes, albeit loosely, alluding to anxieties as an explanation. In this section, I analyse the cultural distress and anxieties behind the events of the period by examining the narratives created by Egyptians on how they perceived and interpreted the apparition of the Virgin Mary. The narrative can be instrumental in identifying the unconscious background helping to understand the psychological need of the cultural unconscious. Moreover, the narrative is part of the historical context and these external factors reveal the distress for which the cultural unconscious is compensating.

In the aftermath of the 1967 war, Nasser struggled in vain to piece together the Egyptian state and to regain the control that he had during the pre-war era. Instead, internal turmoil increased, and one of the backlashes of the military defeat was that religious tensions between the Muslims and Copts intensified. Within the small sample of eyewitness accounts, only a handful of interpretations of why the image of the Virgin Mary had appeared in Zeitoun can be found. Therefore, I consider also interpretations from secondary sources, some of which are not included in the database discussed in Chapter 4. One narrative of the Zeitoun phenomenon is that the Virgin Mary had appeared in order to intervene and save Copts from an impending massacre from Muslims. I found evidence of only one person making this claim. In a short documentary on the Zeitoun apparitions, "The Appearance of the Virgin Mary in Egypt", questions were posed, "Why Zeitoun and why Egypt in the mid-1960s when the Middle-East was a powder-cake? War was in the air, and a massacre had been plotted. The homes of Christians were marked for blood. Peace, it seems, would take a miracle". In answer to this, one interviewee from the documentary, Archdeacon Youssef Kamell, gives his interpretation on why the Virgin Mary appeared, "[t]hey marked every house of the Christians with a red cross, and then appeared the Virgin Mary. And then instead of taking revenge on them she cured them, healing them" (Marian Apparitions of the 20th Century, 1991). However, if a massacre was planned, why was it not documented, and most importantly, why did none of the eyewitnesses from the 22 case studies report it? A reference was found to an episode which may lead to an alternative interpretation of the red cross seen by Kamell. In *When Millions saw Mary* (1980) Francis Johnston documents the experience of Anglican correspondent Ronald Bullivant, who says that he was taken to the house of a leading Muslim near the Zeitoun church. In Bullivant's account he says:

> In the beginning, he was antagonistic and attacked the pilgrims who had to pass close to his house. He would throw stones at them and call on the police to have them arrested. He says Our Lady appeared to him and asked why he behaved this way. She begged him not to continue in this fashion and commanded him to paint the sign of the cross on his house. Although remaining a practising Moslem, he is now convinced of the authenticity of the visions and we saw the forty huge white crosses he had painted all-round the walls of his house.
>
> (Johnston 1980, p. 25)

With the proximity of the Muslim man's house to the church, could it be that Kamell and others, being unaware of the story behind the cross, misinterpret it as an aggressive act against Copts? Could this misinterpretation have stemmed from already existing tensions between both religious groups? Unfortunately, historical information documenting conflicts between Christian Egyptians and Muslim Egyptians in the 1960s was not systematically recorded, and any documentation of conflicts and attacks appear from the 1970s onward. Since this case focuses solely on the period of the appearances, research on Muslim-Copt relations from the 1970s onward was excluded. Nevertheless, accounts of reported incidences relating to conflicts between Muslims and Copts are included.

Cynthia Nelson (1973), a professor at American University in Cairo at the time, documented her experience with the Zeitoun apparitions. It is one of the few documentations on the appearances of the Virgin Mary in Zeitoun, and perhaps the only in-depth analysis of this phenomenon. Nelson chronicles the evolution of the interpretations given by Egyptians from both Muslims and Copts. Regarding the experiences of Copts, Nelson reports that during the 1967 war Copts began to feel great alienation, and she states,

> During the summer after the war, as Egyptians searched their souls and hearts for explanations for the defeat, tensions between Muslims and Copts intensified to such a degree that Nasser made a public speech about the bravery and courage and patriotism of the Christian soldiers

> to discourage the Muslim Brotherhood from casting blame on the Copts. Even close friends, as I was told by one informant, began to doubt each other when it came to the question of religion.
>
> (Nelson 1973, p. 10)

Another report states that just before the outbreak of the June 1967 War, "an ominous slogan could be heard in Cairo: 'First the Saturday people, then the Sunday people'" (Balint 2010). Jews and Greeks were also met with confrontation and were seen as alien and a possible hostile minority, and the departure of most of them left Copts as the main potential exposed target (Pennington 1982, p. 165). Copts were also seen as a potential threat because of their connection to the regime of the pre-1952 Revolution. The Land Reform of the 1960s, for example, "meant nothing else than taking away land from the copts and distributing it among the Moslems. Even land which belonged to the Coptic Church was given to the Moslems" (Ibrahim 1982, p. 66). Since the 1952 Revolution, but particularly after the defeat of 1967, Egyptian Christians were often accused of acting as spies by the Muslim majority and did not command "serious economic or political respect" (Nelson 1973, p. 10). Nelson states that incidents of conflicts and hostilities between Muslims and Christians could be seen, and that on the 4th anniversary of the first apparition of Zeitoun the new Coptic Patriarch delivered a speech "emphasizing the religious sympathy of the Copts for Anwar Sadat", the leader who took office after Nasser's death and changed the constitution which included a clause that stated "the principles of Islamic Shari'a laws shall be a main source of legislation" (Nelson 1973, p. 10; Brown, p. 1058). The new Coptic Patriarch made this speech in an attempt to heal sectarian rifts: "Religion is the first pillar of the homeland and the Virgin's appearance was a great blessing for the entire country because she made men aware that religion is stronger than their laws" (quoted in Nelson 1973, p. 10).

For many Christians, the appearances also represented the fulfilment of a promise made by the Virgin Mary in 1920. The local legend of the church's inception is well-known by many residents of Zeitoun, and as one Copt explains it,

> Ibrahim Pasha Khalil, a wealthy Copt landowner, was building a villa on some land in Zeitoun many years ago. One night he had a dream and the Virgin appeared to him and told him to stop building his villa and instead build her a Church. She promised to return in fifty years and appear at this Church for one year and perform miracles. . . . For most of us Copts this was a sign of the fulfilment of sacred prophecy.
>
> (quoted in Nelson 1973, p. 9)

In 1925 the church was built and, as one investigator of the appearances at Zeitoun says, "*there existed a forty-year tradition that a Marian visitation would eventually take place at the church*" (Rogo 1982, p. 256, italics in original). The area of Zeitoun is also steeped in Marian history, associated in particular to the escape of the Holy Family to Egypt during Herod's persecution. According to one local belief, the Virgin rested a few miles near Zeitoun under a sycamore tree. This tree is sacred to both Muslims and Christians, and pilgrimages are made by women seeking to become fertile. In fact, Egyptians believed that wherever the Virgin rested abundant water and green fertile lands appeared (Nelson 1973, p. 9; Rogo 1982, p. 256). The legend of the Virgin Mary's promise to return could be seen from the perspective of Egyptian Copts as an explanation for the appearances at Zeitoun. It may appear as an obvious and simple explanation, given that the legend was well-known by the locals. From the standpoint of some Copts who felt threatened by their Muslim neighbours, the reason for the Zeitoun appearances may have been the fulfilment of the Virgin's return.

The possible feared impending Coptic massacre by Muslims, the religious tensions between the two groups, and the 40-year old prophecy were narratives associated to the Zeitoun phenomenon created mostly by Egyptian Christians. The first two explanations reflect threats to the safety and stability of Egyptian Christians, while the last one is a prophecy fulfilled. In a time of uncertainty and religious tensions the fulfilment of Mary's promise may have been a comforting explanation, specifically for Egyptian Copts.

The second narrative of the appearances of the Virgin Mary was expressed by both Muslims and Christians, and connects the phenomenon to the 1967 military defeat. Proponents of this explanation believed that the Virgin Mary appeared as a sign of blessing and that victory was near. In Nelson's (1973) report, she identifies this theory as one of the earliest explanations reported by the people she interviewed on site while the apparition was still ongoing. As Nelson reports (1973),

> In the minds of most Egyptians the apparition is connected to the Six-Day War of June, 1967, in which Egypt suffered a military defeat that left the country in despair and its people confronting perhaps the severest crisis in their contemporary history. . . . To most Egyptians the appearance of the Virgin was initially a sign of hope (*bishara kheir* – good things will happen in the future). Specifically, the Virgin had to come to the Egyptians to restore faith in God and give hope and moral support to the defeated, perhaps even to lead the Egyptians to victory over the modern-day Herods [Israel].
>
> (Nelson 1973, p. 8)

One person who had seen the apparition, in an interview with Nelson, recounted a story of a girl in Beirut who four or five years prior to the phenomenon in Zeitoun "had a vision of Mari Guirgis [St George] and He told her that the Virgin Mary would come to Egypt. 'Tell the Egyptians not to worry, I am near them and I won't forsake them'". (Nelson 1973, p. 9). A Coptic bishop saw the apparition as a good omen and

> that the Almighty God would realize victory for the Arabs against the Israelis, who have occupied the holy places in the Holy City of Jerusalem, considered the *most* sacred city by the Copts and, after Mecca and Medina, by the Muslims as well.
>
> (Nelson 1973, p. 6, italics in original)

The apparition at Fatima in Portugal was even linked with the apparition at Zeitoun in the form of a prophetic message given to one of the seers, a shepherd girl, by the Virgin. This message was given to the Pope with the instruction not to open the letter until 1967; it prophesized that Egypt would experience a great defeat and go through much suffering, and that the Virgin would protect Egypt as it had protected the Holy Family when they fled from Herod's persecution (Nelson 1973, p. 9).

It is apparent that Egyptians, both Christians and Muslims, were trying to make sense of the aftermath of military loss. The visions of the Virgin Mary represented hope and a way out from the loss and despair of the times, signalling a future restored to peace in Egypt. Based on Nelson's (1973) analysis of the situation, this narrative seemed to have been the initial prevailing thought of most Egyptians; that is, the Virgin appeared in order to bless Egypt and suggest that victory was near. According to Nelson (1973), "[a] fter the first few months, however, one sensed a shift in the priority of interpretations given to the apparition of 1968" (Nelson 1973, p. 10). While the predominant explanation for the appearances at first was that it represented a sign of victory or blessing, at some point it changed, reflecting increasing tensions intensified by the war between religious and social groups (Nelson 1973, p. 10). There was one interpretation of the apparitions as the "unexpressed millennial dream" of the conversion of Muslims in Egypt, as one Coptic male described it:

> The most beautiful thing to do is to go to Zeitoun and watch the people of all religions participating in Coptic prayers. Imagine, this is the first time in history the Copts could sing their hymns in the streets of Egypt among all the Muslims and shout aloud, "*Umm el Mokhaless* (Mother of the Savior)". This phenomenon has taken place because we Copts are not very united and cooperative among ourselves. We have been oppressed for so many years that finally we are getting the message to unite and for the Muslims to be converted. This moment in time is most significant because the people are starting to lose their faith in God after all the hardships we have suffered. The message came to the Muslims at the right time when they had lost their faith.
>
> (quoted in Nelson 1973, p. 10, italics in original)

This interpretation of the Zeitoun apparitions may have created further friction and tensions between the two religious groups, especially with the conversion of some Muslims to Christianity in the years following the appearances, the conversions adding to further religious rifts. While the "millennial dream" of a Christian Egyptian nation never came to fruition, many Muslims did begin to question the socialist and secular path of their country. Although some of the intellectual elite dismissed the apparitions as the "overactive imagination" of the lower class peasants, Nelson (1973) points out that several of the people who gathered at Zeitoun came from highly educated and middle-class backgrounds, who "highly disillusioned by the 1967 defeat and by continued uncertainty within the country" turned to religion (Nelson 1973, p. 11). Egyptians from across the social and religious spectrum had questioned the direction Nasser took the country after the June 1967 War.

This leads to a third narrative of the Zeitoun apparitions, relating to the idea that Egyptians had forsaken religion for a secular and socialist path. Soon after the military defeat with Israel, disillusionment began to set in with the way Nasser and his regime had governed the country. It was during this time that "[a] wave of religiosity swept through Egypt, encompassing both Muslims and Christians" (Guenena and Wassef 1999, p. 7). As Egyptian researchers Nemat Guenena and Nadia Wassef (1999) write, "[c]laims that the Virgin Mary had appeared above the Cathedral of Zeitoun came alongside a widespread feeling that the defeat was the result of having abandoned faith in favor of human-made ideas and belief systems" (Guenena and Wassef 1999, p. 7). One author, Nazih N. M. Ayubi, argues that religious leaning Egyptians became "politically conscious during or after the defeat of 1967" and that "the soul-searching question echoed all over the country was", "Why were we so utterly defeated?" (Ayubi 1980, p. 489). There were many who believed the military defeat could be attributed to the lack of piety, states Ayubi (1980); that is, "We left God so God left us" (Ayubi 1980, p. 489). For Muslim radicals, argues Wurmser (2001), 1967 was a watershed (Wurmser 2001). Wurmser states that the

> devastating loss of the war made them – as one of the few truly introspective forces in Arab society – look for the ills of their own world, to search for the flaws within. They concluded that the shortcomings of their society resulted from the fact that Islam did not govern the Arab world, and that the latter had become a land of apostasy and profanation.
>
> (Wurmser 2001)

Consequently, proponents of the religious explanation claimed that the Israelis "won the war on religious bases, and Muslims should do the same to win" (Ayubi 1980, p. 489). Soon after the war, Nasser's speeches began to reflect the growing religious sentiment, and when a secularist Nasser, "who had previously spoken very little of religion, said religion should play a more important role in the society, the broken hero was greeted by an exceptionally enthusiastic roar of applause" (Ayubi 1980, p. 489). It should be recalled that Nasser secretly gathered at the church at Zeitoun to witness the visions of the Virgin Mary, which can be seen as perhaps another signal marking the return of religion. Some Egyptians noted that the victorious October 1973 War against Israel was a result of the return to religion (Guenena and Wassef 1999, p. 7).

Overall, the literature points to three main narratives which surrounded the appearances. Moreover, the prevailing narrative changes over time, with some more frequently mentioned immediately after the first apparition, but gradually replaced by other ones (Nelson 1973). The narrative also changes depending on who is telling the story. These changes are to be expected when investigating cultural phenomena, and the larger the group, the more diverse the explanations will be. Against this background, it is important that explanations given by Egyptians in the form of published accounts be included in the researcher's interpretation. In analysis, analysands provide input to the analyst regarding an interpretation of a dream or fantasy. The explanations extracted from historical material or published accounts take on a similar function when analysing a collective phenomenon. The patient's input is a crucial element to the analytical process because it assists the analyst in pinpointing the root of a neurosis or anxiety. The aim of applying individual psychological methods to social phenomena is to try to uncover cultural anxieties. It is at this juncture that the analyst, or in this case the researcher, proceeds with his or her analysis.

The explanations given by Egyptians suggest that underlying anxieties may have existed prior to the first Marian apparition. Two types of underlying anxieties which existed before the first apparition took place could be gleaned from Nelson's (1973) analysis of the Zeitoun apparitions: 1) cultural despair was experienced as a result of the 1967 War, and 2) tensions between religious groups were intensified by the war. The first anxiety is connected to the explanation that the Virgin Mary appeared because it was a sign of victory to come to Egypt and the country was blessed. The second anxiety is connected to the explanation that the Virgin Mary appeared to ease tensions between religious groups, especially between Muslims and Copts. In addition, I propose a third source of underlying anxiety: after the 1967 defeat Egyptians from both religious groups experienced a period of intense existential angst for having forsaken their religious beliefs for secular and socialist ideals. This angst or anxiety is connected to the aforementioned third explanation.

### *Analysing explanations of eyewitnesses*

In the preceding section, I have identified cultural anxieties surrounding the Marian apparitions at Zeitoun along with three main associated sets of explanations proposed by eyewitnesses and bystanders. Two of these sets of explanations refer to anxieties, while a third one refers to a cultural "existential angst". For the sake of simplicity, they will be called cultural anxieties, even though the third one is labelled an angst. The next step in our analysis of the phenomenon under investigation is to examine the three sets of explanations, and the anxieties to which they refer, in relation to the symbols extracted from the case study database using depth-psychological principles, specifically by applying compensation theory.

The first set of explanations refers to the apparitions at Zeitoun taking place because they were a sign of victory and blessing for Egypt. The underlying anxiety is the collective despair experienced by Egyptians as a result of the June 1967 Arab-Israeli War. As the historical discussion reported previously reveals, economic crisis, war, occupation of Egyptian territory under enemy control, social unrest, and loss of faith in a political leader took place during Nasser's time in power and these factors are likely to have contributed to the collective despair. In addition, tensions with the Israeli state were high after the war and a resolution was not in sight: another war seemed imminent (Mansfield 1968, p. 417; Nelson 1973, p. 8). Cynthia Nelson describes in her field notes Copts chanting throughout the evening newly composed songs in honour of the Virgin Mary, "poetry of a political slant emphasizing the Virgin leading the Egyptians to victory" (Nelson 1973, p. 8). I posit that those who expressed collective despair as a result of the war may have projected the role of the Virgin Mary as "protectress" or "intervener" in order to compensate for an impotent Egyptian government. Accordingly, Egyptians subject to this specific anxiety may have associated the vision of Mary to a force that would protect Egypt from further losses endured in the aftermath of the Arab-Israeli War. In the previous chapter, the symbol of the Virgin Mary was amplified and several interpretations were presented. While the variety of interpretations seems to point to *renewal* and *rebirth*, the associated historical and mythological nuances elucidate the significance of the virgin in relation to the historical and external factors. In fact, one amplification which came out of the interpretation is of the Virgin Mary as the "protectress", similar to the Greek Goddess Athena, such that a devoted, pious follower may trust in her protection during peaceless, war-filled times. As a sign of her significance and power, Athena, along with other ancient goddesses, was seen as a warrior and a war-goddess protecting cities from outside, hostile forces and "her hand outstretched over cities and [covered] them with her golden shield" (Kerényi 1978, p. 30). The Virgin Mary, along with many ancient mother goddesses, intervened in the worldly affairs of human beings, and like the Great Spinstress she "weaves the web of life and spins the thread of fate" (Neumann 1963, pp. 227–228). Similar to the qualities of the *Moirae* described earlier, the Virgin Mary is also depicted as the Goddess of Fate holding a thread and spinning the destiny of mankind; the virgin in this role also signifies the redemption of the world. Worshippers who have attained the knowledge of the goddess are successfully able to move from sterility to restoration. Restoration in this case would take the form of a resolution. The increasing frustrations with a dysfunctional Egyptian government which could not find a path out of the consequences of military defeat or regain the power it once held may have left a vacuum. This vacuum was filled not via a rational mode, but by the redeeming goddess of war guised in the image of the Virgin. The Virgin Mary is venerated by both prevailing religious groups in Zeitoun (i.e. the Islamic and the Coptic); in the Koran it is stated: "Allah has chosen you. He has made you pure and exalted you above all women" (quoted in Nelson 1973, p. 9). Mary may thus represent an image that the cultural psyche could have accepted as a mediatory symbol. As the goddess of war, the Virgin could ensure an Egyptian victory over their Israeli enemy and reclaim the dignity they enjoyed before the 1967 War. In Nelson's analysis of the function of Mary in Egyptian culture, she writes, "the Virgin serves as a symbolic political unifier – uniting Muslims and Copts against the Herods; uniting Egyptians with other Arabs in confrontation with the technologically advanced West" (Nelson 1973, p. 11). In addition, Nelson (1973) argues that the attitude of Egyptians who went to Zeitoun "was one of organized communal supplication toward the supernatural of a people seeking divine guidance at a time when there seemed to be no visible way out of a hopeless situation" (Nelson 1973, pp. 8–9). That a powerful ally such as the Virgin could very well grant this is the belief of the faithful and pious, according to the believer/perceiver, of her perceived miraculous powers, including the medical healings which came out of the Zeitoun apparitions, perhaps reinforcing this powerful and archaic belief.

Summarizing, a link has been made between the first set of explanations and the associated collective anxiety with Egyptians projecting the "protectress" or "intervener" aspect of the Virgin Mary. Amplified aspects drawn from the previous chapter include Mary as a war-goddess and goddess of fate. The aforementioned combination of factors contributed to an unusual collective despair, forcing Egyptians to seek answers and a resolution from the supernatural. As can be gleaned from eyewitnesses and interviewees from Nelson's (1973) analysis of the Zeitoun apparitions, Egyptians sought the protection of the Virgin Mary from further events that would have contributed to the already tense situation and instability in Egypt. The hope of Egyptians went beyond protection and also sought the Virgin Mary's intervention by securing military victory over their Israeli enemy. The image of the Virgin is revered by both religious groups, thereby making it easier for many Egyptians to accept. Yet, Mary represents aspects of goddesses which would draw from unnatural powers to bring together and protect those who worship and venerate her.

The role of "protectress" and "intervener" is also activated in the second set of explanations and the associated anxiety. In this case, the underlying anxiety is represented by the intensification, as a result of the war, of the tensions between religious as well as social (worker and student protests) groups. This second set of explanations refers to the apparitions at Zeitoun as aimed at relieving religious tensions between Copts and Muslims as well as the social instability which had arisen from the worker and student protests. As presented in the historical study and the section on the unusual emotion and tensions, relations between Muslims and Copts rapidly began to deteriorate after the war, while at the same time frustrations with the administration of the government surfaced in the form of student and worker protests. Even though none of the 22 case studies[1] provided an explanation explicitly referring to the effect on religious tensions or social unrest, the historical material, as presented earlier, shows that a social crisis had taken place, including the escalation of religious tensions in the country. A common sentiment, as was expressed by Archdeacon Youssef Kamell, was that the Virgin Mary appeared to prevent the persecution of Copts by Muslims. The role of the Virgin as protectress and intervener was already amplified, and such aspects could be applied to the second set of explanations with its associated anxiety. However, two other aspects of the apparitions described by eyewitnesses include references to doves (birds) and the olive branch. The amplification of these images reveals that the symbols of the dove and the olive branch also represent a type of intervention; the intervention is not like the proactive warrior goddess, but instead takes the form of providing a message of hope and peace in an otherwise stalemate. Forty-five percent of eyewitnesses from the case studies reported seeing the image of birds (see Table 4.2, Chapter 4), and some describe them as doves, pigeons, or simply birds which were categorized as a group. The dove, which was amplified in the previous chapter, symbolically reflects the meaning of peace. As was presented in the previous chapter, in Christianity the dove has been associated with purity, innocence, and peace; in fact, winged creatures represented the sublimation of instincts. The virtues which represent the dove are connected to the Christian understanding of the Holy Spirit which is divine inspiration, wisdom, and guidance. Noah sought guidance by sending out the dove; however, in Islam, Mohammed was inspired by the dove; recalled by the Lutheran hymn mentioned previously. The olive branch symbolizes peace, especially when carried by the dove (Biedermann 1992, pg. 101); in Dante's day the messenger bringing good news carried the olive branch (Vries 1974, p. 349). The cultural psyche's response to the impending threat on a group of people or the perceived threat held by Copts of Muslims was the appearance of the mediating symbol, according to compensation theory. Acknowledging it as a symbol of peace by both religious groups, the image of the dove and olive branch may have been understood and acknowledged by the cultural psyche, whether the threat was real or imagined. During a period of social and religious crisis, meaning, but more importantly, guidance is sought after in order to make sense of a chronic chaotic situation. To move past one position into the next, according to the concept of the transcendent function, it would make sense that a luminous dove representing divine inspiration would have been one of the chosen images projected by the Egyptian collective. Jung's concept of the transcendent function illustrates the role that the symbol has in the psyche, while at the same time enhancing our understanding of the cultural unconscious attitude of Egyptians during the period under study. The essential feature of the transcendent function is that it mediates opposites facilitating a transition from one attitude to another, while the ego holding the tensions allows a mediatory symbol to come through (Jung 1943, para. 121; Samuels, Shorter and Plaut 2007, p. 150; Samuels 1985, p. 59). As explained by Jung, the function is a "manifestation of the energy that springs from the tension of opposites and it consists in a series of fantasy-occurrences which appear spontaneously in dreams and visions" (Jung 1943, para. 121). The transcendent function arises from the union of the unconscious and conscious contents or, put another way, the "tendencies of the conscious and the unconscious are the two factors that together make up the transcendent function" (Jung 1958b, paras. 131 and 145). The appearance of the symbol, whether in dreams, fantasies, ideals, or visions, "transcends time and conflict" without taking sides from either direction – the thesis and antithesis tension – offering a way to move from "either-or" to "and", and, moreover, offering a move towards synthesis (Samuels, Shorter and Plaut 2007, p. 150; Samuels 1985, p. 59).

An alternative solution out of the crisis may have not been perceived as being available. Were the apparitions of the dove the resolution for the Egyptian cultural psyche? As Archdeacon Youssef Kamell states in the documentary interview, the Muslims, after marking the homes of Copts with a red cross, were preparing for an attack. When the apparitions took place, previously ill Muslims were cured and healed. Moreover, eyewitnesses reported a sense of unity between religious groups who went to St Mary's Church to witness the apparitions. As Case 2 states, "Some people were reciting verses from the Koran. Some (Greeks) were praying in Greek; others were singing Coptic hymns. It was something above human experience that attracted and captivated us". Case 8 recalls, "Thousands and thousands of people, fifty, a hundred thousand, from villages and towns around put their sheets [sheets refers to blankets and prayer rugs which Mohammedans usually spread on the ground or floor before kneeling to pray] on the street. . . . We never did this before, not publically". The apparition site was filled with people of diverse backgrounds, although more pronouncedly of Copts and Muslims. For a brief period of time, the problems between these two religious groups were set aside, and even the March 30 Manifesto was introduced, a legislation proposal by President Nasser that laid out plans for Egypt post-1967 War, with some intellectuals expressing frustrations that Egyptians were focusing their attention on the apparition rather than the political implication of the legislation (Nelson 1973, p. 8). The images of the doves and the olive branch were possibly the mediatory symbols, not excluding the image of the Virgin, needed to provide the resolution acceptable for Egyptians to move from the point of impending persecution to a state of conciliation and peace between religious groups and the social upheaval which had ensued in the previous months leading up the apparitions.

The 40-year-old legend, namely the promise of Mary's return, is an important part of the Zeitoun narrative and forms part of the cultural psyche, albeit perhaps pertaining to a (religious) sub-culture in Egypt. The legend and other local beliefs connected to the Virgin Mary may have laid down the foundation and predisposed some witnesses of the Zeitoun apparition; that is, when in relation to an unprecedented humiliating military defeat and its consequence an entire group has been made a scapegoat, the group under threat seeks protection and understanding from the extraordinary. In his explanation on why people saw flying saucers, Jung states,

> It is characteristic of our time that, in contrast to its previous expressions, the archetype should now take the form of an object, a technological construction. . . . Anything that looks technological goes down without difficulty with modern man.
>
> (Jung 1959, p. 18)

Similar to the technological fantasies of UFOs, seers, people whose preoccupations are with the ecclesiastical and divine may see visions of the holy. Essentially, the psyche produces a symbol that the conscious mind must understand and acknowledge (Samuels, Shorter and Plaut 2007, p. 32). The legend of the Virgin Mary as well as the local tales of the sycamore tree may have provided "the most favourable basis for a projection" or "for the manifestation of the unconscious background" (Jung 1959, p. 18). Moreover, this belief in the legend and local tales must be part of the attitude of the "overwhelming majority" (Jung 1959, p. 18). The local population, especially Egyptian Copts, having a long-standing knowledge of the area's local legend and beliefs, integrated the compensatory symbols of the Virgin Mary, the dove, the cross, the Christ Child, and other images which referenced the legend and local tales of the Holy Family's relationship to Zeitoun and Egypt.

The third set of explanations refers to the apparitions as a sign that Egyptians had forsaken religion and God. The underlying anxiety was a form of existential angst for abandoning religion in exchange for socialism and a secular form of governance. The people adopting this perspective felt that since the nation had forgone piety, embracing modernity and man-made ideas instead, God had abandoned them; moreover, if they could go back to religion and God via the Virgin Mary, Egypt would be once again blessed and victory secured. An aspect of the Virgin as protectress and intervener is possibly activated under the third set of explanations in that Egyptians viewed Mary's appearance as a sign that she could advocate victory, as a type of saviour, on their behalf in exchange for their piety. Therefore, the amplified aspect could be applied in the interpretation of this explanation and its associated anxiety. There are other images from the database which may elucidate a psychological interpretation for the third set of explanations and the associated collective anxiety such as the image of the illuminated cross. The symbolism of the cross does not only have its roots in historical Christianity. The symbol of the cross, for instance, is associated to the tree. Similar to the Tree of Life, "the cross stands for the 'world-axis'. Placed in the mystic Centre of the cosmos, it becomes the bridge or ladder by means of which the soul may reach God" (Cirlot 1971, p. 69). The cross represents the bridge between two worlds, the human and the spiritual. Given this symbolic meaning, it is possible that Egyptians viewed the appearance of the cross as the way back to God by embracing their religious beliefs. The image of the light, seen by 86% of eyewitnesses from the 22 case studies, also points to the symbolism of finding one's way back to God. Light is the universal symbol "of divinity and the spiritual" (Biedermann 1992, p. 204), and in Christianity, the Saviour is called "the light of the world" (Biedermann 1992, p. 204; Vries 1974, p. 297). The apparition of light as the way back to God could be interpreted as an individual's salvation or an alternate resolution to the crisis they were facing at the time. The description of one apparition by Case 8 is pertinent here, "A thin line or edge of light appeared like the light you see when you open the door of a lighted room". The door opening to a lighted room is like a door opening to another dimension, perhaps to the spiritual realm. It may be an invitation to cross over to this realm from the worldly realm; the cross symbolizes the conjunction of these opposite worlds (Cirlot 1971, p. 69).

The symbols of the cross, tree, and light were images which were reported by several eyewitnesses from the database, and I have argued that they can be seen as representing a return to God or religion. Moreover, interpreting the symbols as a clear message to return to religion, Egyptians began to question their secularist path and socialist mores to which Nasser had led them. Sensing the move towards religion, especially toward Islam, Nasser began to introduce religious undertones in his speeches. This interpretation of the appearances – that is, in exchange for piety God would grant Egypt military victory via the Virgin – was reinforced as a result of the military victory against Israel which was achieved with the October 1973 War.

## My interpretation

Above, I have presented the three main sets of explanations for the Zeitoun appearances which were extracted from the research, each with their associated collective anxiety. The three sets of explanations were contributed by Egyptians and others involved in the event. After examining the three sets of explanations, I argue that they could be seen as a reflection of a singular overarching interpretation. The political environment under the Nasser regime may have created an imbalance between the masculine and feminine elements or the *coniunctio oppositorum*. I posit that the apparitions represent the unconscious feminine attitude, and that the Zeitoun phenomena took place in order to compensate the one-sided masculine attitude which had prevailed under Nasser's rule. In order to understand the society's psychological need for the feminine, a closer look at the overall historical context is needed. While compensation theory is the main theoretical framework, this thesis draws from other depth-psychological concepts (e.g. amplification, cultural unconscious, transcendent function, etc.).

## *Secularist interpretation*

If we recall the state of Egypt under Nasser's rule, the country's prevailing ideology was characterized by a focus on Arab unity and a secularist rule separating religion from government, concentrating on Arab, rather than Muslim, values. For Egyptians, at least for the middle and upper classes, the role of religion belonged to the private sphere of life and "outside the realm of government and politics" (Al Yafai 2012). Secularism prevailed in Egypt during that period. This fact is exemplified by a joke told by Nasser in a speech in 1953 about his meeting with a high-ranking leader of the Muslim Brotherhood requesting Nasser to make mandatory the wearing of the hijab by all Egyptian women; Nasser replies stating that the Brotherhood leader's daughter, who is studying medicine, does not wear a hijab, and if he as the father of this one girl cannot ensure her wearing of it, how can he (Nasser) make ten million women wear the hijab, at which point the crowd roars with approval and laughter (Al Yafai 2012; video also available on Youtube.com). What is significant about this speech is the response from the crowd. The crowd applauds in approval of Nasser's decision to keep religion out of politics and ridicules the Muslim Brotherhood's ideals for an Islamic form of government. However, it could have been that the people in the crowd, embracing the ideals of secularism, were not an accurate representation of the majority of Egyptians.

In order to determine if the Egyptian cultural unconscious was compensating for a repression of the feminine in the form of religion, we would need to analyse if, and to what extent, religious suppression by governmental forces had taken place. Separation of Church and State was the ideology of governance imposed by Nasser's regime, yet it seemed widely accepted at least by the middle and upper classes. However, how did the Egyptian working class and poor feel about this form of governing? One questioned that needs to be considered is, if secularism was widely accepted by all segments of society, could the repression of the religious function even occur? Following a depth-psychological perspective, if all segments of society were consciously secular, it is possible that the desire for a religious society was repressed. Was it imperative for Egyptians to have Islam as the foundation of their laws and government? Whether some segments of society or all were consciously secular and unconsciously religious, we need to determine if the psychological need was there. One way to understand if the desire for a pious society was repressed is to analyse the cultural landscape prior to when the Zeitoun phenomena took place.

If we take a closer look at Egyptian society, we find that Islam was strong, especially in the provincial areas. Even though Nasser was probably aware of the problem, he had never seriously addressed the issue of popular Islam (Warburg 1982, p. 134). Before the Free Officers came to power, the Muslim Brotherhood was the only movement which addressed the economic needs and beliefs of the Egyptian masses (Warburg 1982, p. 134). However, Nasser and the Free Officers began their campaign to co-opt the Islamic establishment through subversion and by taking away their economic independence. Legitimacy was gained by the backing of al-Azhar and the *ulama* or Muslim scholar or leader blessing Nasser's Arabism in the name of Islam. The *ulama* and al-Azhar were expected to play this central role in order to gain respectability and acceptance both in the central government and Egyptian countryside (Warburg 1982, p. 135). A series of reforms in the 1950s further undermined the religious establishment such as the abolition of family *waqfs*, the abolition of *shari'a* courts, and the nationalization of public endowments. The most humiliating blow to the Islamic establishment came in 1961 when the al-Azhar was turned to a government controlled university. Under the government's control, al-Azhar became the channel through which it advocated the support to Pan-Arabism and socialism and to the idea that this ideology was in line with the principles of Islam. The once economically strong religious establishment had become a "servile part of the feared, but remote, center" (Warburg 1982, p. 134).

While on the surface it seemed that the Islamic establishment was curtailing its own status by sanctioning "the secularization of Egyptian society", it was easier for the regime to control the religious leadership in Cairo than to bring under their control the religious functionaries in the rural area (Warburg 1982, p. 137). The regime could not concentrate religious control in the centre. In "*Strong Societies and Weak States: State-Society Relations and State Capabilities in the Third World*", Joel S. Migdal states,

> strategies adopted by even the weakest groups in society, the masses of poor peasants and workers, have help determine the ultimate power of the state. . . . In the final analysis, the ability of the state to garner support through a multitude of institutional channels decides the fate of state leaders and their often ambitious policy agendas.
>
> (Migdal 1988, p. 181)

Nasser and the Free Officers tried to repackage the military coup as a popular revolution, with some success as it appeared that the mass of the Egyptian population was behind Nasser and his regime. However, was this popularity only concentrated in the centre and major cities? The periphery may have also bought into the regime's state ideology, but for many their traditional values and belief system clashed with government policies (Warburg 1982, p. 137). Could Nasser's lack of control of the periphery have also been a religious factor rather than just an institutional one, as Migdal (1988) suggests, relating to the state's ability to transform society? I think the regime's failure to control the religious functionaries in the rural area is a psychological reflection of the cultural unconscious; that is, a strong and uncontrollable psychological need and desire for piety and religious traditions is likely to have existed prior to the June 1967 War, at least for Egyptians living in rural areas. Subsequently, that desire which had been previously neutralized or even suppressed under the secularist and socialist government was exposed following the war and later with the Zeitoun apparitions.

Another way to determine if the desire for a religious society was repressed is by analysing events which occurred *ex-post* military defeat and the Zeitoun phenomena. It seems that cooption of the religious establishment under the Nasser regime was more successful in the cities than in the countryside, and that Egyptian peasants and farmers were less likely to embrace the state ideology of Arab socialism and secularism. By this line of reasoning, one may conclude that Egyptian peasants and farmers should have been the majority in attendance at the Zeitoun apparitions. However, if we examine the 1986 survey, we find that a high majority of respondents, 73 out of 86 survey respondents or eyewitnesses, claimed to be white-collar professionals; for example, 7 respondents marked "Professor", 8 "Engineer", 12 "Accountant", 9 "Businessperson", 6 "Physician", and 4 "Student". Although the 1986 survey may not be entirely representative of the witnesses of the Zeitoun apparitions, it may indicate that there were a high percentage of educated people present at the church. Furthermore, some intellectuals were baffled by the high number of educated people gathering at the church to catch a glimpse of the apparitions, assuming that only the Egyptian peasantry would be attracted by such events (Nelson 1973). In fact, what could be gleaned from the historical material is that the appearance of the Virgin Mary sparked a revival of religion that affected all segments of Egyptian society, including some of the technocrats and intellectuals. As mentioned previously, Nasser's speeches were welcomed by the cheers of the crowds as they began to reflect a renewed religious sentiment, and later when Sadat became president, he changed a clause in the constitution to reflect Sharia law. Had the 1967 war awakened the religious "sleeping giant"? The cultural landscape was transformed as Egyptians embraced the "message" behind the Zeitoun apparitions and as Egypt moved from secularism towards an Islamic form of governance. In fact, after the war and the Zeitoun apparitions, there was a rise in popular Islamic movements, as we will see later.

By taking a look at the religious attitude of Egyptians prior to the 1967 war and the change of religious attitude following the Zeitoun apparitions shortly after the war, I posit that repression of the religious function occurred. The repression of this function in individuals and the collective may occur under authoritarian regimes similar to Nasser's Egypt. In *The Undiscovered Self (1957)*, Jung discusses the psychological implications which a socialist dictatorship has on the masses and the individual. Specifically, Jung's analysis focuses on the aftermath of the WWII, the beginning of the Cold War, and the erection of the Berlin Wall; and that religious experience (as well as self-knowledge) is needed for the individual to protect himself from totalitarian mass society. In a socialist dictatorship, the state assumes many of the roles of the Church: "The State, like the Church, demands enthusiasm, self-sacrifice, and love, and if religion requires or presupposes the 'fear of God', then the dictator State takes good care to provide the necessary terror" (Jung 1957, para. 512). When socialist dictatorships take the place of religions, the result is overcompensation in the form of fanaticism: free opinion is stifled and the opposition is stamped out (Jung 1957, para. 511). These types of tactics took place under Nasser, and even though Nasser and the Free Officers may have had the best intentions for the future of Egypt when they overthrew the king, a few years into the revolution it turned into an authoritarian regime. Fear of Western imperialism and internal power struggles may have forced the new leader to reject a parliamentary democracy and opt for authoritarian rule instead.

As Nasser wrote in *The Philosophy of the Revolution*, "We needed order, but we found nothing behind us but chaos. We needed unity, but we found nothing behind us but dissension" (quoted in Goldschmidt 2004, p. 105). Competing entities were suppressed or eliminated such as the old regime parties and groups like the trade union and communists who helped in the overthrow of the king. For example, initially, the Society of the Muslim Brotherhood received privileges denied to other parties, but after an attempted assassination in 1954 the Egyptian government launched a campaign against the Society jailing its members and wiping out all "its branches, schools, and welfare institutions" (Goldschmidt 2004, p. 116). The Muslim Brotherhood was pushing for the Koran to be Egypt's constitution as well as demanding "veto power over any laws passed by the new regime" (Goldschmidt 2004, p. 106). Nasser was determined to centralize power and strengthen the Revolutionary Command Council, thereby weakening all rival movements.

In a totalitarian state such as this, a rationalistic attitude prevails, lending itself to one-sidedness, creating a split in the cultural psyche. However, the religious function cannot be disposed of by the rationalistic thought of the Zeitgeist (Jung 1957, para. 514). The religious function, which is a natural function,

> is an *instinctive* attitude peculiar to man. . . . Its evident purpose is to maintain the psychic balance, for the natural man has an equally

> natural 'knowledge' of the fact that his conscious functions may at any time be thwarted by uncontrollable happenings coming from inside as well as from outside.
>
> (Jung 1957, para. 512, italics in original)

According to Edward Edinger in *Ego and Archetype: Individuation and the Religious Function of the Psyche* (1992), "[u]nderstood psychologically, the central aim of all religious practices is to keep the individual (ego) related to the deity (Self)" (Edinger 1992, p. 64). As repositories of transpersonal experience and archetypal images, Edinger argues that religious ceremonies provide the individual with "the experience of being related meaningfully to these transpersonal categories . . . [and religion] is the best collective protection available against both inflation and alienation" (ibid., p. 64). If the breakdown of the religious projection takes place, it is possible that the Self is reprojected onto a political system (Edinger 1996a, p. 36). However, Edinger argues that secular or political systems or movements "are never an adequate container for religious meaning" (Edinger 1992, p. 68).

Under the Egyptian dictatorship, as the secularist and rationalistic attitude prevails, the religious function is suppressed or denied expression; consequently, "a general disturbance results" (Jung 1957, para. 544). From this perspective, what could have followed was that the Egyptian psyche reached a point where it sought synthesis, and the "general disturbance" may have been the 1967 military defeat which consequently demoralized many Egyptians and later jolted them out of their political apathy. In order to restore psychic balance or balance the contents suppressed under Nasser's authoritarian regime, the psychological need of the cultural unconscious is an experience with the *numinosum*. In his research on trauma and religion, Jungian Greg Mogenson writes, "[a]s the pain increases so, too, does our sense of relationship to an omnipotent being" (Mogenson 2005, p. 28). Mogenson continues and states that "[a]s the persistence of our suffering mocks our inability to understand it within the categories of our usual existence, our sense of relationship to a wholly other will and purpose grows" (ibid., pp. 28–29). The god-image may manifest as an opportunity for transformation growth or, as discussed next, synthesis may not take place.

What perhaps believers of the message of the Marian apparitions interpreted as the literal return to religion, whether Christianity, Islam or otherwise, may have represented something more profound. Jung's perspective on religion is something beyond creed or dogma; for Jung, religion is an "immediate experience". As Jung states in *Psychology and Religion* (1938/40),

> I want to make clear that by the term "religion" I do not mean a creed. It is, however, true that every creed is originally based on the one hand upon the experience of the *numinosum* and on the other hand upon . . . trust or loyalty, faith and confidence in a certain experience of

> a numinous nature and in the change of consciousness that ensues. . . . We might say, then, that the term "religion" designates the attitude peculiar to a consciousness which has been changed by experience of the *numinosum*.
>
> (Jung 1938/40, para. 9, italics in original)

The *numinosum* cannot be willed by the individual or collective; it controls its subject, causing an alteration in consciousness (Jung 1938/40, para. 6). Moreover, it is an aspect of the God-image which is the image of totality and "the highest value and supreme dominant in the psychic hierarchy, the God-image is immediately related to, or identical with, the Self" (Jung CW 1951d, para. 170). Jung was very interested in religion, and with Victor White, a priest of the Dominican Order, Jung shared a fruitful collaboration dialoguing between psychology and theology (Stein 1999, p. 12). Their friendship eventually soured after White became offended by Jung's *Answer to Job* due to fundamental differences in the concept of the God-image (Edinger 1996b, p. 51). White's God-image was embedded in the metaphysical and the fundamental Christian tenet that God could be defined as *summum bonum* or the highest good (Edinger 1996b, p. 51; Edinger 1996a, p. 50). Jung was not convinced that God was purely good, and he criticized the notion of the *privation boni* principle which states that evil can be defined as the "absence of good" (Stein 1999, pp. 14–15). Jung interpreted Christian doctrine from the perspective of analytical psychology and viewed God as containing both the light and darkness (ibid., p. 15). Moreover, Jung posited an evolutionary process and continuous incarnation of the God-image. In *The New God-Image*, Jungian psychologist Edward Edinger presents the major stages in the evolution of the Western God-image, reviewing the series of transformations it has gone through in the course of recorded history (Edinger 1996b, pp. xiv-xv). Consequently, Edinger states "all manifestations of the God-image [could be understood] as descriptive stages of humanity's experience of the autonomous aspect of the psyche" (ibid., p. xv). The numinous balancing symbol as the symbolic representation of religion, in this case the Zeitoun apparitions, may be the immediate experience with the God-Image or the Self. Therefore, the *numinosum* is a religious experience undeniable by those possessed by it, and possession of it is more important than any religious dogma or creed.

To summarize, under a socialist dictatorship, the religious function is suppressed or denied; seeking synthesis, the numinous balancing symbol is of a religious nature. Denied its instinctive nature and connection with the God-image, the unconscious psyche then seeks to experience the *numinosum*. The Marian apparitions at Zeitoun could have been the *numinosum* or balancing symbol, and the eyewitnesses claiming to have seen the numinous figure of the Virgin Mary may have experienced and been possessed by it. Although the Virgin Mary was a specific image traditionally associated with religious creed, the projected image was more important than its doctrinal significance. Moreover, the Virgin Mary was an image that most Egyptians could accept because the Virgin was a beloved religious figure, for example, by both Muslims and Copts; therefore, it was possible for the cultural psyche to integrate the balancing symbol. Lastly, another indication that the Zeitoun apparitions could have been a numinous balancing symbol is linked to its impact it had on Egyptian society, specifically the religious revivalism that followed.

### *Teleology of the psyche and the destroyer*

So far, I have argued that the religious function was repressed under Nasser's authoritarian rule despite the veneer of popular majority support. Nasser's type of rule can also be compared to Jung's analysis of socialist dictatorships in which a rationalistic attitude prevails, creating a one-sided attitude in the unconscious. The psyche, or in this case the cultural unconscious, seeks change, a shift, or a transformation; therefore, the balancing symbol is produced in order to facilitate the transition from one prevailing attitude to another. Jung called this the transcendent function. Regarding the transcendent function and the aim of the symbol, Jung does not address the "why" it occurs, but rather focused on the "what for?", giving credence to the teleology of the psyche, or that the psyche does not proceed without aim or purpose (Samuels, Shorter and Plaut 2007, p. 150).

The psyche has a potentially destructive function, and in Jungian psychology the regressive tendency can play that role. Jung viewed regression as a way to regenerate the personality by an encounter with the parental imago or God-image, and that this leads to the dissolution or death of the ego in its old form, consequently reducing the tensions of the former way of life (Samuels, Shorter and Plaut 2007, p. 40). According to Jung, the human psyche is divided into two forces or tendencies, progressive and regressive, described by Freud (1920) as Eros and Thanatos. Jung understood these two forces as psychic energy (libido) and that their nature is neutral, as he describes them,

> Progression might be compared to a watercourse that flows from a mountain into a valley. The damming up of libido is analogous to a specific obstruction in the direction of the flow into the potential energy of a reservoir. Thus dammed back, the water is forced into another channel, if as a result of the damming it reaches a level that permits it to flow off in another direction. Perhaps it will flow into a channel where the energy arising from the difference in potential is transformed into electricity by means of a turbine. This transformation might serve as a model for the new progression brought about by the damming up and regression, its changed character being indicated by the new way in which the energy now manifest itself.
>
> (Jung 1948b, para. 72)

Jung saw the death instinct, a psychoanalytic concept conceived by Freud, as a merger, a longing for the abyss, oceanic feelings, and a desire to re-unite with the Eternal Feminine. Jungian Andrew Samuels (1985) describes it as having a purpose "namely to act as a necessary antidote to the pain and anxiety resulting from rupture and separation so that, in the peace and quiet of an integrated state of oneness, the boilers of creativity can be re-stoked" (Samuels 1985, p. 99).

If the Zeitoun Marian apparitions were the numinous balancing symbol which consequently could signify an immediate experience with the God-image, then it would follow that, when considering Jung's conception of the regressive tendency, a death of the old form occurs, reducing the tensions of the former way. The encounter with the God-image or *parental* imago could produce the projection of a mother archetype such as the Virgin Mary as a compensation of the masculine image. When this specific symbol is analysed, that is, the Virgin Mary, I find that there are two aspects contained within it; that is, the aspect of good and evil. In the analysis of the symbols in Chapter 5, the theme of death and the destroyer emerged, specifically, in the virginity aspect of the Virgin Mary. When the virgin aspect was amplified, an association emerged pointing to characteristics of Jung's concept of the *anima*. What emerged in the previous chapter is that the anima could take on a destructive form and appear as the destroyer in an individual's life. Characteristics of the anima include it having a bipolar nature, as all archetypes do; she can appear good one moment and evil the next. When the maiden aspect, also associated with virginity, of the anima is activated, she possesses a daemonic power seducing those in her path. She can act like a trickster by promising renewal and life and the next moment bring misery. Individuals possessed by the anima, if not integrated, could be led to destructive tendencies or events like illness, an accident, or even death.

If the virginity aspect of the Virgin Mary was activated and could bring with her destructive elements, could war have also been one of them? Several documented apparitions are surrounded with the theme of war, such as Marpingen's Franco-Prussian war (Blackbourn 1993), Medjugorie's Bosnian War, Fatima's WWI, among others. The Zeitoun apparitions took place ten months after the 1967 June war. Of course, not all apparitions are connected with the theme of war as some are connected with religious hostilities, modernity, and a reaction to secularism. However, for those that are connected with the theme of war, war could be a representation of the terrible mother archetype. The terrible character of the Feminine rules over desire and seduction which leads to sin and destruction, and in addition, Terrible Goddesses like Athena, goddess of war, contain the aspects of love and death in one (Neumann 1963, p. 172). The great Mother Goddesses of ancient Egypt also contained two opposing aspects in one. Hathor or Neith and Mut or Bast were goddesses which gave and sustained life and at the same time, were goddesses of savagery, blood-lust, and destruction. Both

Neith and Hathor were goddesses of war (Neumann 1993, p. 55). Also, warlike figures accompanied the Great Mother following her destructive aspect (Neumann 1963, p. 302). In my opinion, it is possible that the Virgin Mary of Zeitoun along with the Virgin Mary of Fatima, Medjugorie, and other apparitions with the theme of war were manifestations of the Great Mother accompanied by her warlike element. The dual nature of the manifestation of the Feminine contains good and evil elements, and I argue that the Virgin Mary also contains this dual aspect which the destructive aspect could manifest as war.

The virginity aspect of the Virgin Mary may not only represent death and destruction, but she is also associated with the Triple Goddess representing the life-death-rebirth triad. In addition, the triad represents time or the past-present-future, and when this aspect of the Feminine is activated, the Triple Goddess intervenes in the matters of human affairs (see Chapter 5). Earlier, Athena as goddess of war is discussed, but within that context she plays the role as the "intervener"; however, as death and destroyer the aim could be to destroy old paradigms and structures. In the Baltic folk tradition, there exists the image of the Destroyer and Regeneratrix. She may appear as a "beautiful woman or nightmarish creator", and as the Ragana, she "reminds us that nature is mortal and that there is no life without death . . . she is essentially concerned about regeneration" (Gimbutas 1989, pp. 209–210). Following the idea of the teleology of the collective psyche, death or destruction of the old takes place in order for a renewal to begin. The destruction of unwanted social structures could have translated into the destruction of the state's ideology of secularist and socialist values of 1960s Egypt, and the removal of old structures and patterns clears the way for something new in its place. The symbolic meaning of the Virgin Mary of Zeitoun could be seen as an unconscious desire for change, and most importantly, an opportunity for renewal. What I think is important about the destructive aspect of the Virgin Mary is that it represents the potential for transformation, similar to how the virgin represents latent energy as amplified in Chapter 5; it contains the possibility of the union of masculine and feminine aspects which can result in the birth of the third.

The destructive aspect of the Feminine is similar to the anima; it is the "chaotic urge to life". The integrated anima (maiden-mother, Kore-Demeter) could intervene and move individuals from meaninglessness and stagnation to creativity, meaning, and renewal and act as an instrument for forced change; that is, the anima presents a choice for the dissolution of the old form, reducing the tensions of the previous path of life. When the anima presents itself in a vision, the psyche is ripe for the death of the old and ineffective patterns and ways of existence. The anima could be an energy which is neither good nor evil, but utilizing her energy for the good can manifest human love and cultural development. The pertinent question is, how did the Egyptian cultural unconscious integrate the anima? The anima and the

Terrible Mother represent this crucial role, and later in the chapter, I discuss how Egypt was transformed years after the appearances at Zeitoun.

### *The Virgin Mary pointing the way towards God/Self via religion*

I have argued that the natural inclination of the collective psyche, from a depth-psychological perspective, is to proceed with purpose and aim; and that the destructive function or regressive tendency is a way for the psyche to move forward in order to break the tension of opposites that it finds itself in. In the previous chapter, the amplification method revealed that the symbolic meaning of the Virgin Mary is represented by fecundity, fertility, and renewal, but could the symbolic meaning, similar to the images of the cross, tree, and light, also be interpreted as *the way towards God*? In depth-psychological language this could represent the way towards the *self* and the path towards *individuation*.

The projected feminine symbol, such as the image of the Virgin Mary, could signify the pointing the way towards God, and within the historical context could translate into a transition towards religion. Associations of the projected feminine regarding religion had been made. In *Psychology and Religion* (1938/40), Jung states, when analysing a dream of one of his patients, that "the anima is the mysterious allusion to religion" (Jung 1938/40, paras. 71–73). This may not always be the case, but applied here, the negative or destructive aspect of the anima could lead man towards a path of destruction; conversely, the positive aspect of the anima may reveal to one the "mysterious", and this aspect of her has a "religious tinge" (Jung 1951a, para. 356). If the apparitions of the Virgin Mary are associated with religion – that is, it points the way towards religion – then the appearances can be seen as promoting religion. If this is the case, what is the *positive* feminine trying to convey? Why was the introduction of religion via the Zeitoun apparitions important for the Egyptian cultural psyche?

Jung felt that individuals were naturally religious, and that the religious function was just as powerful as the instinct for sex (Samuels, Shorter and Plaut 2007, p. 131). If the religious function is suppressed in an individual or society, the psyche is devoid of its natural and religious state, according to Jung's definition of religion. The experience with the *numinosum* could move the individual from the rational to the irrational; in this case, the psyche under secularist rule may be associated with the rational, the irrational being its opposite. In Jungian psychology, the opposites are always reconciled by the unifying symbol. The research material for this case points to a general increased interest in religion following the appearances at Zeitoun, as was presented earlier. Critics believed that the only ones to gather and believe in the Marian apparitions were the "Upper Egyptian peasants"; however, in her investigations, Nelson noted that the great majority of gatherers were "middle-class workers and semi-professionals, many of whom are highly educated but who are also highly disillusioned . . . by continued uncertainty within the country. *They have turned to religion*" (Nelson 1973, p. 11, italics added). As discussed earlier, the appearances seemed to have appealed to both segments of Egyptian society, the educated and non-educated. The gatherings, especially of the educated and middle-class, could point to the psychological need of the religious function deprived by the secularist-leaning society. As described previously, the Virgin Mary plays the role as the "intermediator". She is not the representation of religion, but as the "intermediator" between man and God, she may direct the way to bridge the two worlds or psychological states.

On a differentiated level, the appearances may seem to represent a return to religion; however, at an unconscious level the teleology of the psyche is to seek balance reducing the tensions of opposites moving closer to the Self. Symbolically, the images of the Virgin Mary, the cross, and other images could also represent the *mandala*, the symbol of totality and the Self. Twenty-two percent of eyewitnesses from the case studies reported seeing the image of the Virgin Mary "standing or kneeling in front of the cross". The image of Virgin Mary bowing to the cross is significant in that the cross forms four parts when it is encircled. In many traditions, the symbolism of the cross is joined with the circle. For example, the four arms of the Celtic cross represent the four elements, Water, Fire, Air, and Earth, and they coincided with the division of Ireland into four provinces, and in African art, "the cross has cosmic significance, as its totality, since it indicates the cardinal points" (Chevalier and Gheerbrant 1994, pp. 254–256). As presented earlier, Jung described the symbol of the cross as the "most perfect symbol" and associates it to the Self, as it is a totality and wholeness symbol. Moreover, the Cross of the Passion signifies Christ's suffering and death (ibid., p. 252), and the symbol of the cross could personify the suffering that many Egyptians were experiencing during this period. At the same time, the cross is a symbol of transformation as it is associated with Christ's Resurrection. Subsequently, the Cross of Resurrection signifies Christ's victory over death (ibid., p. 252). As stated previously, compensatory symbols appear because they relieve tensions between the conscious and unconscious. The symbol of the cross could have helped Egyptians to bear their own "cross" as the symbol of the cross turns into the Paradise of the Elect, transforming into the symbol of eternal glory "acquired by sacrifice and culminating into ecstatic bliss" (ibid., p. 253). Therefore, the cross could symbolize man's transition from this world to paradise or the divine.

In addition to the cross, 14% of eyewitnesses described circular lights hovering or flying around the image of the Virgin Mary. These circular images could be seen as mandala images. Jung studied the symbolic meaning of mandala images, interpreting them as an expression of the Self (Jung 1950b, para. 634). In individuals, this motif "is the premonition of a centre of personality, a kind of central point within the psyche, to which everything is related, by which everything is arranged, and which is itself a source of energy" (Jung 1950b, para. 634). In interpreting one of the mandalas from his paper entitled "Concerning Mandala Symbolism", Jung describes aspects of it as "self-generated", "creative energy", and "generative power" (Jung 1950b, para. 640). The circle is the second of the four fundamental symbols along with the cross, centre, and square (Chevalier and Gheerbrant 1994, p. 195). The circle symbolizes cosmic heaven, and in particular, "the dynamic instrumentality of Heaven within the cosmos" (ibid., p. 195). Jung argues in *Flying Saucers* (1959) that the mandala images emerge out of chaos and disasters. As symbols of wholeness and salvation, mandala images similar to the ones seen by Zeitoun eyewitnesses may personify the need for order. The circle is the symbol of time, and in earlier times it was used "in order to measure more accurately its passing" (ibid., p. 197). When the apparitions first took place, Egyptians were coping with political, social, and economic instability. The Sinai Peninsula and the Gaza Strip were annexed by the Israel as the result of the June 1967 War, with Israel refusing to return the occupied territories. As a representation of the circle, the triumphal arch symbolizes a path through which "only the victorious hero is allowed to pass" (ibid., p. 197); this need for victory against the Israelis was felt and expressed by many Egyptians. In addition, frustrated workers went on strike during an economic crisis prompting government forces to react with excessive force. As the circle symbolizes "aspirations towards a higher world or a more elevated plane of existence" (ibid., p. 197), for many Egyptians during this time of unusual crisis, the appearance of flying circular objects in the sky may have been perceived as their salvation.

Amplified, the symbolism of virginity takes on a similar meaning as the mandala. The symbolism of the mandala is in line with the meaning of the virgin aspect of Mary; that is, the virgin is latent energy, pure, and not yet revealed, expressed, or manifested. Similar to the ascetics and pagans who worshipped their god and goddesses respectively, the psychological need behind the ritual practices were for the worshippers to become renewed and reborn. The virgin aspect of Mary also revealed during the amplification process an association with primordial goddesses with parthenogenetic or self-generated abilities such as Nyx, Gaia, and Chaos. The apparition of the Virgin Mary alone itself *does not* represent the Self; however, one interpretation of the apparition relates to the symbol of the Self since its association with mandala images forms a part of the apparition narrative.

The symbol of light may, as amplified in the previous chapter, signify a return to God. God separates light from darkness, declaring in the Book of Genesis, "Let there be light", becoming the primal symbol of duality and giving birth to life and life forms. The unity of light and darkness may reflect unity and in turn transform into "grace". Grace, according to Karingadayil (2011), is a symbol of salvation and a gift of God "designed to assist and bless human beings" (Karingadayil 2011, pp. 119–120). Grace supplies a person with "a new supernatural nature equipped with new powers" of faith and hope empowering and elevating him or her; thus grace, "becomes the chief element in [one's] redemption" (ibid., pp. 119–120). Egyptians entered a period of self-reflection in the aftermath of the June 1967 War, and many believed that abandoning their religious principles led to the devastating military defeat (Guenena and Wassef 1999, p. 7). This widely felt sense of being punished by God for rejecting religion for modern ideals and secularism may reflect the dark feelings of the existential angst, contents which may have constellated in the cultural unconscious. As mentioned previously, "sinners" are blocked from heaven, and the function of grace is to guide one to renewal, rebirth, and balance. Christ the Saviour is called "the light of the world", and he was born to save man from his sins (darkness) as well as being associated as a Holy Warrior who engages in war against sinners. The darkness or sin may symbolize the cultural anxiety of Egyptians at this time, while the mediating symbol of light, containing both darkness and light aspects, presents a way out of the current situation. Choosing the light aspect of the symbol signifies a movement, thus breaking the tensions of the opposites. For many Egyptians, this was a move towards piety, as I discuss next.

In a society where disillusion and disappointment with the current government was prevalent, Egyptians sought meaning. The religious enthusiasm which took place after the June 1967 War and especially after the first months of the Zeitoun apparitions returned, to some extent, a sense of purpose and meaning to the country. From a Jungian perspective, the uniting symbol of the Zeitoun apparition signifies the potential to become whole, feeling a sense of purpose and feeling that life makes sense again. Demonstration of this is seen, for example, in the belief by Egyptians that the Virgin Mary appeared as a sign of military victory.

To summarize, in this specific case, the apparition of Mary can be interpreted as representing a move towards religion, and in depth-psychological language, I argue, the projected positive feminine image symbolizes the way towards the Self. The religious function is denied expression under the Egyptian dictatorship. As a compensation, it seeks synthesis with the *numinosum* of a religious nature, in this case the image of Mary. The image of Mary as virgin and other apparition images are associated with mandala images similar to representing the Self. As will be seen in the next section, the appearance of the Virgin Mary is significant in its role as the feminine counterbalancing the masculine.

## Coniunctio *and the father image*

As argued previously, the apparition of the Virgin Mary at Zeitoun symbolizes a way towards the Self under the conditions of a prevailing masculine attitude expressed as secularism. This is one interpretation of the Zeitoun apparition when observing the phenomenon through the lens of the religious function of the psyche. President Nasser has been described as a charismatic and strong leader, and he was also often referred to as the *father* of modern Egypt (Flower 2002). For most of his rule, Nasser maintained his charisma and projected an image of strength; however, it was said that he was never the same after the June 1967 War, and that from then onwards his charisma began to wane. It was Nasser's actions which led to the demise of his country along with the idea of an Egyptian "utopia". He became a fallen leader whilst still holding office. Large groups demonstrated their support immediately after the military defeat as people marched insisting that Nasser remain their leader.

By applying depth-psychology, Nasser as the public leader is associated with the father image, and one way of examining the father image is in relation to the primal scene: by doing so, it could paint a picture of the collective's psychological state. In the primal scene,[2] according to Andrew Samuels (1993), the image of the father and mother suggests "*a self-regulated diagnostic of the person's psychopolitical state at any moment*" (Samuels 1993, p. 167, italics in original). The image of the copulating parents is a metaphor for a *coniunctio oppositorum*, Latin for conjunction of opposites (Samuels 1993, p. 168). When the primal scene is reflected as fertile – that is, the projection of it – it is vital, and the "psyche is trying to express its multifarious and variegated nature – and also its oneness and integration" (Samuels 1993, p. 168). Conversely, if the primal scene is one-sided it can be disharmonious, reflecting a pattern of exclusion and defeat (Samuels 1993, p. 167). The Egyptian state was slowly rebuilding itself after decades under colonialism, and Nasser had placed Egypt on this path. However, as mentioned in the previous section, his regime was oppressive, especially against members of the Muslim Brotherhood who were banned as a political party shortly after Nasser took control, and freedom of speech was stifled along with capitalism. Imbedded in the psyche, according to a depth-psychological view, is a self-regulatory function which compensates one-sided tendencies; there is similar function in the *coniunctio* in that the mother and father images need to be in balance and union. Following this line of theory, a one-sided tendency in the Egyptian cultural unconscious is constellated as sustained political oppression continues; and consequently, under the right conditions, social revolutions and unrest appear. The father image as represented by Nasser via his actions created disharmony by excluding, instead of adopting, an environment of inclusion, especially of competing political groups. In a way, the father-leader of Egypt had failed it. If we consider that the symbol of utopia[3] represents the self in this case, then it may be argued that the integration of the self was stifled for Egyptians as a collective. The *hieros gamos*, or sacred marriage, is a representation of integration and individuation, and amplification of this concept is presented in Chapter 5. Applying this concept to the case under discussion, the father image, as was just identified, may have transitioned to a state characterized by a lack of harmony and balance, as Nasser moved away from his original principles of democracy heading towards centralized power and dictatorship, creating one-sidedness in the cultural political psyche. The cultural psyche seeks release from the contents constellated in the unconscious. The military defeat, though not a creation from the cultural unconscious, but from the leader, became an impetus for Egyptians to demand a change in course and direction for the country. The father-leader, having ruled with absolute control, manages to clamp down on the growing social movement appearing in major cities throughout the country. As the father-leader, Nasser may also personify the *senex* archetype. Latin for "old man" (Hillman 1989, p. 208), the senex contains qualities such as balance, wisdom, and farsightedness (Samuels 1989, pp. 34–35). However, in its pathological or pure state, the senex becomes excessively cautious, authoritarian, and obsessional (ibid., 1989, p. 35). Moreover, the senex has been associated as "the sick father", "an archetypal metaphor for a situation of stagnation and decay in the psyche and its need for rejuvenation" (Colman 2000, p. 522).

Despite Nasser being a beloved leader, at the same time he was an oppressor and curtailed the basic freedom rights of his people. There may have existed an internal conflict within the Egyptian people; that is, on the one hand you loved your father for providing a roof over your head, and on the other, you despised him over his rigid rules. One way of understanding this internal conflict is to direct our analysis toward the cultural unconscious of Egyptians. If the Egyptian psyche was consciously generally satisfied with the socio-economic and political atmosphere pre-June 1967 War, but on the unconscious level dissatisfied, how would the cultural unconscious react? Given its teleological nature, I argue that it would bring about its balance. It is here that we look to Jung's understanding of the dynamics of the psyche via the destructive function or regressive tendency. As Jung describes it,

> [t]his death is no external enemy, it is his own inner longing for the stillness and profound peace of all-knowing non-existence, for all-seeing sleep in the ocean of coming-to-be and passing away. Even in his highest strivings for harmony and balance . . . he seeks death.
>
> (Jung 1952a, para. 553)

Similar to the individual, the cultural psyche seeks death so that it can bring destruction of the old and bring forth the new. The military defeat was the beginning of the end of Nasser's rule. It would be a stretch to suggest that the June 1967 War was the manifestation of the destructive function since it was Nasser who embroiled Egypt into the war.

As the father image is dominant in the *coniunctio*, the psyche responds by producing the compensating feminine image. I argue that, after a sustained period of anxiety and confusion following the war, coupled with the prevailing masculine attitude, activation of the mother archetype occurs as its manifestation. Mother Mary emerges to become the compensating figure in the *coniunctio*. The apparition at Zeitoun was a numinous experience for the people who witnessed it as well as for the Egyptian nation. The appearances captured the attention of the nation, such that public discussions seemed to focus more on this phenomenon than on the coming March 30 elections. While a high percentage of eyewitnesses from the case studies and survey used language such as "Blessed Virgin" or "Virgin Mary" to describe the apparition, 14% of the eyewitnesses referred to the apparition as "Blessed Mother". Interestingly, none of the survey participants used language to describe the apparition as "mother". Nonetheless, the 14% is just as significant as would be, for example, a figure playing a minor role in a dream. The figure is still examined in individual analysis, and its significance is explored via amplification. Moreover, a notable aspect which emerged under the amplification process was the Virgin's association with "mother". Mary's predecessors – Cybele, Demeter, Isis, Ishar, among others – were *virgin mother* goddesses who, similar to the virgin archetype, were one-in-themselves; that is, self-generated beings, part of the cycle of life-death-rebirth, not controlled by man-made laws (as discussed in detail in Chapter 5). Similar to the myth of Demeter and Persephone, the perception of the figure of the Virgin Mary contains the dual aspect of maiden (virgin) and mother, which are made whole through the reunion to become "one-in-herself". This union represents the process of transformation, and the transformative character of Demeter/Persephone and Virgin Mary compels tension, movement, and change. In order to seek polarity between the masculine and feminine principles, ancient cultures engaged in the rituals of the *hieros gamos*, and this was a transformative experience in which the initiate received immortality and ever-lasting renewal. A modern equivalent of the *hieros gamos* is the Assumption of Mary, and the union of Mary and Jesus represents the union of masculine and feminine principles; as they become one, duality is transcended and the *coniunctio oppositorum* takes place. The manifestation of the *hieros gamos* is found in myths, folklore, and books, but it could also manifest in the psyche of the individual via dreams and in society as well.

In the Egyptian psyche, the emergence of a leading mother figure in a context characterized by a dominating father figure reflects the widespread desire for transformation and unity prevailing in Egypt during the period under study. In Jungian analyst Warren Colman's (2000) paper, "Tyrannical omnipotence in the archetypal father", he argues that the father's need to control the mother leads to tyrannical behaviour and suppression of the feminine, downgrading the role of the mother in patriarchy societies (Colman 2000, p. 536). This sets the stage for the son to overcome the archetypal tyrannical father, and the assistance of the mother is needed who is a threat to the father as she has the means to inflict "the defeat of omnipotence and [to restore] mutuality and procreativity" (ibid., p. 536). Symbolically, the visions of the Virgin Mary may personify the need for the mother's ability to defeat the tyrannical father and restore imbalances created by his authoritarian rule over Egypt such as the imposition of secularist rule. The visions of the Virgin Mary may not have occurred if the feminine principles had been acknowledged and respected in Egypt, yet the feminine may have emerged in other forms such as a movement for a loosening of tyrannical policies and more freedoms.

In the next section, I explore the question of whether there was transformation and unity in Egypt, and more specifically, if synthesis and integration took place as a result of the emergence of the feminine.

### *Synthesis and integration: was it achieved?*

The aim of this section is to determine whether the numinous symbol of the feminine can be seen as having contributed to the integration and synthesis of the Egyptian cultural psyche.[4] If integration of the feminine symbol took place, how would it manifest itself in the external world? The function of the symbol is to allow the way forward of the mind of the individual; however, in some cases, balance is not always attainable. Accordingly, I propose an analysis of whether the symbol was integrated by the Egyptian cultural psyche. As presented previously, the transcendent function mediates opposites, thereby assisting a transition from one attitude to another. The psychological need for this process takes place when a standstill exists; Jung described it as "a suspension of the *will*" occurring "when there is full parity of the opposites, attested by the ego's absolute participation in both . . . for the will can no longer operate when every motive has an equally strong countermotive" (Jung 1923b, para. 824, italics in original). Jung's theory on the suspension of the will is similar to the worshipper's encounter with the virgin archetype which arose from the amplification process presented in Chapter 5; that is, an encounter with the virgin goddess offers a release from stagnation, or the banality of life, invigorating one's life with meaning, creativity, and vitality. As a consequence of the standstill, "a damming up of vital energy results", and in order to break the "insupportable condition" a new content is produced by the tension of opposites; that is, the new content emerges "constellated by thesis and antithesis in equal measure and standing in a *compensatory* relation to both"; thus, a middle ground is created in which the opposites can be united and which transcends them (Jung 1923b, paras. 824 & 825, italics in original). The new content puts an end to the division "forcing the energy of the opposites into a common channel", and consequently, the "standstill is overcome and life can flow on with renewed power towards new goals" (Jung 1923b, paras. 827).

In answering the question as to whether the mediating symbol of the Virgin Mary and its associative images facilitated the synthesis of opposites of the Egyptian cultural psyche, historical events which took place post-Zeitoun apparitions are taken into account. The enquiry focuses first of all on answering the above-mentioned sets of explanations posited by eyewitnesses: 1) the apparitions were a sign of victory and blessing, 2) the apparitions took place to ease religious tensions, and 3) the apparitions signalled a return towards religion/backlash against secularism.

At first glance, the answer to the above question would be a "yes" to all of the three explanations given by eyewitnesses. If the emergence of the symbol alleviated anxiety arising from the collective despair as a result of the June 1967 War, then the result is a society which is blessed with a victory against the enemy, the Israelis. That is, there was a move from one situation to another. Egyptians gained back all territories lost in 1967 with the October 1973 War. As mentioned earlier in the chapter, one interpretation of the apparition by some eyewitnesses related to the fulfilment to a promise made by the Virgin Mary that if Egyptians returned to God she would grant them victory over their Israeli enemy (Ayubi 1980, p. 490). Under this interpretation, the Virgin Mary is associated with the "intervener" and ancient war-goddesses. In the previous chapter, one aspect of the child archetype considered is the child hero, and perceived as semi-divine, he liberates the world from monsters (Cirlot 1971, p. 45). Moreover, the image of the child hero may indicate the conquest of anxiety "and the attainment of inner peace" (Chevalier and Gheerbrant 1994, p. 190). The function of the child hero is to overcome the darkness (Jung 1951b, para. 284), and the manifestation of this image may point to the possibility that one may alleviate such darkness and anxieties. The triumph of the war could represent a concrete outcome which points to the cultural psyche attaining balance between the conscious and unconscious state, relieving anxiety brought on by the collective despair of the time. The victory represents a blessing that was given by the virgin war-goddess fulfilling the desired role projected by advocates of this interpretation. Since it is difficult to establish that synthesis of opposites took place on the cultural level, the October 1973 victory may suggest that synthesis was achieved.

The image of the Virgin Mary as "protectress" and "intervener" is also projected by individuals and eyewitnesses in the second set of explanations. For those adopting this perspective, the Virgin grants immediate relief in preventing the massacre of the Copts. That is, the new content breaks the "insupportable condition" releasing the tension of opposites, which are united and transcended. In this case, the "insupportable condition" is represented by the cultural anxiety associated to increased tensions between Muslims and Copts following the military defeat of 1967. The vision of the Virgin Mary as well as signs such as the doves and the olive branch were images that both groups could have found relatable due to clear references found in their respective religious texts. Since the conscious needs to acknowledge the projected symbol to achieve integration, it is plausible that those advocating the second set of explanations accepted the mediating symbol and moved from a warlike attitude to an attitude of peace. This is exemplified by the harmonious environment which ensued when the apparitions began. The atmosphere of unity and peace was described by people who gathered at the Church site and claimed seeing several religious groups, especially Muslims and Copts, participate in prayers and setting aside their differences. The image of the dove, for example, signifies purity, innocence, and peace in Christianity; in particular, the flying dove represents not only peace, but the Holy Spirit (see Chapter 5). The dove as the Holy Spirit is associated with the totality of the Self (Jung 1948a, para. 276); thus, the symbol of the dove represents unity and wholeness. Jesus is attributed the saying, "Be ye therefore wise as serpents, and harmless as doves" (Matthew 10:16). The Dove of Peace, Aphrodite, is the bringer of peace (Walker 1983, p. 253). Two doves led Aeneas to the Golden Bough, "which was to safeguard his return from the underworld", and the dove is also associated with the Moirai, the fates of life, destiny, and death (Vries 1974, p. 144). When the dove is holding the olive branch, it symbolizes peace, harmony, and refound happiness (Chevalier and Gheerbrant 1994, p. 190). Athena with the olive branch symbolizes "renewed life" (Vries 1974, p. 144). In Japan, the olive symbolizes friendship (ibid., p. 716). The dove also symbolizes rescue and protection, for example, Odysseus's weapon against the Cyclops was an olive, and later he grasped an olive before the ship going down at Charybdus (Vries 1974, p. 350). In this respect, I argue that at least some synthesis was attained and the cultural psyche integrated the mediating symbol to at least some as an allegedly imminent massacre, to which Archdeacon Youssef Kamell in the previously mentioned short documentary referred, was not only avoided, but the symbol became a unifying agent between the two religious groups.

Unfortunately, tensions increased between the Copts and Muslims in the months following the initial apparitions due to a claim that mass-conversions of Muslims to Christianity were taking place (Nelson 1973). As explained earlier, there were eyewitnesses who interpreted the Zeitoun apparitions as fulfilling a millennial dream of the conversion of Muslims in Egypt. This claim prompted a shift from an interpretation that united the two groups in victory and blessing to strained relations and suspicion. While a massacre did not take place, relations between the two religious groups deteriorated throughout the years especially into the 1970s, prompting the suggestion that the integration and healing was not attained, or that it was attained but only in regards to avoiding the heinous act of mass murder.

Finally, according to the third set of explanations, the apparitions signalled a return to religion or a backlash against secularism. Supporters of this interpretation argue that the Virgin Mary represented a sign that Egyptians had forsaken their religious beliefs by embracing modernity, secularism, and socialist ideas and signalled a need to return to a pious society. The anxiety associated with this explanation was an "existential angst" triggered by the act of turning away from a vision of an Islamic state and instead embracing a secular one. The outer reactions of the psychological tension can be seen by an increase in religious discourse, exemplified by the introduction of religious rhetoric in Nasser's speeches and later by the inclusion of the principles of Islamic Shari'a laws in the Egyptian constitution incorporated by President Sadat (Brown 2000, p. 1058). Within the aforementioned events of the late 1960s, a move closer towards a religious attitude may signify synthesis and integration of the cultural psyche as repressed feelings surrounding socialist ideas and secularism are released. As the Muslim movement swept throughout Egypt in the 1970s and 1980s and aimed to reverse the secularist governmental structure introduced by Nasser and to some extent maintained by Sadat, we see that religion begins to be included in the political area, perhaps signalling integration by the Egyptian cultural psyche.

However, a glimpse into Egypt's future following the apparitions points to possible *enantiodromia*, as extremist elements of Islam began to overshadow the country; for example, the rise of the Muslim movement in the 1970s aiming to overthrow the "impious regime" and the assassination of Sadat by militant Muslims (Goldschmidt 2004, pp. 180–183). Jung defined *enantiodromia* as a psychological law in which sooner or later everything runs into its opposite or "running contrariwise" (Jung 1943, para. 111). Egypt not only embraced religion in the 1960s, but it went a step further. Instead of achieving the balancing of the opposites – secularism and religion – Egyptian society moved towards the exact opposite as certain segments of society imposed Islamic rule by force (i.e. assassination of Sadat). Moreover, it seems that the repressed contents, instead of achieving integration, expressed itself in inferior ways as the rise of the Islamic militant movement took place that, by the mid-1990s, had already "made attempts at the assassination of two Ministers of the Interior and has developed . . . into an open confrontation with Coptic Christian minorities as well as secular writers and intellectuals" (Shukrallah 1994, p. 15). While secularization was accepted in the major cities, it is possible that the Egyptians residing in the periphery or rural areas harboured a desire for piety and religious tradition. Perhaps similar to the apparitions in Marpingen and Ezquioga, the Zeitoun apparitions were co-opted by religious and political groups. Thus, Nasser moved from his Pan-Arabism rhetoric in his speeches to including religious language as well as interacting with Coptic leaders and bishops. The *enantiodromia* may reflect the psychological need of some elements of Egyptian society to hold on to its religious tradition and values albeit in an extreme form.

In the interpretation proposed herein, I argued that the Zeitoun apparitions represent the feminine principle compensating the one-sided masculine attitude which prevailed in the cultural unconscious of Egyptians. This interpretation is tied in with the third set of explanations referred to previously, as religion can be seen as representing the external indicator of the compensating feminine aspect. That is, whereas in the third set of explanations religion is the external factor which indicates compensation against secularism, in my interpretation religion is used as an external factor to indicate compensation against the masculine attitude. Thus, within this interpretation religion becomes a symbolic meaning to express the feminine principle, while from the perspective of the third set of explanations religion is an indicator that points to possible integration.

One way to assess whether synthesis and integration of the numinous symbol occurred is by taking a closer look at the images. Earlier, I argued that the disharmonious *coniunctio* is reflected in the dominance of the father figure represented by Nasser's authoritarian regime. The symbol of the harmonious *coniunctio* suggests oneness and integration. It was only a small percentage of eyewitnesses (9%) who described the image of the Virgin wearing a crown, but the crown image may signify the elevation of Mary's role or the feminine from suppression to the restoration of balance. As Baring and Cashford (1993) argue, the placing of the crown over Mary's head is a celebration of the *hieros gamos* or sacred marriage (Baring and Cashford 1993, pp. 604–607), representing the union of the masculine (Jesus) and feminine (Mary) principles. One way to interpret the coronation, expanding on Colman's (2000) work, is that the Christ as the son of Mary crowns her after defeating and usurping the tyrannical father. The son is transformed and renewed after the mother becomes pregnant with him again and he is reborn (Jung 1952b, para. 491). As discussed in the previous chapter, the myth of the coronation of Mary represents a step in the path towards individuation, and the role that the Virgin Mary plays is reflected in the *coniunctio*; and a marriage taking place in a heavenly place free from devastation and impurities. Jung argues that behind the popular movement of the Virgin Mary was the most powerful motive for dogma of the Assumption of Mary reflecting the psychological need of the collective (Jung 1958a, para. 748). The psychological need of the feminine could also take place on a cultural level, specifically, in the Egyptian cultural unconscious. As Baring and Cashford suggest, a "new 'incarnation' of the myth of the goddess and her son-lover" manifest when people are ready to deepen their understanding by searching for a new revelation, and the numinosity of the image brings about "a transformation of the image of the deity in a particular culture at a particular time" (Baring and Cashford 1993, p. 607). The symbol of the *coniunctio* along with the coronation of the Virgin Mary may reflect the suppression of the feminine in Egyptian society and the symbol of the sacred marriage may signal an attempt to restore it.

In addition to the symbol of the *coniunctio* and the crown, the child image signifies 'potential future' (Jung 1951b, para. 278). Fourteen percent of eyewitnesses from the case studies reported seeing the image of Jesus as a child. The symbol of the child can take on many meanings, one of them being represented by the mediator and bringer of healing (ibid., para. 278). When the child archetype is activated, it prepares the individual for a future change of personality and in "the individuation process, it anticipates the figure that comes from the synthesis of conscious and unconscious elements. . . . It is therefore the symbol which unites the opposites" (Jung 1951b, para. 278). The appearance of the child image may signal synthesis of the masculine and feminine principles, while at the same time it could also be an early symbol signifying the start of the individuation process.

This interpretation also suggests that Nasser's authoritarian regime reflected and contributed to the prevailing one-sided masculinity. The opposite of this form of government would be a democracy; however, it was never achieved, and in this respect, synthesis did not occur. In fact, President Hosni Mubarak was sworn in after Sadat's assassination and his rule lasted 30 years, ending with his resignation following the demonstrations during the Egyptian Revolution in 2011.

The manifestation of a numinous symbol does not assure the projector that synthesis and integration of the new content was achieved, even within my short analysis in the context of the three sets of explanations advanced by eyewitnesses as well as the proposed interpretation. Another way to analyse the Zeitoun apparitions consists in expanding the time period to the present time. Indeed, the visions at Zeitoun may represent just one mediatory symbol in the line of many other integrations as the psyche advances along the path of individuation. The apparitions at Zeitoun were the first collective visions in Egypt; however, there were three more mass visions of the Virgin Mary which took place in Egypt: in 1986, 2000, and 2009. From a depth-psychological perspective, the reoccurrence of this phenomenon may suggest that the cultural psyche still has not fully integrated the feminine principle.

## Conclusion

This chapter attempts to weave together the historical material as introduced in Chapter 3, including the socio-economic and political instabilities of 1960s Egypt, with the "inner-world" factors represented by the common themes and symbols extracted from eyewitness published accounts. The first part of the interpretation aimed to determine whether the Zeitoun visions had a *psychological* case for a causal basis, or *emotional tension*, "having its cause in a situation of collective distress or danger, or a vital psychic need" (Jung 1959, p. 7). I determined this by analysing the cultural distress and anxieties behind the events of the period as well as by examining the narratives created by Egyptians on how they perceived and interpreted the apparitions of the Virgin Mary. Following this examination, I identified three sets of explanations proposed by eyewitnesses and bystanders and the underlying anxieties associated with the explanations. In the second part of the interpretation I offered my interpretation, and argued that the political environment under the Nasser regime may have created an imbalance between the masculine and feminine elements of the *coniunctio oppositorum*. Moreover, I posited that the apparitions represent the unconscious feminine attitude, and that the Zeitoun phenomenon took place in order to compensate the one-sided masculine attitude which had prevailed under Nasser's rule.

The chapter concluded by posing the question whether integration and synthesis of the feminine mediating symbol of the Marian apparitions had occurred. I argued that in specific cases integration did occur, represented for example by the claims of physical healing, the military victory of the October 1973 War, and the prevention of the Coptic massacre. At the same time, a glimpse into 1970s Egypt indicates that extremist elements of Islam began to overshadow the country, pointing to possible *enantiodromia*. Furthermore, I argued that the cultural unconscious of Egyptians has not fully integrated the feminine principle, a view supported by the persistent struggle of Egypt to move away from authoritarian regimes as well as the fact that mass visions of the Virgin Mary in Egypt continue to take place in the early 21st century.

## Notes

1 The 22 eyewitnesses in the case studies do not provide any explanation for the appearances. However, eyewitnesses from Nelson's (1973) analysis do, but these eyewitnesses were excluded from the 22 case studies' database because these interviews did not provide a description of their experience.
2 Here Andrew Samuels uses Freud's concept of the primal scene.
3 According to Jung, projections of modern man "is now confined to personal and social relationships, to political Utopias and suchlike" (Jung vol. 13 para. 395). For modern people the projection of the self is manifested in political parties, social organizations, and, as in our case, an (Egyptian) Utopia. Moreover, Jung states that the idea of utopia goes back to the early image of the archetypal dream of paradise, or Golden Age, "where everything is provided in abundance for everyone, and a great, just, and wise chief rules over a human kindergarten" (Jung 1972, p. 85).
4 Since this is an investigation on the cultural psyche, my analysis focuses on whether synthesis of opposites was achieved by the Egyptian cultural psyche and not on individual eyewitness which the latter may be easier to establish.

# Conclusion

This short conclusion is divided into two main parts; the first summarizes the main argument of the research, while the second offers suggestions for further research.

The present study introduced the Zeitoun Marian apparitions which took place in the late 1960s. It was 1968 when the Virgin Mary of Zeitoun began her appearances against the backdrop of turmoil, protests, and revolts taking place across the globe. Egypt did not represent an exception in this regard. Indeed, it had suffered a humiliating military defeat with its Israeli neighbours only nine months earlier, causing the Egyptians to question their political leadership, the strength of the Egyptian military, Nasser's vision of Pan-Arabism, and the secularist direction he had taken the country. The first apparition began with two Muslim mechanics noticing what appeared to be the figure of a woman dressed in white on top of St Mary's Church in Zeitoun (a district of Cairo, Egypt). Correcting the mechanics' initial assumption that the woman was planning to jump and commit suicide, a woman nearby gave out a cry of joy and said, "Our Lady, Mary" and asked the Virgin for her blessing (Zaki 1982, pp. 4–5). Just a few days before this event, Nasser announced the March 30 Program which proposed liberalizing policies. Now, however, instead of focusing on the March 30 Program, Egyptians were more captivated by the appearances of the Virgin Mary. International newspapers covered the story of the Zeitoun appearances, and the news spread to other parts of the Middle East, with some commentators even comparing the figure to that of Fatima and her connection to the Koran (Nelson 1973). The visions of the Virgin Mary during these first few months united Muslims, Copts, and other religious minorities, especially in their common belief that the Virgin was a sign of blessing and victory to come. The reverberations of the Zeitoun apparitional events were felt for several years, also thanks to the religious revivalism of the 1970s and later to the continuing mass appearances of the Virgin Mary in Egypt in 1986, 2000, and 2009.

By analysing all major aspects of the event at length, I tried to understand the significance of the Zeitoun apparitions. Why the Virgin Mary? Why did the appearances occur at that specific place and time? In order to answer these questions, the first and logical step was to collect published accounts of the seers from as many sources as possible. This led to the development of an overall understanding of what people saw and to reconstruct the sequence of events characterizing the apparitional phenomenon at Zeitoun. Creating a database to summarize and sort out the descriptions of the testimonies assisted in extracting the common themes of symbols of the event. Realizing that the statements of the visionaries were rich and colourful in their descriptions and that these visions had a profound impact on eyewitnesses, I tried to integrate these aspects in the data analysis implemented in Chapter 4. The database was a useful tool, for example, in identifying and separating the aspects of the descriptions of the apparition mentioned with a higher percentage from those mentioned less frequently. The database was also useful because it allowed me to group and categorize similar descriptions. This process was also instrumental in minimizing any subjectivity or bias in the selection of specific aspects characterizing the descriptions. Moreover, following this empirical approach also helped me to organize the testimonies in a systematic and structured format.

Jung's amplification method is applied in interpreting the extracted symbols and themes. This method allows one to look for patterns using comparative material, and the associations found in mythology, fairy tales, and religion which assist in the understanding of the archetypal images. The central figure to emerge from the material was the Virgin Mary, but the illuminating finding was the virgin archetype and the virginity aspect associated with Mary. Following the interpretation of the symbols and common themes, I examined the symbols associated to the main historical events surrounding the apparitional event at Zeitoun. The historical context included the entry of President Nasser's regime into the Egyptian political stage, the introduction of legislative policies, the economy pre-and post-June 1967 War, and the worker and student uprising following the aftermath of the military defeat.

I argue that there is a *psychological* case for the Zeitoun phenomenon "having its cause in a situation of collective distress or danger, or a vital psychic need" (Jung 1959, p. 7), and that an *unusual emotion or tension* existed prior to the appearances of the Zeitoun visions. The psychological projection or visions of the Virgin Mary must have had a psychological cause behind them. The narratives created by Egyptians are examined, which form part of the historical context, and how they perceived and interpreted the visions of Mary which can be instrumental in identifying the unconscious background which may allow an understanding of the psychological need of the cultural unconscious. The aim was to assess the distress for which the cultural psyche is compensating.

Cultural anxieties identified surrounding the Marian apparitions at Zeitoun connected with three main associated sets of explanations proposed by eyewitnesses and bystanders. The next step in this process involved an examination of the three sets of explanations, and their associated anxieties. This allowed for the identification of symbols specific to their respective anxiety. The aim of this method was to include the seer's input in a similar way as an analysand's input is taken into consideration in the analytical process because it assists the analyst in pinpointing the root of a neurosis or anxiety. The first set of explanations referred to the apparitions at Zeitoun taking place because they were a sign of victory and blessing for Egypt, and the associated underlying anxiety was the cultural despair experienced by Egyptians as a result of the defeat in the June 1967 Arab-Israeli War, the economic crisis, the occupation of Egyptian territory under enemy control, and social unrest. I posited that the seers projected the "protectress" or "intervener" aspect of the Virgin Mary as many adopting this perspective sought a force that would protect Egypt from further losses endured in the aftermath of the Arab-Israeli War.

The role of "protectress" and "intervener" is also activated in the second set of explanations in which the underlying anxiety is represented by the intensification, as a result of the war, of the tensions between religious groups (especially between Copts and Muslims) as well as unrest among social groups (notably in the form of worker and student protests). Not only was the protectress and mediatrix aspect of the Virgin activated, but the mediating symbol of the dove and the olive branch were also manifested.

Finally, the third set of explanations proposed by eyewitnesses and bystanders were examined, according to which the apparitions were a sign that Egyptians had forsaken religion and God, and the associated underlying anxiety was a form of existential angst for abandoning religion in exchange for socialism and a secular form of governance. From the perspective of this set of explanations, I posit that an aspect of the Virgin as protectress and intervener was possibly activated as Egyptians may have viewed Mary's appearance as a sign that she could advocate victory, as a type of saviour, on their behalf in exchange for their piety. Other possible mediating symbols to emerge were the cross, tree, and light, as they represent a "bridge or ladder by means of which the soul may reach God". (Cirlot 1971, p. 69).

Following an examination of the three sets of explanations, I offer my interpretation of the Zeitoun phenomenon. I speculate that the three sets of explanations could be seen as a reflection of a singular overarching interpretation, and that the political environment under the Nasser regime may have created an imbalance between the masculine and feminine elements of the *coniunctio oppositorum*. I argue that the apparitions represent the unconscious feminine attitude, and that the Zeitoun phenomenon took place in order to compensate in the cultural unconscious of Egyptians the one-sided masculine attitude which had prevailed under Nasser's rule. In order to examine this hypothesis, I analysed the material, drawing on different concepts of Jungian psychology.

First, it is argued that the religious function was repressed under Nasser's authoritarian rule and compared Nasser's type of rule to socialist dictatorships as analyzed by Jung in *The Undiscovered Self* in which a rationalistic attitude prevails under these societies, creating a one-sided attitude in the unconscious. Under the conditions of a socialist authoritarian regime in Egypt, the suppressed religious function, denied its instinctive nature and connection with the God-image, sought synthesis with the numinous balancing symbol of a religious nature. The denial of this connection may be expressed in other ways such as joining a political movement or organization, as some Egyptians did with the worker and student movements. Adopting Jung's perspective on the teleology of the psyche, I next examine the destructive aspect of the symbol of the Virgin Mary and posit that the activation of the Virgin could bring with it warlike elements as demonstrated by previous Marian apparitions and the wars associated with them. I posit that the destructive element represents the destruction of unwanted social structures and the potential for transformation, and moreover, that it contains the possibility of the union of masculine and feminine aspects which can result in the birth of the third. Then, I speculate that the apparition of Mary can be interpreted as representing a move towards religion, and in depth-psychological language the projected positive feminine image symbolizes this move. The Virgin Mary is not the representation of religion, but rather, as the "intermediator" between man and God, she directs the way in order to bridge the two worlds or psychological states.

The final step of my research uses and expands the concept of the *coniunctio*. Nasser as the public leader is associated with the father image, and a way of examining the father image is in relation to the *coniunctio* in order to gauge society's psychological state. The image of the copulating parents is a metaphor for a *coniunctio oppositorum* (Samuels 1993, p. 168). When the image is reflected as fertile – that is, the projection of it – it is vital, and the psyche expresses oneness and integration (Samuels 1993, p. 168). I argue that the *coniunctio*, as projected by the Egyptian cultural unconscious, was one-sided and disharmonious, reflecting a pattern of exclusion and defeat. The self-regulatory function in the psyche compensates one-sided tendencies; there is a similar function in the *coniunctio* in that the mother and father images need to be in balance and union. Following this line of theoretical reasoning, I argue that a one-sided tendency was created as sustained political oppression constellated in the Egyptian psyche, and consequently, under the right conditions, social revolutions and unrest appeared. The father image as represented by Nasser via his actions created disharmony by excluding, instead of adopting, an environment of inclusion especially of competing political groups. The father-leader of Egypt failed in its role to maintain balance, as Nasser moved away from his original principles of democracy and headed towards centralized power and dictatorship, creating one-sidedness in the cultural political psyche. The Egyptian psyche sought release from the contents constellated in the unconscious. The psyche responded by producing the compensating feminine image. I argue that, after a sustained period of anxiety and confusion following the war, coupled with the prevailing masculine attitude, activation of the mother archetype occurred as its manifestation. Mother Mary emerged to become the compensating figure in the *coniunctio*.

I ended my research examining whether synthesis and integration of the feminine mediating symbol of the Marian apparitions occurred. I applied the depth-psychological concept of the transcendent function which mediates opposites, thereby assisting a transition from one attitude to another; thus, a middle ground is created in which the opposites can be united and which transcends them (Jung 1923b). The new content puts an end to the division "forcing the energy of the opposites into a common channel", and consequently, the "standstill is overcome and life can flow on with renewed power towards new goals" (Jung 1923b, paras. 827). My assessment includes posing the question as to whether synthesis and integration occurred from the perspective of the three sets of explanations proposed by eyewitnesses. In the context of the first set of explanations, the triumph of the October 1973 War could represent a concrete outcome which points to the cultural psyche attaining balance between the conscious and unconscious state, relieving anxiety brought on by the collective despair of the time, specifically, the consequences of the June 1967 War. From the perspective of the second set of explanations, I posit that integration occurred as tensions were relieved between Muslims and Copts as the environment moved from a warlike attitude to an attitude of peace; however, relations between these two religious groups deteriorated months later as rumours that mass-conversions of Muslims to Christianity were taking place. In the context of the third set of explanations, I argue that a move closer towards a religious attitude may have signified synthesis and integration of the cultural psyche as repressed feelings surrounding socialist ideas and secularism were released. However, a glimpse into Egypt's future brings into question this assessment, as the apparitions point to a possible *enantiodromia*, as extremist elements of Islam began to overshadow the country. In assessing whether synthesis and integration occurred in the interpretation I offered, I argue that synthesis did not occur as the father image(s) of the *coniunctio* never succeeded in moving from an authoritarian regime towards democratic government which, as stated previously, was Nasser's goal in his first two years in power. The mass visions which continue to appear in Egypt over the decades following the 1968 apparitional event raise doubts as to whether the feminine principle has been fully integrated by the Egyptian cultural unconscious; as argued in Chapter 2, the cultural unconscious is an autonomous entity, and I speculate that, similar to an individual, its teleological aim, in part, is integration.

I chose to investigate the Virgin Mary of Zeitoun because it had not been previously systematically research and analysed. The collective aspect of the

Marian apparition appealed to me particularly because of its potential to examine specific socio-political and economic aspects of the case. One of the values of researching this phenomenon is the usage of the empirical material to identify the common themes and symbols, which in my opinion was an essential step in the methodological approach I adopted for this purpose. A challenge I met at the onset of this study was the limited number of available published accounts in relation to the thousands of people claiming to have seen the apparition. I wonder if a larger sample size would have yielded different results. For example, the case studies revealed a higher percentage of people reporting seeing one or more birds; however, in the 1986 survey a smaller percentage mentioned the image of the bird in their descriptions of the events. The main contribution of the present study is the application of Jungian depth-psychological principles, including the theoretical framework imbedded in *Flying Saucers* (1959), which was the main theory I planned to apply when I began this project. The application of other Jungian concepts such as the religious function and the *coniunctio* were not part of my original vision, but I am pleased that they emerged during the interpretation process as I think they enriched the overall interpretation of the Zeitoun apparitions. Nonetheless, the objective was to present a methodological approach to interpret mass visions of the Virgin Mary from a Jungian perspective, and it is my hope that this was accomplished.

## Further research

I think that there is value in applying a depth-psychological approach to investigating mass visions of the Virgin Mary, and here are some pointers for further research.

One of the benefits of a Jungian approach in studying mass visions is that it can uncover the unconscious contents of the cultural psyche within a society. Due to the constraints of this book, I could not conduct a comparative study between the late 1960s apparitions in Egypt and the three mass Marian apparitions which took place in 1986, 2000, and 2009 in Egypt. The 2009 apparitions in Warraq-al Hadar would have been of particular interest not least due to the revolution known as the Arab Spring which started 13 months after the apparitions took place. From a Jungian perspective, unconscious anxieties and tensions could have led up to the events of the Egyptian Revolution of 2011. One of the questions I would address in analysing this case is, why did the apparition occur before a major transformation took place in the country, and not after like the case of the Zeitoun apparitions? That is, collective anxiety in Zeitoun may have had time to constellate in the unconscious before the mediating symbol emerged, while it is unclear why the apparitions at Warraq-al Hadar occurred at that specific time and place. More importantly, how do the two apparitions relate to one another, taking into account the cultural psyche of the Egyptians over the past century?

In Chapter 4, I presented both qualitative and quantitative material as the primary sources of this case. An alternative approach to analysing the material would have been a purely qualitative one. Such an approach was for example adopted by Alschuler (2006) in his study of the political consciousness of oppressed peoples, by analysing four personal testimonies of people who had lived under oppression and achieved liberated consciousness and psycho-political healing. In his study, Alschuler applies the "case study" method by analysing three published accounts (see Chapter 2). Within the 22 case studies of the present work, there were a few long and detailed accounts of the seers' experiences. Analysing a few cases applying Jungian depth-psychology may have still yielded equally interesting insights.

Another way to examine the mass visions of the Virgin Mary at Zeitoun could have been the application of Jung's theory of synchronicity. This theory could allow for an examination of the connection between the cultural psyche and the historical events associated to the apparitions. This approach would arguably also allow for a discussion of the reality of the appearances. An alternative perspective to explore the mass apparition phenomenon using Jungian theory is represented by the application of the "cultural complex". More specifically, an application of the latter concept to the case under study would include an examination of the psychological nature of the conflict between Egyptian Christians and the Islamic aspects of the Egyptian culture in relation to the Zeitoun apparitions taking place on top of a Coptic church. Analysing the apparitions from this perspective could shed some light on the tensions between the two religious groups, Copts and Muslims, representing a cultural complex that may stem from the Arab conquest of Egypt in the 7th century, a time when the majority of Egyptians were Christian. Such an examination could also provide insights on how the Coptic minority deals with conflict in their society, which might be relevant in interpreting the Marian apparitions which took place in Egypt in the late 20th and early 21st centuries.

A final avenue for future research consists in expanding the analysis of the cultural psyche to the collective. It is clear from the secondary sources that the visions of the Virgin Mary were also seen by non-Egyptians. In the Introduction, I briefly described the cultural revolutions that were unfolding across the globe in the year when the apparitions took place. Did the transformative events of the Zeitgeist in 1968 influence Egyptians to demand change from outdated forms of governance like Nasser's authoritarian rule prompting the student and worker uprisings which were never seen before under his rule? Would a wider amplification into the collective reveal that a universal archetype was being activated? A comparative examination of the Zeitoun apparitions and feminism may be worth exploring. Marina Warner's (1976) work shows that the figure of Mary is shaped by social and historical change. In Chapter 1, I provide an overview of Marian apparitions which were recorded before and after WWII. Behind the messages and the social and historical circumstances stands the archetype operating according to the psychological needs of the people of that era. The messages of the Virgin have changed with history. Has the image of the Virgin Mary changed? In the Victorian era, women (and children as well) did not have the same rights that people nowadays enjoy in most countries of the world. Women, especially, had limited access to education, lacked property rights, and were denied the vote. They were under the protection and control of their fathers and later their husbands. A woman was not "one-in-herself". The Mary of the 20th century continued to predominantly appear to women and children, and similar to the 19th-century visionaries, most visionary women led traditional and conventional lives as mothers and wives. The main difference between the two Marys, i.e. that prevailing in the 19th century and that emerging from the 20th-century apparitions, may lay in the message; that is, while 19th-century seers often claimed that the message received from Mary was to pray for the salvation of the Church against republican and secular forces, the messages reported specifically from the middle of the 20th century onwards most often could be seen as pushing the role of Mary to the centre stage as Co-Redemptrix and Mediatrix. The psychological meaning behind the 20th-century image of the Virgin Mary may be related to the desire or need for a stronger or integrated animus in the figure of the Blessed Mary.

Admittedly, a certain degree of subjectivity, difficult to avoid, characterizes the present study, detectable for example in the amplification of the common themes and symbols reported by eyewitnesses, based on comparative material mostly derived from Western mythology, literature, and symbols. Different insights might be gleaned using alternative comparative material. An Egyptian researcher studying this case, for example, may have access to different material (which was unavailable to me), leading perhaps to a somewhat different interpretation of the Zeitoun apparitions, although not necessarily incompatible with the one offered in the present analysis.

Studying mass visions of the Virgin Mary strongly supports the view that there is an underlying meaning to these phenomena that is not clear and apparent on the conscious level. Moreover, the psychological meaning behind the visions points to a neglected aspect of a society oppressed and repressed by external forces. The theme that emerged from the analysis of the Zeitoun apparitions is the psychological need for the feminine, which, in my opinion, translated into a drive towards religion in the mind of many Egyptians. From a Jungian perspective, this meant a religious experience with the *numinosum* needed at a time of cultural distress and the search for meaning in the midst of chaos. The populist movements emerging out of the United States and several Western European countries in recent years have markedly influenced the political landscape, arguably even determining events such as result of the U.K. referendum to leave the E.U. ("Brexit") in June 2016 and the result of the November 2016 U.S. presidential elections, leading to a crisis in several traditional mainstream political systems and power centres representing the establishment in these countries, challenging existing multilateral trade and security agreements, and threatening to stop and reverse progress achieved in international collaboration and integration, as several of these countries are subject to increasing pressures pointing away from internationalism towards isolationism. The changes are already being felt in the United States with the Trump Administration's attempts to impose a travel ban from several Middle East countries and the increasing deportations of Mexicans, causing widespread fear within the Muslim and Mexican-American communities. Fear and anxiety may be constellating in several of these societies, and perhaps in the foreseeable future when tensions reach a boiling point, a feminine mediatory symbol may emerge.

The Virgin's appearance brings with her the archaic forces of destruction of old structures and patterns and the promise of renewal and rebirth; the energy of this force, albeit hibernating in the unconscious, is never anachronistic, and the energy of the Virgin Mary remains, in my opinion, much needed in the 21st century.

# Bibliography


Adams, Michael Vannoy. (2008). The Archetypal School. In *The Cambridge Companion to Jung*. Ed. Polly Young-Eisendrath and Terence Dawson (2nd edn). Cambridge: Cambridge University Press, 107–124.

Adams, Michael Vannoy. (2009). Imaginology: The Jungian Study of the Imagination. In *Archetypal Psychologies: Reflections in Honor of James Hillman*. Ed. S. Marlon. New Orleans: Spring Books.

Adler, Gerhard. (1961). *The Living Symbol: A Case Study in the Process of Individuation*. London: Routledge and Kegan Paul.

Adly, Amr. (2014, March 24). *The Problemic Continuity of Nasserism*. Trans. Amir Beshay. The Tahrir Institute for Middle East Policy, Washington, D.C. https://timep.org/commentary/problematic-continuity-of-nasserism/.

Alschuler, Lawrence R. (2006). *The Psychopolitics of Liberation: Political Consciousness from a Jungian Perspective*. New York, NY: Palgrave Macmillan.

Al Yafai, Faisal. (2012, November 3). The Death of Arab Secularism. The National.

An Official Statement from Pope Kyrillos VI Declares: The Virgin Appeared in Zeitoun Church. (1968, May 5). Al-Akhbar (4946).

*The American Heritage Dictionary*. (2001). (4th ed.).

Anderson, Benedict. (1991). *Imagined Communities: Reflections on the Origin and Spread of Nationalism*. Revised edition. New York, NY: Verso.

Ayubi, Nazih H. (1980. December). The Political Revival of Islam: The Case of Egypt. *International Journal of Middle East Studies* 12(4), 481–499.

Bair, Deirdre. (2003). *Jung: A Biography*. New York and Boston: Back Bay Books Little, Brown & Company.

Balint, Benjamin. (2010, February 5). *A Barometer of Religious Intolerance*. Haaretz. Washington D.C.: Hudson Institute.

Baring, Anne and Cashford, Jules. (1993). *The Myth of the Goddess: Evolution of an Image*. London: Arkana Penguin Books.

Barnett, Michael N. (1992). *Confronting the Costs of War: Military Power, State, and Society in Egypt and Israel*. Princeton, NJ: Princeton University Press.

Bartholomew, Robert E. and Goode, Erich. (2000, May/June). Mass Delusions: Prominent Cases over the Last 5 Centuries. Skeptical Inquirer 24(3).

Bayat, Assef. (1993, December). Populism, Liberation and Popular Participation: Industrial Democracy in Egypt. *Economic and Industrial Democracy* 14, 65–87.

Biedermann, Hans. (1992). *Dictionary of Symbolism: Cultural Icons and the Meaning Behind Them*. Trans. James Hulbert. New York, NY: Facts on File Inc.

Blackbourn, David. (1993). *Marpingen: Apparitions of the Virgin Mary in Bismarkian Germany*. Oxford: Clarendon Press.
Brady, Thomas F. (1968, May 5). Visions of Virgin Reported in Cairo: Coptic Bishop Among Those Who Tell of Apparition. The New York Times.
Briggs, Robin. (1996). *Witches and Neighbours: The Social and Cultural Context of European Witchcraft*. London: Harper Collins Publishers.
Bromley, David G. and Bobbitt, Rachel S. (2011). The Organizational Development of Marian Apparitional Movements. *Nova Religio: The Journal of Alternative and Emergent Religions* 14(3). 5–41.
Brown, Scott Kent Ii. (2000). The Coptic Church in Egypt: A Comment on Protecting Religious Minorities from Nonstate Discrimination. *Byu Law Review* 1049.
Bush, Ray. (2011, December). Coalitions for Dispossession and Networks of Resistance? Land, Politics and Agrarian Reform in Egypt. *British Journal of Middle Eastern Studies* 8(3).
Carroll, Michael P. (1986). *The Cult of the Virgin Mary: Psychological Origins*. Princeton, NJ: Princeton University Press.
Carter, Nancy C. (1979). Demeter and Persephone in Margaret Atwood's Novels: Mother-Daughter Transformations. *Journal of Analytical Psychology* 24, 326–342.
Chevalier, Jean and Gheerbrant, Alan. (1994). *The Penguin Dictionary of Symbols*. Trans. John Buchanan-Brown. London: Arkana Penguin Books.
Christian, William A., Jr. (1973, January). Holy People in Peasant Europe. *Comparative Studies in Society and History* 15(1), 106–114.
Christian, William, Jr. (1981). *Apparitions in Late Medieval and Renaissance Spain*. Princeton, NJ: Princeton University Press.
Christian, William A., Jr. (1987, February). Tapping and Defining New Power: The First Month of Visions at Ezquioga, July 1931. *American Ethnologist Frontiers of Christian Evangelism* 14(1), 140–166.
Cirlot, J. E. (1971). *Dictionary of Symbols*. Trans. Jack Sage. (2nd edn). London and Henley: Routledge and Kegan Paul.
Colman, Warren. (2000). Tyrannical Omnipotence in the Archetypal Father. *Journal of Analytical Psychology* 45(4), 521–539.
Committee Ordered to Collect All Documents About the Transfiguration and Miracles. (1968, May 6). Al-Ahram.
Corbett, Lionel. (1996). *The Religious Function of the Psyche*. London and New York, NY: Routledge.
Coury, Ralph M. (1982, November). Who Invented Arab Nationalism? Part 2. *International Journal of Middle East Studies* 14(4), 249–281.
Dala, Farhad. (1998). *Taking the Group Seriously*. London: Jessica Kingsley.
Danielson, Robert Eugene. (2007, June). Nasser and Pan-Arabism: Explaining Egypt's Rise to Power. Diss. Naval Postgraduate School, Monterey, California.
Dargin, Justin. (2011, May 11). In the Moment: Revolutions End When the Flags Go down, and Then What? Al-Arabiya News.
Demolition Man. (1993). Dir. Marco Brambilla. Warner Bros. Film.
DeVincenzo, Victor. (1988). The Apparitions at Zeitoun, Egypt: An Historical Overview. *The Journal of Religion and Psychical Research* 11(1).
Donnelly, James S. (1993). The Marian Shrine of Knock: The First Decade. *Éire-Ireland* 28(2), 54–99.

Dougherty M. (1998). Duccio's Prayer: Mediating Destruction and Creation with Artist in Analysis. *Journal of Analytical Psychology* 43, 479–492.

Dreher, Anna Ursula. (2000). *Foundations for Conceptual Research in Psychoanalysis*. Trans. Eva Ristl. Psychoanalytic Monograph 4. London and New York, NY: Karnac Books.

Edinger, Edward F. (1992). *Ego & Archetype: Individuation and the Religious Function of the Psyche*. Boston and London: Shambhala.

Edinger, Edward F. (1996a). *The Aion Lectures: Exploring the Self in C.G. Jung's Aion*. Deborah A. Wesley. Toronto, Canada: Inner City Books.

Edinger, Edward F. (1996b). *The New God-Image: A Study of Jung's Key Letters Concerning the Evolution of the Western God-Image*. Ed. Dianne D. Cordic and Charles Yates, M. D Wilmette, IL: Chiron Publications.

Echeverria, Loreto and Perry, Nicholas. (1988). *Under the Heel of Mary*. London and New York, NY: Routledge.

Elide, Mircea. (1961). *Images and Symbols: Studies in Religious Symbolism*. Trans. Philip Mairet. London: Harvill Press.

Eliade, Mircea. (1965). *The Two and the One*. Trans. J. M. Cohen. London: Harvill Press.

Freud, Sigmund. (1920). Beyond the Pleasure Principle. In The Standard Edition of the Complete Psychological Works of Sigmund Freud, Volume XVIII (1920–1922): Beyond the Pleasure Principle, Group Psychology and Other Works, 1–64, London: Vintage Classics, 2001.

Freud, Sigmund. (1923). A Seventeenth-Century Demonological Neurosis. In *The Standard Edition of the Complete Psychological Works of Sigmund Freud*. XIX (1923–1925): *The Ego and the Id and Other Works*, 67–106. London and New York: Penguin, 2003.

Fritz, D. W. (1980). The Animus-Possessed Wife of Bath. *Journal of Analytical Psychology* 25, 163–180.

Flower, Raymond. (2002). *Napoleon to Nasser: The Story of Modern Egypt*. London: Author House.

Gimbutas, Marija. (1989). *The Language of the Goddess*. New York, NY: Thames and Hudson.

Goldschmidt, Arthur, Jr. (2004). *Modern Egypt: The Formation of a Nation State*. Boulder, CO: Westview Press.

Gray, Richard M. (1996). *Archetypal Explorations: An Integrative Approach to Human Behavior*. London and New York, NY: Routledge.

Greenblatt, Stephen. (1990). Psychoanalysis and Renaissance Culture. In *Idem, Learning to Curse: Essays in Early Modern Culture*. London: Routledge.

Greeley, Andrew M. (1977). *The Mary Myth: On the Femininity of God*. New York, NY: The Seabury Press.

Guenena, Nemat and Wassef, Nadia. (1999). *Unfulfilled Promises: Women's Rights in Egypt*. New York, NY: Population Council.

Gusain, Raju. (2013, June 23). Superstition or Co-Incidence? Locals Believe Kali Avtaar Dhari Devi Unleashed the Floods for Revenge. India Today.

Hafny, Qadri. (2013, October 9). The Legacy of the 1973 October War in Egypt and Israel. Al Arabiya Institute for Studies.

Hall, Nor. (1980). *The Moon and the Virgin: Reflections on the Archetypal Feminine*. New York, NY: Harper & Row Publishers.

Harding, M. Esther. (1971). *Woman's Mysteries: Ancient and Modern*. Boston and Shaftesbury: Shambala Publications Inc.
Harris, Ruth. (1999). *Lourdes: Body and Spirit in the Secular Age*. London: The Penguin Press.
Hart, David L. (2008). The classical Jungian School. In *The Cambridge Companion to Jung*. Ed. Polly Young-Eisendrath and Terence Dawson (2nd edn). Cambridge: Cambridge University Press, 95–106.
Hazelton, Lesley. (2004). *Mary: A Flesh-and-Blood Biography of the Virgin Mother*. New York and London: Bloomsbury Publishing.
Heisig, James W. (1979). *Imago Dei: A Study of C.G. Jung's Psychology of Religion*. Lewisburg, PA: Bucknell University Press.
Henderson, Joseph L. (1984). *Cultural Attitudes in Psychological Perspectives*. Toronto, Canada: Inner City Books.
Henderson, Joseph L. (1990). The Cultural Unconscious. In *Shadow and Self: Selected Papers in Analytical Psychology*. New York, NY: Chiron Publications, 32–55.
Hibbard, Scott and Layton, Azza Salama. (2010, October). The Origins and Future of Egypt's Revolt. *Journal of Middle Islamic Law and Culture* 12(3).
Hillman, James. (1989). *A Blue Fire*. Ed. T. Moore. New York, NY: Harper Perennial.
Hogenson, George B. (2004). Developmental Aspects of Analytical Psychology. In *Analytical Psychology: Contemporary Perspectives in Jungian Analysis*. Ed. Joseph Cambray and Linda Carter. Hove and New York, NY: Brunner-Routledge, 32–55.
Horwitz, Alan V. (2010). How an Age of Anxiety Became an Age of Depression. *The Milbank Quarterly*. 88(1), 112–138, [online]. www.ncbi.nlm.nih.gov/pmc/articles/PMC2888013/].
Horsfall, Sara. (2000). The Experience of Marian Apparitions and the Mary Cult. *The Social Science Journal* 37(3), 375–384.
Hossain, Shaikat. (2012). The Internet as a Tool for Studying the Collective Unconscious. *Jung Journal: Culture & Psyche* 6, 103–109.
Ibrahim, Fouad N. (1982). Social and Economic Geographical Analysis of the Egyptian Copts. *Geojournal* 6(1), 63–67.
James, Laura M. (2012). Egypt: Dangerous Illusions. In *The 1967 Arab-Israeli War: Origins and Consequences*. Ed. W. M. Roger Louis and Avi Shlaim. Cambridge: Cambridge University Press.
Jillani, Anees. (1991, April). Nasser, Saddam and Pan-Arabism. *Pakistan Horizon* 44(2), 75–88.
Johnston, Francis. (1980). *When Millions Saw Mary*. Chulmleigh, Devon: Augustine Publishing.
Johnson, Peter. (1972, July). Egypt under Nasser. *Middle East Research and Information Project(MERIP)* 10, 3–14.
Jung, C. G. (1902). On the Psychology and Pathology of So-called Occult Phenomena. In *Collected Works, Vol 1*. Princeton, NJ: Princeton University Press. (1975).
Jung, C. G. (1923a). Definitions. In *Collected Works, Vol 6*. Princeton, NJ: Princeton University Press. (1971).
Jung, C. G. (1923b). Psychological Types. In *Collected Works, Vol 6*. Princeton, NJ: Princeton University Press, 1971.
Jung, C. G. (1934). The Soul and Death. In *Collected Works, Vol 8. The Structure and Dynamics of the Psyche* (2nd edn). Princeton, NJ: Princeton University Press, 1969.

Jung, C. G. (1936). The Method. In *Collected Works, Vol 12. Psychology and Alchemy* (2nd edn). Princeton, NJ: Princeton University Press, 1968.

Jung, C. G. (1936/37). The Concept of the Collective Unconscious. In *Collected Works, Vol 9i. The Archetypes of the Unconscious* (2nd edn). Princeton, NJ: Princeton University Press, 1991.

Jung, C. G. (1937). The Work. In *Collected Works, Vol 12. Psychology and Alchemy* (2nd edn). Princeton, NJ: Princeton University Press, 1968.

Jung, C. G. (1938/40). Psychology and Religion. In *Collected Works, Vol 11. Psychology and Religion.* New York, NY: Pantheon Books, 1958.

Jung, C. G. (1940). Psychology and Religion. In *Collected Works, Vol 11. Psychology and Religion: West and East.* New York, NY: Pantheon Books Inc, 1958.

Jung, C. G. (1943). On the Psychology of the Unconscious. In *Collected Works, Vol 7. Two Essays on Analytical Psychology* (2nd edn). Princeton, NJ: Princeton University Press, 1977.

Jung, C. G. (1948a). A Psychological Approach to the Dogma of the Trinity. In *Collected Works, Vol 11. Psychology and Religion: West and East.* New York, NY: Pantheon Books Inc, 1958.

Jung, C. G. (1948b). On Psychic Energy. In *Collected Works, Vol 8. The Structure and Dynamics of the Psyche* (2nd edn). Princeton, NJ: Princeton University Press, 1969.

Jung, C. G. (1948c). The Spirit Mercurius. In *Collected Works, Vol 13. Alchemical Studies.* Princeton, NJ: Princeton University Press, 1967.

Jung, C. G. (1948d). General Aspects of Dream Psychology. In *Collected Works, Vol 8. The Structure and Dynamics of the Psyche* (2nd edn). Princeton, NJ: Princeton University Press, 1969.

Jung, C. G. (1950a). Concerning Rebirth. In *Collected Works, Vol 9i. The Archetypes of the Unconscious* (2nd edn). Princeton, NJ: Princeton University Press, 1991.

Jung, C. G. (1950b). Concerning Mandala Symbolism. In *Collected Works, Vol 9i. The Archetypes of the Unconscious* (2nd edn). Princeton, NJ: Princeton University Press, 1991.

Jung, C. G. (1951a). Psychological Aspects of the Kore. In *Collected Works, Vol 9i. The Archetypes of the Unconscious* (2nd edn). Princeton, NJ: Princeton University Press, 1991.

Jung, C. G. (1951b). The Psychology of the Child Archetype. In *Collected Works, Vol 9i. The Archetypes of the Unconscious* (2nd edn). Princeton, NJ: Princeton University Press, 1991.

Jung, C. G. (1951c). Christ, a Symbol of the Self. In *Collected Works, Vol 9ii. Aion, Researches into the Phenomenology of the Self* (2nd edn). Princeton, NJ: Princeton University Press, 1978.

Jung, C. G. (1951d). The Historical Significance of the Fish. In *Collected Works, Vol 9ii. Aion, Researches into the Phenomenology of the Self* (2nd edn). Princeton, NJ: Princeton University Press, 1978.

Jung, C. G. (1951e). The Sign of the Fishes. In *Collected Works, Vol 9ii. Aion, Researches into the Phenomenology of the Self* (2nd edn). Princeton, NJ: Princeton University Press, 1978.

Jung, C. G. (1952a). Symbols of Transformation. In *Collected Works, Vol 5. Symbols of Transformation* (2nd edn). New York, NY: Pantheon Books, 1956.

Jung, C. G. (1952b). The Symbolism of the Mandala. In *Collected Works, Vol 12. Psychology and Alchemy* (2nd edn). Princeton, NJ: Princeton University Press, 1970.

Jung, C. G. (1952c). The Lapis-Christ Parallel. In *Collected Works, Vol 12. Psychology and Alchemy* (2nd edn). Princeton, NJ: Princeton University Press, 1970.

Jung, C. G. (1952d). Basic Concepts of Alchemy. In *Collected Works, Vol 12*. Psychology and Alchemy (2nd edn). Princeton, NJ: Princeton University Press, 1970.

Jung, C. G. (1952e). Introduction. In *Collected Works, Vol 12*. Psychology and Alchemy (2nd edn). Princeton, NJ: Princeton University Press, 1970.

Jung, C. G. (1954a). Archetypes of the Collective Unconscious. In *Collected Works, Vol 9i. The Archetypes of the Unconscious* (2nd edn). Princeton, NJ: Princeton University Press, 1991.

Jung, C. G. (1954b). The Philosophical Tree. In *Collected Works, Vol 13*. Princeton, NJ: Princeton University Press, 1967.

Jung, C. G. (1954c). Transformation Symbolism in the Mass. In *Collected Works, Vol 11. Psychology and Religion: West and East*. New York, NY: Pantheon Books Inc, 1958.

Jung, C. G. (1954d). Concerning the Archetypes, with Special Reference to the Anima Concept. In *Collected Works, Vol 9i. The Archetypes of the Unconscious* (2nd edn). Princeton, NJ: Princeton University Press, 1991.

Jung, C. G. (1954e). On the Nature of the Psyche. In *Collected Works, Vol 8. The Structure and Dynamics of the Psyche* (2nd edn). Princeton, NJ: Princeton University Press, 1969.

Jung, C. G. (1957). *The Undiscovered Self*. Princeton, NJ: Princeton University Press, 2010.

Jung, C. G. (1958b). The Transcendent Function. In *Collected Works, Vol 8. The Structure and Dynamics of the Psyche* (2nd edn). Princeton, NJ: Princeton University Press, 1969.

Jung, C. G. (1958a). *Answer to Job. 50th Anniversary Ed*. Princeton, NJ: Princeton University Press, 2002.

Jung, C. G. (1959). *Flying Saucers: A Modern Myth of Things Seen in the Skies*. London and New York, NY: Routledge Classics.

Jung, C. G. (1972). *Man and His Symbols*. London: Aldus Books.

Kamell, Youssef G., John P., Jackson and Rebecca S. Jackson. (1996). *A Lady of Light Appears in Egypt: The Story of Zeitoun*. Colorado Springs, CO: St. Mark's Avenue Press.

Karingadayil, Santhosh Thomas. (2011). *From Darkness to Light: The Concept of Salvation in the Perspectives of Thomas Aquinas and Śankara*. Frankfurt: Lang.

Kanovsky, Eliyahu. (1970). *The Economic Impact of the Six-Day War: Israel, the Occupied Territories, Egypt, Jordon*. New York, Washington and London: Praeger Publishers.

Kerényi, Karl. (1978). *Athene: Virgin and Mother in Greek Religion*. Putnam, CT: Spring Publications Inc.

Kimbles, Samuel. (2003, August). Joe Henderson and the Cultural Unconscious. *The San Francisco Jung Institute Library Journal* 22(2), 53–58.

Knox, Jean M. (2001). Memories, Fantasies, Archetypes: An Exploration of Some Connections Between Cognitive Science and Analytical Psychology. *The Journal of Analytical Psychology* 46(4), 613–635.

Kselman, Thomas A. (1986, July). Marian Piety and the Cold War in the United States. *Catholic Historical Review* 72(3), 403.

Kselman, Thomas A. (2001, April). Lourdes: Body and Spirit in the Secular Age. *The Catholic Historical Review* 87(2), 337–339.

Laskier, Michael M. (1995, July). Egyptian Jewry under the Nasser Regime. *Middle Eastern Studies* 31(3), 573–619.

Layard, John. (1972). *The Virgin Archetype*. New York, NY: Spring Publications.

Les Apparitions Miraculeuses De La Vierge Marie Au-Dessus De L'église Copte 'Notre-Dame' À Zeitoun: Confirmees Hier Par S.S Le Pape Kyrillos VI. (1968, May 5). *Progres Dimanche* 20(17).

Louis, W. M Roger and Shlaim, Avi. (2012). *The 1967 Arab-Israeli War: Origins and Consequences*. Cambridge: Cambridge University Press.

Lu, Kevin. (2013, March 7). Can Individual Psychology Explain Social Phenomena? An Appraisal of the Theory of Cultural Complexes. *Psychoanalysis, Culture, & Society* 18, 386–404.

Main, Roderick. (2004). *The Rupture of Time: Synchronicity and Jung's Critique of Modern Western Culture*. Hove and New York, NY: Brunner-Routledge.

Main, Roderick. (2006). Religion. In *The Handbook of Jungian Psychology: Theory, Practice and Applications*. Ed. Renos K.Papadopoulos. London and New York, NY: Routledge, 297–323.

Mansfield, Peter. (1968. October). Egypt Since June 1967. *The World Today. Pub. by Royal Institute of International Affairs* 24(10), 414–420.

Manuel, Paul Christopher. (2002). The Marian Apparitions in Fátima as Political Reality: Religion and Politics in Twentieth-Century Portugal. Minda de Gunzburg Center for European Studies. Cambridge, MA: Harvard University. Working Paper 88.

Margry, Peter Jan. (2009). Marian Interventions in the Wars of Ideology: The Elastic Politics of the Roman Catholic Church on Marian Apparitions. *History and Anthropology* 20(3), 243–263.

Martin, Richard P. (2003). *Myths of the Ancient Greeks*. New York, NY: New American Library.

Matter, E. Ann. (2001). Apparitions of the Virgin Mary in the Late Twentieth Century: Apocalyptic, Representation, Politics. *Religion* 31, 125–153.

Migdal, Joel S. (1988). *Strong Societies and Weak States: State-Society Relations and State Capabilities in the Third World*. Princeton, NJ: Princeton University Press.

Migdal, Joel S. (2001). *State in Society: Studying How States and Societies Transform and Constitute One Another*. Cambridge: Cambridge University Press.

Miller,E. and K. Samples. (1992). *The Cult of the Virgin*. Grand Rapids, MI: Baker Book.

Mogenson, Greg(2003). The Serpent's Prayer: The Psychology of an Image. In The Jung Page [Online]. www.cgjungpage.org/index.php?option= com_content&task= view&id=277&Itemid=40 [2012, February 12].

Mogenson, Greg. (2005). *A Most Accursed Religion: When a Trauma Becomes God*. Putnam, CT: Spring Publications Inc.

Montalban, Ricardo. *Marian Apparitions of the 20th Century: A Message of Urgency*. (1991). Nar. Ricardo Montalban. Marian Communications Ltd.

Mor, Ben D. (1991, November). Nasser's Decision-Making in the 1967 Middle East Crisis: A Rational-Choice Explanation. *The Journal of Peace Research* 28(4), 359–375.

Nasr, Seyyed Vali Reza. (2001). *Islamic Leviathan: Islam and the Making of State Power*. New York, NY: Oxford University Press.
Nelson, Cynthia. (1973, September). The Virgin of Zeitoun. *World Review, Council on Religion and International Affairs* 16(9), 5–11.
Neumann, Erich. (1963). *The Great Mother: An Analysis of the Archetype*. Trans. Ralph Manheim. (2nd edn.). Princeton, NJ: Princeton University Press.
Neumann, Erich. (1993). *The Origins and History of Consciousness*. Trans. R.F. Hull. Princeton, NJ: Princeton University Press.
Palmer, Father Jerome, O. S. B. (1969). *Our Lady Returns to Egypt*. San Bernardino, CA: Culligan Publications.
Papadopoulos, Renos K. (2006). Jung's Epistemology and Methodology. In *The Handbook of Jungian Psychology: Theory, Practice and Applications*. Ed. Renos K. Papadopoulos. London and New York, NY: Routledge Taylor and Francis Group, 7–53.
Perry, Paul. (2003). *Jesus in Egypt: Discovering the Secrets of Christ's Childhood Years*. New York, NY: Ballantine Books.
Pennington, J. D. (1982. April). The Copts in Modern Egypt. *Middle Eastern Studies* 18(2), 158–179.
Pope Kyrillos Declares: The Apparition of the Virgin Is a Truth. An Official Papal Statement Affirms Her Apparition Many Times in Zeitoun Church. (1968, May 5). Al-Ahram (29731).
Rigoglioso, Marguerite. (2010). *Virgin Goddess of Antiquity*. New York, NY: Palgrave Macmillan.
Roper, Lyndal. (1994). *Oedipus and the Devil: Witchcraft, Sexuality and Religion in Early Modern Europe*. London and New York, NY: Routledge.
Rogo, Scott D. (1982). *Miracles: A Parascientific Inquiry into Wondrous Phenomena*. New York, NY: The Dial Press.
Samuels, Andrew, Shorter, Bani and Plaut, Fred. (2007). *A Critical Dictionary of Jungian Analysis*. London and New York, NY: Routledge.
Samuels, Andrew. (1985). *Jung and the Post Jungians*. London: Boston & Henley, Routledge & Kegan Paul.
Samuels, Andrew. (1989). Analysis and Pluralism: The Politics of Psyche. *Journal of Analytical Psychology* 34, 33–51.
Samuels, Andrew. (1993). *The Political Psyche*. London and New York, NY: Routledge.
Segal, Robert A. (1998). *Jung on Mythology*. Selected and Introduced by Robert A. Segal. Princeton, NJ: Princeton University Press.
Shafik, George. Apparition of Virgin Still Being Seen. (1969, April 11). The Egyptian Gazette.
Shamdasani, Sonu. (1998). From Geneva to Zürich: Jung and French Switzerland. *Journal of Analytical Psychology* 43(1), 115–126.
Sharp, Jeremy M. (2009, May 12). *Egypt: Background and U.S. Relations*. Congressional Research Service Report for Congress. Washington, D.C.
Shukrallah, Hala. (1994, Summer). The Impact of the Islamic Movement in Egypt. *Feminist Review* 47, 15–32.
Singer, Thomas. (2016). Introduction. In *Europe's Many Souls: Exploring Cultural Complexes and Identities*. Ed. Thomas Singer and Joerg Rasche. London and New York, NY: Spring Journal Inc.

Singer, Thomas and Kimbles, Samuel L. (2004). Introduction. In *The Cultural Complex: Contemporary Jungian Perspectives on Psyche and Society*. Ed. Thomas Singer and Samuel L. Kimbles. London and New York, NY: Routledge.

Stein, Murray. (1999). *Jung on Christianity*. Selected and Introduced by Murray Stein. Princeton, NJ: Princeton University Press.

Stephenson, Craig E. (2009). *Possession: Jung's Comparative Anatomy of the Psyche*. London and New York, NY: Routledge.

The Patriarch Announces the Appearance of the Virgin Mary at the Church in Zeitoun. (1968, May 5). Al-Goumhouryia.

The Transfiguration of the Virgin at Zeitoun Exceeds Her Transfiguration at Fatima and Lourdes and Spain. (1968, May 5). Watani.

Tonsi, Ahmed. (2012, September 27-October 3). Nasser in 2012. Al-Ahram Weekly (1116).

Turner, Edith and Turner, Victor. (1982). Postindustrial Marian Pilgrimage. In *Mother Worship*. Ed. J. Preston, 145–173. Chapel Hill: University of North Carolina Press.

Varghese, Roy Abraham. (2000). *God-Sent: A History of the Accredited Apparitions of Mary*. New York, NY: The Crossword Publishing Company.

Ventresca, Robert A. (2003. Winter). The Virgin and the Bear: Religion, Society and the Cold War in Italy. *Journal of Social History* 37(2), 439–456.

Virgin Mary Appeared at Zeitun – Kyrillos. (1968, May 5). The Egyptian Gazette 89(28345).

Vries, Ad de. (1974). *Dictionary of Symbols and Imagery*. Amsterdam and London: North-Holland Publishing Company.

Von Franz, Marie-Louise. (1996). *The Interpretation of Fairy Tales*. Revised edition. Boston and London: Shambhala Publications Inc.

Walker, Barbara G. (1983). *The Woman's Encyclopedia of Myths and Secrets*. New York, NY: Harper One.

Warburg, Gabriel R. (1982. April). Islam and Politics in Egypt: 1952–80. *Middle Eastern Studies* 18(2), 131–157.

Warner, Marina. (1976). *Alone of All Her Sex: The Myth and the Cult of the Virgin Mary*. New York, NY: Vintage Books.

Warner, Marina. (2013). *Alone of All Her Sex: The Myth and the Cult of the Virgin Mary*. Oxford, UK: Oxford University Press.

Wheelock, Keith. (1960). *Nasser's New Egypt: A Critical Analysis*. New York, NY: Frederick A Praeger Inc. Publisher.

Wojcik, Daniel. (1997). *The End of the World as We Know It: Faith, Fatalism, and the Apocalypse in America*. New York and London: New York University Press.

Wolf, Eric R. (1969). Society and Symbols in Latin Europe and in the Islamic Near East: Some Comparisons. *Anthropological Quarterly* 42(3), 287–301.

Woodman, Marion. (1985). *The Pregnant Virgin: A Process of Psychological Transformation*. Toronto, Canada: Inner City Books.

Wurmser, Meyrav. (2001). *The Roots of Islamic Radicalism*. Washington, D.C.: Hudson Institute.

Zaki, Pearl. (1982). *Our Lord's Mother Visits Egypt*. Cairo: Privately Printed by the Author.

Zimdars-Swartz, Sandra L. (1991). *Encountering Mary: Visions of Mary from La Salette to Medjugorje*. New York, NY: Avon Books.

## Webliography

Miracle Hunter, www.miraclehunter.com/marian_apparitions/index.html.
www.stmaryztn.org.
zeitun-eg.org.

# Index

Note: Page numbers in *italics* indicate a figure and page numbers in **bold** indicate a table on the corresponding page.

For Product Safety Concerns and Information please contact our EU
representative GPSR@taylorandfrancis.com
Taylor & Francis Verlag GmbH, Kaufingerstraße 24, 80331 München, Germany

www.ingramcontent.com/pod-product-compliance
Ingram Content Group UK Ltd.
Pitfield, Milton Keynes, MK11 3LW, UK
UKHW022126190926
475702UK00013B/1677
* 9 7 8 0 3 6 7 4 8 9 3 2 8 *